JOHN CHAMBERLAIN was born in New Haven, Connecticut, and studied at Yale University. He is the author of *The American Stakes, MacArthur, The Roots of Capitalism,* and *The Enterprising Americans.* He is at present a columnist for King Features Syndicate.

FAREWELL TO REFORM

☆

JOHN CHAMBERLAIN

FAREWELL TO REFORM

THE RISE, LIFE AND DECAY OF THE PROGRESSIVE MIND IN AMERICA

QUADRANGLE PAPERBACKS
Quadrangle Books / *Chicago*

First QUADRANGLE PAPERBACK edition published 1965 by Quadrangle Books, Inc., 180 North Wacker Drive, Chicago 60606.
Manufactured in the United States of America.

Foreword to the Second Edition

THIS book was completed almost a year ago, and in consequence the final chapter has a certain pre-election tone. Were this chapter being written at the moment, it would, perforce, take on a different outline. The criticism of the "social planners" would note that George Soule, the shrewdest of the advocates of a "planned society," has abandoned his romantic position of 1932. "What we have . . . created," says Mr. Soule of the New Deal formulae, "is not a reformed industrial system, but a mixture in which problems will be precipitated with greater clarity, an arena in which sides may be chosen and significant conflicts waged." In summary, the era of syndicalism—of owners' syndicates, workers' syndicates, farmers' syndicates, and even consumers' co-operative syndicates—is upon us. The class war is here.

Certain reproaches have greeted the author of this book since the advent of Franklin D. Roosevelt in Washington. The Democratic Party, it is urged, represents a new flowering of the old liberalisms of the pre-war decade. In spite of the front pages, however, I must persist in the use of the sub-title, "rise, life and decay of the progressive mind in America." The "farewell" must stand as a "farewell," not an *Auf Wiedersehen*. I see nothing in the long-term predictions of the last chapter that needs alteration. The "reforms" of the New Deal will not lead to reform as it is carefully defined in this book; they will not help to maintain "freedom of contract," freedom from monopoly, freedom of competition. Rather do they bear out the thesis; they tend to congeal capitalism. In making this point once more, I note with some amusement that I stand both with Ralph West Robey, financial editor of the conservative *New York Evening Post,* and with John Strachey, the English Marxist critic. In other words, both conservatives and radicals know how capitalism works; it is only the liberal, who has mistaken an adjective for a credo, that is deluded.

Why won't the New Deal work? What will be the rôle of Franklin D. Roosevelt in the coming war of the syndicates? A rising price level, brought about consciously through currency manipulation and production by quota, will, I predict, force him more and more to the Right. If this happens, the "brain trust" will go the way of Louis D. Brandeis in the Wilson administrations—the Brandeis whose proposed banking reforms were so sedulously ignored. What Roosevelt, a catastrophe President, might have done had the conditions of March 4 continued, he cannot do if the Farm Relief Act and the Industrial Recovery legislation have any effect. He cannot, given a price rise, given farm shortages (and wheat is already at a dollar) make any important alterations in the economic system, such as nationalizing the banks. He can merely "freeze" certain variables, by dictating hours of labor and wages, the result of which will be to make the working of the market more cumbersome. A really free market demands roller-bearing movement of all its variables. And when the next inevitable depression is upon us, business men will have more difficulty in getting out from under. They will find the system more congealed than ever.

There is no clause in the control legislation of the sort that J. Franklin Carter proposed a few years ago—a clause that would permit, nay, compel, the Government to "take over," Norman-Thomas fashion, the majority stock in recalcitrant industries. Supporters of the New Deal argue that a licensing provision means "control." This may fairly be questioned. To begin with, Justice Brandeis's Oklahoma Ice opinion, arguing that a State has the right to limit the number of businesses operating in a given field, was a minority opinion of the Supreme Court. If enforced despite precedent, a licensing provision will become the football of the "vested interests," so dear to the heart of the mordant Veblen. If the populace, under the stimulation of rising prices and increased prosperity, cries out against "radicalism," we may expect a gradual usurpation of the control of any enforceable licensing clause by big business itself. Big business has circumvented the intent of the Sherman and Clayton Acts; it can circumvent the intent of any other act, given a modicum of prosperity as the basis for the necessary buttressing of popular psychology. Nor does the fact brought out by Berle and Means—that ownership is often divorced from "control"—affect this judgment. When I speak of "big business," I am speaking of "control," whether by bankers or by the few remaining Henry Fords of industry.

The reason why Roosevelt will either become conservative or be ground between two stones is to be found in an elementary study of the workings of mass psychology. He is committed by his own moves to a return of prosperity; thus he becomes part of the American Tradition which reached its apotheosis in Calvin Coolidge. A return of prosperity must move him to the Right, for the cry, "Don't tamper with improving business," must be too strong for so adept a politician to ignore. If, however, any upturn proves illusory, a President who has gambled on bulling the market will find himself in the position of Herbert Hoover in 1932. He will become the effigy of a people's devil, to be scourged alike, though for different reasons, by both radical and conservative voters.

As for the possibility of creating fair prices, plus fair wages, plus a "fair" return on the investment, how is the administration to get around the logical objections voiced by John Strachey? (And to those who say, "You mustn't be too logical," my answer is, to paraphrase Lawrence Dennis, "Then why use words, which are the tools of logic?") How to settle the rights of competing substitute industries, how to prevent inter-industry (as distinct from intra-industry) competition?

There must be bureaucratic choice of the *status quo* here (i.e., control of the Government by the most powerful in industry).

Only the old game of push and haul can determine the relative rights of bus lines and railroads. Only the game of pressure politics can settle matters when cotton goods commence to compete with silk goods and both with rayon goods. Coal, natural gas, petroleum, and hydro-electricity must compete with each other, despite intra-industry codes formulated for the use of General Hugh S. Johnson. And individual monopolies in different fields must lead to pressure for trading advantages abroad—with what effect on the economic organization of other countries also pressing for trading advantages, or striving to maintain favorable balances of trade?

I put some of these objections in the form of questions, for they are for the future to decide upon. But the future can decide only one way if labor does not awake, organize, and go into pressure politics on its own. Labor must face the implications of the syndicalist era, or be content with the position of industrial serfs under what John T. Flynn calls Guild Fascism. With hours set at a maximum, wages at a minimum, and prices kept level, the only way of cutting costs within an industry will be by the road of technological improvement, i.e., by labor-saving devices. Labor will have to remain constantly awake if it is to seize the advantage of technology for itself. In other words, for every improvement in processes, labor must strike for shorter hours and increased pay. Can labor do it?

And the farmer? Still a Populist, he is playing for a price rise that will prevent any fundamental change in the business mechanism of the country. Cotton option plans, reduction of wheat acreage, all of these devices, cannot succeed under even a partially free capitalism. For no one can foresee what used to be called Acts of God. A wheat and cotton reduction, planned one year and capped the next by a famine or a blight, would send commodity prices skyrocketing—with what effects on a partially planned economy? It would be the old pre-war problem of the "high cost of living" over again. Then, too, as Louis

Hacker points out in his recent John Day pamphlet, "The Farmer is Doomed," acreage limitation is not synonymous with crop reduction, for extensive farming can give way to intensive farming, with a resultant great increase in soil productivity.

And what, to continue in this pessimistic vein, is to prevent a newly prosperous farmer from taking his money into Wall Street, once the mortgage is liquidated; or what is to prevent the automobile manufacturer from putting the money gained from the automobile-buying farmer into excess plant and indirectly into the watering of securities? If the President has found a way to "control" the investment process without being controlled, in turn, by an intrenched finance capitalism, then we have yet to learn the trick. And if he can control Wall Street, the first hint of it would be to send the market tumbling in the rush to get out. Even if the export of capital be prohibited, what is to prevent masters of money from buying "international" commodities, such as cotton in America, selling them abroad, and hoarding their funds in real capitalist countries, such as France, Holland, Switzerland and Belgium? Of course, the shipment of commodities could be regulated, too, subject to control in the interests of direct exchange for rubber, coffee, and other necessities which we do not ourselves produce. But who said "dictatorship is not the American way of doing things"?

However we look at it, Franklin D. Roosevelt is caught in the act of gambling on a "return to prosperity." And, as the savior of a nation from the vices of capitalism, it may be predicted that he will not be able to stand prosperity. For prosperity is a concomitant, given the psychology of capitalism, of a rising market. And what goes up, as credit is created by the banks, must come down, as credit is withdrawn by the banks. And reformers of capitalism, once they have created the psychology leading to an upturn of the credit cycle, must inevitably change mentally or be replaced at the top by the Coolidges and Hoovers. Reformers cannot stand prosperity.

JOHN CHAMBERLAIN

CONTENTS

☆

FAREWELL TO REFORM

☆

CHAPTER ONE

A Pattern of the Nineties

☆

THE nineties saw the last full-throated attempt of the American dirt farmer to seize a government he had not wholly owned since Jackson's day, and had owned not at all since the Civil War had ended. It was an attempt rendered the more desperate because of the sudden and confusing transformation of American economic life. In the old days, the dirt farmer—as distinct from the Southern-planter aristocracy that depended upon slave labor—had been a self-sufficing person; he didn't borrow exorbitantly at the banks to buy costly farm machinery; he produced for use, not for profit. Within his own neighborhood he could find simple craftsmen to take care of his wants; he didn't have to go to Brockton for shoes, to Lowell for his clothes. But the revolution in transportation broke heavily into the primitive division of labor of pioneer America. The farmer suddenly discovered that he was implicated, to an extent undreamed of in the days of true isolation, with banks, with railroads, and with all the manufacturers who went into politics in the interest of controlling prices through discriminatory tariffs and favorable monopolies.

And so the farmer, after the Civil War, in the seventies, eighties and nineties, found himself dragged into politics as a matter of self-defense. He made a bad job of it, first and last. For the nineties, in spite of all the Populist clamor for the righting of a deranged balance, witnessed, toward their close, the final steps in the unchecked burgeoning of a flushed business enterprise. This enterprise had swept across the continent in the pioneer's wake, or even before him. It had, quite early, gobbled up choice sections of land to be held out of use for speculative purposes. It had corrupted legislatures in the interests of its railroad and traction lines, and had monopolized coal, copper and the oil of Pennsylvania, Ohio and California. Business, in the years following Appomattox, had only to compete in a local market behind high tariff walls; agriculture had to compete in a world market. It was *laissez faire* for the farmer and paternalistic aid for industry. It meant, simply, that the farmer had to buy his shoes, clothes and implements at a high price level, and pay for them with money earned from crops sold at a low price level. Is it any cause for wonder, then, that his howls were mistaken by Eastern editorial writers for revolution, for anarchy and for socialism?

With the farmer, as the nineteenth century ran out, went the small shopkeeper and the small shipper. When it is once fully understood that the conflict of the nineties, which saw Bryan go down before McKinley, and the subsequent and similar battles of La Follette, Roosevelt and Wilson for the common man in the next decade, were not stirrings of red revolution, but merely a struggle between small and large capitalists, the significance of the movements that will be detailed in this book becomes plain. It is quite true, of course, that expanding industry kicked up its socialist threat, and that this threat made itself felt in Congress, but dissatisfied workers were constantly being drawn off into enterprises of their own, and the lines of labor formed only to break again when an immediate objective had been won. The minor victories of labor were often more apparent than real; so bland folk, after the election of 1900, were willing to sit back with the knowledge that they hadn't given many concessions, after all.

Even large groups of the farmers seemed less fearful in 1900 that big business might fail to work its magic in their favor. A series of lucky breaks, as will be apparent, lulled some of them into a sudden sense of false security. And in the dull dog days of the Summer of 1901—before Czolgosz, the deluded boy who had been listening to and perhaps misinterpreting Emma Goldman, had put a bullet into McKinley at an exposition in Buffalo—the United States was definitely committed to the welfare of the plutocracy. It is to this benign period that all inherent conservatives look back when they speak of normalcy. The country was not even troubled, as yet, by the mock-menace of the Roosevelt scowl. Never had the sun shone so broadly upon the politicians of the acquisitive instinct. At last, after the bread lines and bank failures of the early nineties, the strikes of two decades and the abortive onslaughts of Grover Cleveland upon the swollen Civil War tariffs (which, like the war taxes of the nineteen-twenties, lived on as an ironical reminder that peace is never with us), the nation seemed to be moving ahead in a way to please the crassest Hamiltonian. The Spanish War, incited chiefly as a rabble-rousing crusade for the benefit of the newspaper circulation of Hearst and Pulitzer, and against the sober wishes of both Andrew Carnegie and J. P. Morgan, had proved to be a blessing to the very people who had refused to plump for it; the "splendid little war" for Cuba *libre* had stilled, so far as could be heard in the editorial offices that had deplored Bryanism, all the bubble and seethe of the Western unrest, and had opened the way for a consolidation of business that had been undreamed of in the philosophy of the cruder pirates of Jay Gould's age. There was still a Sherman Anti-Trust Act, but judicial decisions had rendered it flabby, and "illegal" trusts had only to be made over into legal holding companies to escape the teeth of a law which, in any event, didn't particularly interest either McKinley or his Warwick, Mark Hanna. Besides, as the great Pullman strike of 1894 had shown, the anti-trust laws were two-edged; they could be used against union labor even more effectively than against corporations and combinations of corporations.

It had taken a long time to reach this point of beatitude. But the consummation had been implicit in the Civil War and its consequences. First had come the time of gobble, made possible by the sudden disappearance of the planter opposition to the manufacturing interests in Congress. The Western farmer, often of moral New England origin, mistook his natural ally, the Southern slave owner, for an enemy; and while he was fighting to rid America from chattel bondage, the manufacturing interests ran away with the Republican Party. When the soldiers were setting out to stake that Western farm they had voted themselves (it was the least that was coming to them for having fought in the Wilderness or for having suffered the hell of Libby prison), the men who stayed at home were sniffing the breezes of the future. These men included Morgan, the banker; Armour, the packer; Jay Gould, railroad man and gambler; Carnegie, the industrialist, and countless others who resembled their more famous prototypes in intention, if not in ultimate success. The adopted party of these men, the Republican, was to have its new birth of freedom, inanely enough, as the "party of good crops." Robert Ingersoll called it that, even as it was betraying all the interests of the Western agrarians, in a speech that denounced the Democratic Party of the weevil and the Colorado beetle. And under the Republican ægis there flourished the many hosts of privilege, and America passed into the cynical seventies, the decade that saw the exposure of the Tweed Ring and the scandals of Crédit Mobilier. Panic came in 1873, induced by overbuilding of the West, and the business depression did not let up until crop failures in Europe and the closing of the Black Sea ports by the Russo-Turkish War raised the price of the American agricultural surplus. And in the seemingly more placid eighties, as William Allen White has said, evolving what might be termed the dialectical materialism of the beard, "... American men ... still were skulking behind the barricade of their whiskers ... so much sham and cupidity were rampant in the land that men did not dare to show their naked faces."

These hairy grandparents of ours were caught between two worlds and thus corrupted by the necessity of dividing allegiance between the pristine idealism of the party of Lincoln and the nascent industrialism. They were interested in just three things: high tariffs and allied favors to what was to become the ogre of Big Business; the uses of waving the "bloody shirt" in keeping the agrarian South from returning to the seats of political power (and this out of no great friendship for the freed slave); and the troublesome question of the currency. This last was the only subject upon which there could be two Republican opinions, and that was because silver and gold and the crops of the West never remained the same in relation to each other. In the matter of the tariffs and the protection of the Republican majority at the Southern polls, the rank and file of the party of Lincoln were of one accord. For a time the politics of grab reigned prosperously, in spite of Anti-Monopoly parties and the granger and greenback agitation. President Hayes checked the tide of privilege when he removed the Southern States from the grasp of the carpetbaggers; and the agitation for Civil Service Reform—or "Snivel Service," as the Stalwart politicians called it—struggled upwards in the eighties. But Carl Schurz and George William Curtis and the rest of the "man-milliners and carpet knights of reform" (so Roscoe Conkling christened them) could do little to modify fundamental injustices. Nor could the veterans of the social trenches—men like Peter Cooper and Wendell Phillips—do much more.

The Cleveland era in American history, which followed the darker days of Republican supremacy, was little more than a plateau on which social forces canceled each other. Cleveland himself championed no ism; he had no theory of government beyond a diurnal conception of duty and common sense learned in a preacher's household. He made the last stand for an idealism that was chained to no definite social philosophy, but merely to the abstract and tricky doctrine of Righteousness. But he symbolized an urge towards honesty in a society that had looked too long upon economic debauch, and that was shortly to look upon the rising sun of Progressivism. He left behind him a few ringing phrases; he denounced the "communism of pelf"; and his trenchant sentence aimed at the high-tariff men, "It is a condition which confronts us, not a theory," accurately pilloried the idiocy of abstracting from the pockets of the American consumer to pour a gigantic surplus into the national treasury. This surplus, made up largely of the overweening duties on imports, was to make President Harrison's one administration notorious for its billion-dollar disposal of pork. Most of it came out of the pockets of the farmer.

If Cleveland formulated no dynamic political credo, if he fashioned no Wilsonian doctrine of the New Freedom, if he made no La Follette speech of '97, he at least did not countenance monopoly. But he did very little constructively; the creation of the Interstate Commerce Commission in 1887, which marked the first success in the effort to get the railroads under the control of the people, was more the work of the small shipper and the farmer, irrespective of party affiliation, than it was the handiwork of any particular Cleveland democracy. "His Obstinacy," Grover of Buffalo, merely stood, a picture of touching and genuine moral protest, in the path of the Blaines, soft-voiced and devious; the Oakes Ameses, who could put stock where "it would do the most good"; the Randalls and the "Pig Iron" Kelleys of industrial Pennsylvania, with their everlasting prolongation of Civil War tariff levies that, even in the admission of Henry Clay Frick, the steel-master, put all the trumps of prosperity in the hands of the employers.

Cleveland, in the eighties and nineties, was the spearhead of a thrust that was less Democratic, in the Jacksonian sense, than it was of the Manchester liberal brand. Modern critics like to stress the alliance between Republicanism and *laissez faire,* but in truth the Republican Party is only for the free workings of Adam Smith's eighteenth-century, mercantile and hypothetically just God under circumstances that are favorable to the most wealthy segments of the population. The true apostles of *laissez faire* in the eighties and nineties were the Cleveland Democrats. Many of them were also followers of E. L. Godkin, the liberal editor of the *Nation,* who had the bad grace to sneer at the Populists and at the first critics of the cut-throat practices of the Standard Oil Company. And behind these anti-protective tariff men who believed that industry should take care of itself, raise its own infants, and bury its own dead, were the American disciples of Herbert Spencer, men like William Graham Sumner of Yale.

WILLIAM GRAHAM SUMNER has become a legend. Those who knew him, and those who studied under him, light up at recollection of days spent listening to this American pioneer in sociology. He was a great mind-opener in a day of great mind-openers; with Robert Ingersoll he helped give the *coup de grâce* to a theology that resisted to its last breath the onslaught of the evolutionists on the truth of *Genesis.* If we except personalities like Clarence Darrow, H. L. Mencken and Arthur Garfield Hays, who let their libertarianism remain in the emotional stage, Sumner must stand as the last great exemplar of the breed in the United States. And as a libertarian he stood between two dominant American forces, that of Charles Beard's "politics of acquisition and enjoyment," and its counter-principle, the force that made for the experiment in social democracy that came after 1904.

The most powerful of these forces—need we say it?—was the first, the one represented by men whose philosophy, when it was consciously formulated, derived, ironically enough, from the same source as Sumner's own: Herbert Spencer. But when Andrew Carnegie and Senator Nelson Aldrich, to name two representatives of this specific wing of the Spencerian parade, bit off the philosopher of evolution, they fixed upon its Darwinian phase, that of the struggle of species: they stressed the survival of the fittest, allied it to the Calvinistic doctrine of the elect, and had something perfectly congruous to the Presbyterian, the New England Puritan, and the Hamiltonian mind. The protective tariff, to these men and to their ally, William McKinley, seemed a logical and just instrument to be wielded by the elect in the interests of promoting the prosperity of the fittest. If good resulted for the top dog, the same good would seep down, in the form of increased wages, to the dog on the bottom. But Sumner, who also believed in the survival of the fittest, considered that *natural* evolution was the only evolution that was justified; interference with Adam Smith's Invisible Hand by man-made law only put emery in the works.

Thus Sumner, whose own political philosophy was firmly grounded in Spencer, came to cross lances with men who themselves flaunted the banner of the synthetic philosopher. A storm raged about him at Yale; he was continually annoying the "Pittsburgh millionaires" who made New Haven an educational stamping ground for their sons in the early years of the twentieth century; and when he denounced the acquisition of the Philippines and spoke caustically of the "conquest of the United States by Spain" two members of the Yale corporation, rich men, actually tried to put a muzzle on him. But this stubborn dissenter went his way, hitting right and left in his slow, methodical manner, always fighting fairly. Meanwhile, as he was moving out of political economy into the virgin field of sociology—an evolution that resulted in his magnificent overview of all societies that is established and documented in his *Folkways*—the Lester Wards, the John R. Commonses, the Richard Elys, the Henry Demarest Lloyds and allied souls stole the show. Sumner's libertarianism, his championship of complete *laissez faire* as against the status economy of the guild system of the Middle Ages, with no governmental interference whatsoever with natural laws of competition, was seen to have little grounding in the reality of 1890, no matter how desirable it may have been in the realm of the abstract. Sumner was, politically speaking, a solid rock whose fate it was to be ground to pieces between contending glaciers. He was caught between the champions of privilege, who rejected his free trade, and the social reformers, the anti-freedom-of-contract men, who demanded more and more governmental regulation, more and more of the State in business.

Sumner began as an Episcopal clergyman. He broke out of this in the period that witnessed the conquest of evangelism by Darwin. He began, too, as an admirer of certain portions of the Bill of Rights, and he never got over this early grounding in eighteenth-century doctrine. Always he stood for the "inalienable right" of "free speech." His theory of government was the old Jeffersonian one—"anarchy plus the street constable," but unlike Jefferson, he countenanced its grafting upon an industrial society. The rock of modern society, as he conceived it, was private property; he posited "the free man in the free society," an atom able to rise with ability. In this he was close, very close, to an American Humanist, Mr. Paul Elmer More, who has said that "to the civilized man, the right to property is more important than the right to life." And this "right to property" depends on the "freedom of contract" that has been guaranteed in the Bill of Rights and buttressed by the Fourteenth Amendment—an amendment which was devised, or so people were led to believe, to protect the emancipated Negro, not the capitalist.

The sacredness of freedom of contract and all the honored prerogatives of the free man in the free society—whereby the scales were weighted, as things were constituted in the America of the late nineteenth century, in favor of men like George Pullman and Henry Clay Frick—are argued in Sumner's *The Challenge of Facts* and *What Social Classes Owe to Each Other* with a cogency, a tough-fibered consistency, that cannot be gainsaid once the initial assumptions are granted. These assumptions seemed all too natural in the eighties and nineties, before the meaning of the census report of 1890 had sunk in; perhaps they seem all too natural to-day.

We have called Sumner a libertarian. Yet he did not believe in the "natural rights" of man, in the sense that Rousseau did. These rights—the right to a living, the right to the paternal care of the state—were, he argued, a hardship upon the "Forgotten Man" who was the good citizen, who paid his taxes, kept his house and business in order, exercised a due frugality, and raised his children to go in Roman ways of staunchness, decency and sobriety. Abandon *laissez faire,* said Sumner, and you force the superior man, the "forgotten man" who has no need of legislation, to shoulder "duties" when the logical time has come for him to enjoy rightfully the fruits of his labor and care. You penalize thrift and diligence, and ultimately make poverty desirable—since, by having nothing and expending no energy, the shiftless man can call upon the thrifty to "support" him.

All this sounds completely rational on the face of it. But, as it must seem to a disillusioned world, there is more trust in Sumner than in all of Rousseau. For the nature of power—the power of the "superior" man—is that it becomes corrupt; it seeks to entrench itself by fair means and foul; it will not observe the rules laid down by the libertarian rationalist. It obeys its own inner compulsion; it has laws of its own.

What balked Sumner as a political scientist was his inadequate definition of the State. Sensible as he was on most points, he failed to be realistic here. For what is government? It is, as Laski says, merely a function of that group or groups which are in a position to make the most effective demands upon it. Sumner wanted to devise laws to guarantee civil liberty against the tyranny of majorities. But he skimped ways and means, a matter in which he could have learned much from the principles of Matthew Stanley Quay, the Anti-Saloon League, and the protective-tariff lobby. Government, he failed adequately to see, is a fulcrum, not an entity—a fulcrum by which men in organized groups get predatory leverages which enable them to better themselves at the expense of the less powerful, the less wary, the less worldly sagacious. When he came to analyze specific uses and abuses of this leverage, Sumner saw clearly enough. He arraigned, for example, the rotten borough system of his adopted State of Connecticut, which enabled the small town of eighteenth- and early nineteenth-century building to dominate the larger city populations in politics. But he did not write as if he saw that government is, and always has been, merely a function of power. The hope that a "civilized minority"—a phrase which the Menckenites must have devised after a total immersion in Sumner—could throw up legal bulwarks against mob oppression was, even in the nineties, a forlorn hope, to say the best for it.

Meanwhile, during all the wars of Sumner's days as a political scientist and before, what was actually happening? By using the government as a fulcrum, the railroad men had gotten vast sums from the public treasury and vast acres from the public domain by legislative fiat such as the Pacific Railroad Act. Civil War currency legislation had enabled certain classes to use the government as a fulcrum to pry loose from the pockets of the small settler in the West cash that was not contemplated in the original mortgage papers. Such instances of currency legislation as the resumption of specie payments in 1879 (which Sumner approved), and the demonetization of silver in 1873, had decreased the number of dollars per capita in the land, and forced the settler to pay in dearer coin. By making secret agreements with the railroads—and what was this but exercising "freedom of contract"?—the oil and coal winners in the rebate wars of that early phase of *laissez faire* were enabled to squeeze out smaller, less powerful, or less crooked competitors. The protective tariff—"the biggest job" of all, as Sumner was perhaps the first to make known to the college generations of the eighties and nineties—was simply another flagrant example of using the government as fulcrum for a predacious wrench. In brief, the "ins" were "in" through politics, through original grants in colonial days, through preëmpting sites that were destined to become valuable and making their claims good under the law, through monopolizing natural resources, and so forth. These "ins," many of them, had once been "out," and they had fought wars and revolutions, had intrigued and bribed and cajoled, had broken treaties with the neighboring red men, to get "in."

I wish to be fair to Sumner. No one has flayed "jobbery," "the vice of plutocracy," with more effective epithets, with more forceful moral indignation, than this ex-clergyman. He did not believe in "the politics of acquisition and enjoyment" when the rules were voided. He considered that labor should take care of itself *by organizing;* in this he was a first-cousin of the syndicalists, and on the side of the future, as was his natural enemy in the nineties, the intransigent socialist, Daniel De Leon. "Industrial war," Sumner said with acumen in 1889, after the publication of Edward Bellamy's *Looking Backward* had emphasized the groanings of the industrial structure in the eighties, "is, in fact, an incident of liberty... a sign of vigor in society. It contains the promise of a sound solution." What he did not see was that labor, if it were to cope with court decisions, and with the "government by injunction" that was shortly to be employed against Debs, must perforce interfere by political pressure with the sacred "freedom of contract" that prevented minimum-wage legislation, fixed hours of labor, and so on. The single workman, without benefit of union, could not cope at the factory door with those who had wealth and stores to tide them over periods of distraught business, as Woodrow Wilson (who was just as much a libertarian as Sumner in his early days) came to realize when he walked out of Princeton into New Jersey politics. In other words, the "jobbery" of plutocracy, which Sumner gave many a verbal lacing, must be balanced by the "jobbery" of the underdog; in an industrialized world we must all live off each other, or not live at all. The answer to the "vice of plutocracy" was "jobbery for every one"—as Lester Ward, whose *Dynamic*

Sociology was put forth in 1883 as an answer to Herbert Spencer's *Social Statics,* perhaps realized. By this "jobbery," and by this alone, the "outs"—the small farmer and shipper, and the common laborer—could become, to some extent, "ins": rebates must be voided by interstate commerce legislation and regulation, as was attempted in 1887. The disinherited could, by combining, force a disgorging of the natural resources which the possessors had gone into politics originally to get; and just this happened, on a certain scale, in the days of Roosevelt's conservation legislation and administration.

But the libertarian that was Sumner stood by the old guns; he hoped to reverse the tide that was running viciously towards plutocracy, and restore primitive *laissez faire* and democracy. He did not see that the inevitable result of competition was combination *by means of jobbery.* In spite of his common-sense views on war, his intelligent analyses of the uses of dogma and "flags" (later to be incorporated into the *Folkways*), his sturdy objections to our irresponsible incursion into colonialism after the Spanish-American War (an incursion which, in William James's memorable phrase, caused the United States to "puke up its ancient soul"), Sumner wore his blinders—the "mores" of expansionist America had prevented him from taking an overview, in the manner of the philosopher, or identifying himself with one or another of the "going" concerns of plutocracy or social democracy, in the manner of the politician. He failed to realize that if you posit "the right to property" (and by this I do not mean to call into question the right of every man to his toothbrush) as the basis of society, you posit incentives to getting property, and jobbery is at once unleashed. The two are inseparable, now and forever.

In his later days, after a breakdown in health in the nineties had impelled him to confine himself more strictly to sociology—or "Sumnerology," as his students came to call it—the rugged libertarian came to see the problem of "freedom of contract" versus the status economy of a fixed society like that of the Middle Ages in broader perspective. "We see," he remarked in a late paper, "Mores of the Present and Future," "in the status and outlook of the present time, these facts: underpopulation of the globe and increasing control of natural forces give easier conditions for the struggle for existence. This means the most to those who have inherited the least. *It is, however, obviously a temporary advantage, for the human race will, in a few generations, find itself face to face with overpopulation and harder conditions."* Thus the old man brought the perspective of the æons he so loved to study to bear upon what he had himself written, as polemics, in his battles with the politicians of the eighties and nineties.

In one way, Sumner was a forerunner of the muckrakers of the next generation. His diagnoses of society agreed with theirs; his prescriptions did not. But his heart, if not his prescriptive logic, was in the right place; once he was convinced of the justice of his decision, he went stolidly ahead, in spite of university corporations, of pruderies in Prospect Street and even of the denunciations of powerful men like McKinley, whose demagogy about "the influence of the professors in some of our institutions of learning, who teach the science contained in books, and not practical business," was a javelin undoubtedly hurled at the head of Sumner. Academic freedom owes much to this man who refused to be budged by pressure, and it is scant cause for amazement that he has left his devoted disciples, such as A. G. Keller. Character is attractive to character, irrespective of logic.

The libertarian went into his last phase as he had lived all the other phases of his life, persistently avid for more facts, dogged to the end. In 1908, when he had lost the use of his right hand for some months, he trained himself to compose with his left. A laggard body was whipped on by a magnificent intellectual will. And a year later a great and stalwart spirit, author of "the first grand essay on the nature of human society ever written by an American," as Thomas Beer has said, died of his labors, an enemy to the end of fluffy white dogs, the white man's burden, and the mulcting of one's neighbors by law. His successor, Keller, carries on, adding women and house cats to the dogs of Sumner's maledictions, but otherwise fighting the lost battle of the "free man in the free society."

OF COURSE, during the nineties, it was not at all apparent to the commonalty that this battle of the free man in the free society had been lost; it is not apparent to most people now. We have become latterly accustomed, through reading such titles as *The Tragic Era, The Age of Hate, The Brown Decades, The Great Barbecue* and *The Gilded Age,* to sneer at William Dean Howells for choosing to portray in his novels "the smiling aspects of life that are the more American." The Gilded Age, we say, was vulgar, raffish and cannibalistic; it had no taste; it marked a national low in culture; decent people were swamped by the trends of the times. And so some of them were. But there were "smiling aspects" in the years leading up to and including the nineties, in spite of the growth of slums and the origin of "the submerged tenth," in spite of the evils of sweat shops and child labor, in spite of the heavy architecture of Richardson and the deliquescence of taste that spawned the blight of golden oak, antimacassar and what-not. When Julian Street and Booth Tarkington, to take two typical nostalgics, look back upon the nineties, they do not remember the red lining of the day's news, or the menace of corporate industry, or the oppression of the Southern share cropper and Middle-Border farmer. They do not remember unemployment, pauperism and bank failures. They do not recall books like Henry Demarest Lloyd's *Wealth Against Commonwealth* or Bellamy's *Looking Backward.* What they remember is a delightful way of life—the life of the small town in Meredith Nicholson's *Valley of Democracy* that extended from the Alleghenies to the treeless plains beyond Omaha and Kansas City. The average man got along very well by himself, in spite of labor troubles and the menace of anarchists of the deed such as Johann Most, or the cut-throat tactics of a Rockefeller. Small business men and doctors, lawyers and craftsmen, the good folk of Howells' novels and even the prototypes of the Magnificent Ambersons of Mr. Tarkington's belated creation, all of them lived in their roomy houses set about by lawns and maple trees. In the East the so-called petty bourgeoisie swarmed to the seashore in Summer. They read the popular books, from *Ben Hur* to Winston Churchill's early romances; they made a beginning at lawn tennis; baseball was widely played; they welcomed the bicycle; their sons raised chrysanthemum heads of hair and played football. In brief, they enjoyed themselves with the enjoyment of a blessed naïveté.

The traditional connotations of the nineties are, of course, golden, naughty and gay. They connote loitering on front porches and serenading and bouts of close harmony; and they were, as Thomas Beer has pointed out, a time of "primary sophistication" in letters. Perhaps the best way of describing them is to say that they were all things to all men. To Henry Mencken, watching the newsstands in Baltimore, they were "electric"—the electricity being furnished by foreign batteries as Percival Pollard brought home new geniuses from France and Germany, as Vance Thompson uncovered his French portraits, as Huneker ran through the seven arts, and as Zola and Tolstoi and the Morrison of *Tales of Mean Streets* introduced the spirit of realism that Howells liked to talk about. To the less intellectually avid citizen the period was one of happy sampling. The very songs of the nineties proclaim it to have been the true age of innocence. It was the time of "The Lark" and "The Purple Cow," the tandem bicycle and the leg-of-mutton sleeve. College poets were exploring the delightfully easy possibilities of French verse forms. So far as America was concerned, imperialism hadn't dawned. The gruff opposition of Grover Cleveland had postponed the gulping of Hawaii; and the more sinister implications of Rudyard

Kipling's jingo music, which was to stir the literate youth of the land as the decade ended, were unrealized in the mid-nineties. The American West was still a gleam in the mind of the small boy, and to the average citizen the significance of the vanishing frontier, which was to push Manifest Destiny across the Pacific, had not become obvious. The West was merely an excuse, to this average citizen, for the draughtsmanship of Frederick Remington, who was making the Indian and the cowpuncher familiar to the readers of the pleasant magazines of the period. These pictures of Remington were merely one facet of the high noon of the magazine illustrator. A. B. Frost was drawing his cracker-barrel sages and humorous bumpkins; Kemble was looking on the sunny side of Negro life in his darky types. Local color, in the hands of the illustrator, was as warm and genial and healthy as it was in the stories that had been sired by Bret Harte. And in the broad-shouldered, clear-eyed Gibson girl and the jutting-chinned Gibson man (built along the bumptiously adolescent lines of Richard Harding Davis) there was nothing but purest health. The next decade was to see a vogue for the book of the Gibson girl, until the glazed charms of Leyendecker's beauties riding in rickety airplanes were to pave the way for the exit of the clean line, and the entrance of the glucose enticements of the magazine cover nymph of to-day.

To ramble through the popular literature of the nineties that surrounded the pleasant draughtsmanship in the magazines, one would scarcely come to know there were troubles afoot. There was a smattering of native realism, and the taste for it was to have an abortive growth, but Harry Thurston Peck, who employed his off-hours in editing *The Bookman,* couldn't quite stomach *Jude the Obscure.* To him it was "the studied satyriasis of approaching senility." Culture was talked about in sepulchral tones by Hamilton Wright Mabie, a pale echo of Arnold who is remembered chiefly by Mencken's strictures; and William Dean Howells was growing mildly socialistic. The taste for foreign importations that went to make up Mr. Beer's "primary sophistication" proved as short-lived as the demand for native imitations of Zola and Flaubert. Theodore Roosevelt, turned literary commentator, was all for a specious Americanism in letters; *The Bookman* for February of 1896 proclaimed his emphatic, almost physical, concern for the patriotic note in his review of a text by Brander Matthews. This American note, when Roosevelt came to reveal it, was something along the lines of Longfellow's ballads; and it is hardly cause for wonder that Theodore Roosevelt was perturbed in the next decade by Upton Sinclair's *The Jungle* and Frank Norris's *The Octopus.*

But the deeper movements of the nineties, as no one sufficiently emphasizes outside the political biographies, were toward an abyss. These years were hungry years. In 1894 it was estimated that the number of tramps in the country had doubled since 1870; social wrongs were being agitated; Jane Addams opened her Hull House in Chicago in 1889; and large charity organizations—inevitable concomitants of the agitation by the socialists and the anarchistic followers of Johann Most—had made their appearance in the larger cities. To understand the starveling aspects of these years one could do no better than board a train (preferably one of George Pullman's new vestibule trains, for the sake of the contrast between progress and poverty) and travel to Chicago in the year 1893. If one will take the precaution to arrive early, and if one will remain through 1894, the succession of four events, explored and imagined through all their implications, will yield forth the secret of the decade. A little prescience, made easy by hindsight, a little posthumous crystal-gazing...and future and past become magically clear. We have only to listen to a historian quote some figures from the census of 1890; we have only to follow the bearish figure of Grover Cleveland to the fair grounds of the Columbian Exposition; we have only to mingle with those earliest sons of the wild jackass, the free silver hordes, as they vociferate in the Palmer House lobby, or complain of the lack of spittoons in the First

Methodist Church, where they have gathered to elect a permanent chairman. And as the year of 1894 comes and goes we have only to sniff into our nostrils the smoke from the burning trains in the Chicago railroad yards, and wait for the blanket injunction that will put an end to the Debs rebellion, quash the Pullman strike and incidentally create the Social Democratic (more familiarly known as the Socialist) Party of 1900.

It was on January 12, 1893, that a certain paper by Frederick J. Turner was read before the American Historical Association in Chicago. To a community a-quiver with preparations for the World's Fair, which was to prove to an excited and admiring country that a metropolis built on beef, grain and converging traffic lines could, nevertheless, make culture burgeon as never before, this was hardly remarkable; and probably few historians paid any attention to it. But the paper has been compared, in cultural significance, to Emerson's notable address on "The American Scholar," delivered long ago when wolves were howling beyond Fort Dearborn; and one of the highest compliments that has been paid John Bach McMaster, an older historian, has been that he *almost* hit upon the Turner theorem in the eighties. For once the stricture pronounced by Henry Adams—that "historians turned to the collection of facts as the geologist turned to the collection of fossils," with no attempt at interpretation—was wrong.

The Turner paper, called "The Significance of the Frontier in American History," contained in its title, no less than in its body, the suggestion of one of those fertilizing concepts that have so much to do with the way we dramatize ourselves. It meant simply that there was a shortage of free land, except in arid districts, in sight. The mobile, wayfaring American of the westward push would have to settle down, if not in 1893, at least by 1910 or 1920. To the sons of an isolationist America who passed down the midway at the World's Fair four months later to gape at the Duke of Veragua, Christopher Columbus's own descendant and representative at the Exposition that carried his name, the paper meant nothing in any conscious sense. But the crowd, too, as well as the paper, was symbolic of a turn in the tide. The America of extension was dying; the America of intension, symbolized by the swelling civic spirit that moved through perverted Græco-Roman channels into the creation of the synthetic marvels of the Exposition, was born on a national scale—but hardly in a form that would have pleased the philosophers of the eighteenth-century enlightenment.

The most eminent of these philosophers, Rousseau, had predicted that pioneer conditions would automatically produce simple democracy—government built on the delegation of authority by equal integers. But no one, unless it be the Italian Laria, had speculated on what a *moving* frontier might mean to a nation. To this question Professor Turner addressed himself. There was much suggestion of the part which open lands to the West had played in the development, or rather the continuity, of democracy in the United States. But the most significant item in the paper was as juiceless as a timetable: it consisted of the repetition of part of a bulletin issued by the Superintendent of the Census for 1890. The bulletin reported that settlements were now so scattered over the Western region that "there can hardly be said to be a frontier line."

This was not a remarkable fact in itself; other nations had gotten along without a ninety-eighth or a hundredth meridian. But the psychic damage of a hundred years of the wilderness safety valve was done; American thought was literally built on that land. Even Eastern Hamiltonians, such as Senator Aldrich of Rhode Island, derived much of their assurance from its presence; if the common man was discontented in New York or Pittsburgh, there was plenty of room for him elsewhere.

The West had been the *ignis fatuus* of America. Yet, in 1893, it was two short steps, in some cases only one step, away from the condition that Turner recognized as the end of pioneering. The primary stage of pioneer life, that of the Indian and the hunter, had finally come to an end when Geronimo and his Apaches were defeated in the Southwest and after General Nelson Miles had put down the last of the redskin revolts in the Dakotas. The second phase, that of the pastoral ranch life which so attracted the Roosevelt who was eventually to fail because he couldn't decide whether he was a Westerner or an Easterner, was still in existence—in spots. But nationally speaking, it was done; barbed wire and the railroad empire had cut across the Chisholm cattle trail; and the West that Teddy knew at Medora was on its way into the fiction of his friend, Owen Wister. In 1889 a starter's pistol sent the Oklahoma land rush on its way, and "rugged individualism" was compelled at last to fall back upon Herbert Hoover's favorite phraseology—that of the rule-bound track meet.

Beyond the hunting and the pastoral stages, Professor Turner recognized two agricultural phases that preceded the final Dead Sea of central manufacturing organization. The first of these phases, that of unrotated crops of corn or wheat, was already disappointing the settler in his sod hut on the dry plains of Kansas or Nebraska; but both phases—this, and the individual intensive farming that grows up in its stead—were to have a tenacious, unintegrated, unbridled life before the Farm Board theorists were to make unsuccessful primary attempts to bring the farmer into reciprocal relationship with the national industrial orbit.

THE tribulations of the border farmer were made palpable to Chicagoans with the gathering, on August 1, 1893, of a free-silver convention in their midst. To it flocked the sons of the West whom Joseph Medill's *Tribune* persisted in calling wild, if not demonstrably insane. The chief butt of Mr. Medill's urban ridicule was "Bloody Bridles" Waite, the Populist Governor of Colorado, whose welcome to Chicago was a ribald cartoon showing him spurring a startled horse (who doubtless believed his oats depended on the gold standard) through a stream of gore, and waving a long sword on which was inscribed "Free Silver." Although this incendiary had proclaimed "our weapons are the ballot and the honest count," the *Tribune* and the *Evening Post* had marked him for a revolutionist dog. "...It is better infinitely that blood should flow to the horse bridles than our national liberties be destroyed," Waite had proclaimed; and the *Tribune,* in answer, placed at its mast-head: "The horse's bridle—it shall and must be preserved bloodless." In this the *Tribune* paralleled the sarcasms of Charles A. Dana's New York *Sun.*

Waite was a symbol of the rising Populist forces. With him, at Chicago, were other Populists: Carl Browne, "a wild-eyed crank all the way from Bloody Gulch or Dead Man's Hollow"; Ignatius Donnelly, the Minnesota romancer who had grown old in the service of fiat money; Jacob Coxey, who, with Browne, would shortly upset and amuse a country with his petition in boots to Washington; General James B. Weaver, who had carried the young Populist standard in 1892; and, not least, the musical William Jennings Bryan, then known as a rising free-trader. Predictions of dire starvation were heard in the Palmer House lobby, where an argument among three or four would quickly turn into a harangue before a hundred. Carter Harrison, Chicago's obliging mayor, greeted the Populists by calling them lunatics, but it was obvious that he meant it well. "Some of you may be wild," he admitted, "but such lunatics as you are have been in the world since the flood, and conservative money-bags have railed against you and your ideas." And Mr. Harrison showed his complete sympathy with the followers of Waite by scenting a British plot: "...When in a few years [after 1849] California began to send gold abroad, England was about to demonetize gold and make silver the money of the world, and yet to-day when you propose to make silver do the work of the world you are called lunatics." Meanwhile, outside the Methodist Church in which the silverites had gathered for Harrison's welcome, the wags were hawking parodies of the silver literature; their pamphlets demanded the free coinage of copper, nothing less.

The silverites talked and wrangled; "white heads were shaken and snowy beards were wagged," and demands were sent up to the skies for "the white metal." The reporters made it a symphony in white. Then the gathering of "ex-statesmen" (as the *Tribune* called them) broke up. On August 4, Governor Waite of Colorado "hung up his bridle, put away his bucket of blood and went out to the fair." Carl Browne, flourishing a rusty sword, and flaunting Indian buckskins which had paid "no tariff tax," carted his strange wagon out to the lake front to set up his "financial panorama"—a mechanism of fourteen oil paintings, done by his own hand, that "gave an insight into the great financial conspiracy of 1861-65." The pictures must have impressed Coxey, the quarry owner from Massillon, Ohio, for henceforward Coxey and Browne were teamed in their efforts to save the country from the bloated bondholders.

It is easy to deride the Populists, who were later to pool forces with Bryan and the Democrats in 1896. Historians have made it a fashion to laugh at their apostolic gestures, their Western *brio,* their vituperative condemnation of the idle rich whose châteaux, designed by Richard Hunt, lined the main thoroughfares of the "gold bug" capital, New York. But behind conventions, such as that presided over by "Bloody Bridles" Waite in Chicago, was a reality that could not be scoffed away. The gathering of the silver forces in the city of the World's Fair had no immediate relevancy to the political situation, since Cleveland had hardly assumed office, and there was no ticket to be put in the field. But the irony visited upon the heads of Waite and his brethren by the urban press was evidence of a growing rift in an America to which "class" distinctions were supposedly anathema. The panic of 1893 was already a dismal fact, made dramatic to Chicagoans at this very moment by the failure of the packer and speculator, John Cudahy; and the growing agitation for the repeal of the Sherman Silver Purchase Act of 1890 was frightening the silver miners of Colorado, and the farmers all over the West and South.

The miners had the more palpable reason to be fearful. For when India had closed her mints to silver, and when the European countries had abandoned bimetallism, the silver balance had turned against the United States; the Treasury had become the only market to which the miners might take their product. The Sherman Act insured the purchase of 4,500,000 ounces of the metal each month—practically the entire output of the mines. Remove this market, and ruin stared the silver owners in the face.

The farmers' reason for fearing a repeal of the enacting clause of the Silver Purchase Act was more complex. With them, it was 1789 all over again; the peasant fighting for freedom from economic bondage to absentee controllers. Their troubles dated back to the Civil War, which had effectively scotched Southern agrarianism as a power and made the road clear for the development of a different sort of agrarianism in the West. The Homestead Act, passed in the sixties, portioned out to every willing Union soldier a homestead of one hundred and sixty acres. With the rush to the plains went a crying need for capital, and no sooner had a young man gained clear title to his acres than he was forced to mortgage them to Eastern and foreign creditors. Industry boomed after the war; the railroads became earth-hungry monsters: expansion was in the air. The floods of money which the war had loosed upon the country went into the building of the new West; and the important thing was that the money was cheap.

The Civil War had more than doubled the country's supply of dollars, and the breed of smart men who had stayed home from the fighting reaped the benefit. When deflation set in, the smart men were in the driver's seat. A peculiar situation favored the creditor class, for when industry was growing, when expansion was more firmly in the saddle than ever before, the gold mines of the world became positively niggardly. Simple figures tell the story: in 1866 the gold mines of the world produced metal worth $129,614,000, while in 1890 the figure had shrunk to $118,848,700. During this period the United States had seen the specie resumption of 1879, designed to liquidate the greenbacks; but, more important, the annual increase in the American population had almost doubled—more and more people pressing upon the land and reaching, nay, straining, for the valuable gold dollar. The act of 1873 had, as we have seen, demonetized silver, and by 1878 the number of dollars per person in the country was half what it had been in 1865. The debtor class, the farmers of the Missouri Valley and elsewhere, who had stocked their lands, built homes and planted orchards on borrowed money, found itself ground between two millstones: that of the pressing creditor and that of the disappearing dollar bill. Never was there more need of an "elastic" currency. As the mortgages fell due, and as the productivity of the silver mines of the Western country increased, and as gold dwindled to the tune of a mounting population, the farmers began to work out the equation. The answer, logical enough in terms of the given situation, was free silver, "the dollar of our daddies," the "honest dollar." So rapid was the increase in American silver production—from some eleven million dollars' worth in 1865 to fifty-seven million in 1890—that two acts, the Bland-Allison of 1877 and the Sherman of 1890, were thrown as sops to the clamorous West.

The seventies, eighties and nineties saw a growth of Grangers, Greenbackers, Farmers' Alliances and Populists, all pointing to the tremendous Bryan push of 1896, as more mortgages—the twenty year variety—fell due. Meanwhile prices had been falling for a generation. At the beginning of the nineties corn was selling at ten cents a bushel in Kansas; it was cheaper to burn than coal. The cry "ten-cent corn and ten-per-cent mortgages," went up. The sanguine hopes of the early eighties, when the first concentrated attack on the "Great American Desert" of Western Kansas and Nebraska was made, were turned to gloom as the successive droughts parched the grain, and as the snows piled up and froze the cattle. A by-stander at the Missouri bridge at Omaha in 1890 might have counted thousands of creaky covered wagons—going east! Only seventeen counties in Kansas maintained their original population when Mary Ellen Lease, the Carrie Nation of the Populists, announced that her home State had better stop raising corn and start raising hell. The towns suddenly seemed all overbuilt; farms were put up for sale because of delinquent taxes. In the South the share cropper found himself in similar trouble; he had given the storekeeper a lien on his crop, and was finding it impossible to meet his obligations and make a living profit.

Populism has been called "crude," even by Westerners like William Allen White. Just why, it is difficult to determine. Jerry Simpson may have gone without socks (although this has been denied), and Senator Peffer of Kansas may have worn incredible whiskers. And the campaign slogans may have abounded in admonitions to "rob the plutocrat who puts chains and shackles around your limbs," to crush the "Rothschilds," the "gold bugs," "the bloated bondholders" and the "money power." But crude as all this may have been, it was no more crude than the monkey dinners of the Eastern rich, the social-secretary fandango of Ward McAllister and the antics of Harry Lehr. All America was crude.

But, as Louis Hacker has perhaps been the first to point out, the farmers were at least "modern." They may have formed their alliances in schoolhouses behind locked doors, with grips, passwords and the rest of the mummery beloved of the American joiner, but their political platforms were evidence of sound thinking. Discount their repetition of "Coin" Harvey's fallacious theories of money, discount their silver panacea, and still the Populist platforms did the spade work for the social thinking of the Rooseveltian decade. The Southern Farmers Alliance, meeting in December of 1889, at St. Louis, adopted a set of resolutions, in which the Northwestern Alliance concurred, that called for the free coinage of silver, abolition of national banks, an expanded currency, government ownership of railroads and telegraphs, prohibition of trading in grain futures, and a limitation of revenues to legitimate expenses. This last was an attack on the protective tariff. In addition, the Southern Alliance advocated a sub-treasury plan which hinted at government subsidy for agriculture. This plan was a scheme for financing agricultural marketing and for granting short-term credits with government funds. Government warehouses and elevators were to store "non-perishable" products, such as grains, tobacco, cotton and wool—and the farmers were to get certificates of deposit. These certificates of deposit were then to be used as collateral for legal tender notes up to eighty per cent of the market price of the products stored.

Here was a plan to set up a commodity basis for credit. It would have removed the farmer's dependence on gold for the fixing of prices; it would have freed him from the domination of Eastern bankers; it would have handed over the surplus accruing from the protective tariff to the farmer as credit—and thus would have righted an old wrong. It would have been a "job," as William Graham Sumner might have said, but it would have canceled the jobbery of the manufacturers.

Later Populist resolutions demanded a graduated income tax, a postal-savings bank, government loans on real estate, the popular election of United States Senators, the initiative, the referendum, the Australian ballot, a single term for the President, the enforcement of an eight-hour law for government employees, the abolition of private detective agencies and restriction of immigration. Surely, the Populists were on the side of the Rooseveltian and the Wilsonian future. But the concentration on the one issue of free silver, which the heightened tension of 1896 brought about, spelled eclipse to the Populist thinking for seven or eight years, and it was not until after the Spanish-American War that it began to sink in, so far as the majority of the electorate was concerned.

As THE farmers were howling for justice, and capturing the government of half a dozen farm States, Jacob Coxey went home to Massillon, Ohio, from Chicago, and Carl Browne followed him. A *beau geste* was in the making, and it was to have an important issue in its repercussions after Debs and the American Railway Union joined the Pullman Company employees in the strike of 1894.

When Coxey went to Chicago he was already an ingrained reformer. But he was also a well-to-do business man, worth about $200,000. As a boy he had worked in the rolling mills; later he became a dealer in scrap iron. In 1881 he walked out of the ranks of labor and purchased a quarry, from which he prepared sand for use in steel and glass works. He also became the owner of a Kentucky stock farm, and made a hobby of raising blooded horses.

But Coxey didn't go back on his early affiliations. His affluence, which was sufficient to make him the best of gold bugs, did not compromise his sympathies; he remained, and still remains in 1932, a partisan of the underdog. Tradition was behind him here, for his father had belonged to the Greenback wing of the Democratic Party, and in 1876, when the Democrats nominated Tilden, the young Coxey became a definite Peter Cooper Greenbacker. In 1885, seeing want all about him, he ran for the State senate of Ohio on a money-inflation issue. It was only natural that, with the rise of the People's Party, Coxey should write himself down a Populist.

Coxey in the nineties had his own program. He became sponsor of the Good Roads Association, proclaiming a demand for a Good Roads Bill that would require the Secretary of the Treasury to issue five hundred million dollars in legal tender notes to be spent on good highways. The work was to be done under the Secretary of War: depression, *c'est la guerre*. Workers were to be employed at a dollar and a half per eight-hour day (Coxey tied one idealistic notion to another), and twenty million were to be spent each month. He predicted an end to the depression should his ideas be put into operation. When city reformers objected that the bill favored the country districts, Coxey retired to his study. He would work it out along equitable lines, and the result was his Non-Interesting-Bearing Bond Bill, which would authorize any State, county, or township that needed public improvements to issue non-interest-bearing bonds to the extent of half the assessed value of the property within the locality's limits. These bonds were to be deposited with the Secretary of the Treasury as security for legal-tender notes, which, in turn, were to be put to use in paying for the construction of roads, courthouses and schools. The principal of the loan was to be repaid without interest by taxes, and the legal-tender notes were to be retired as the tax installments went into the treasury.

Coxey, in his own way, was thus a practical man. He had a plan—and a plan not so different from the ones acted upon by impeccable folk in the present period of depression. He wanted to make buildings the basis for money, as banks, since his time, have made trade acceptances the basis for money. But there was a catch in it under the financial dispensation that pertained in the days before the Federal Reserve System was inaugurated, or the Aldrich-Vreeland Currency Bill passed. Coxey not only flouted the reigning metaphysics of gold, but of all metals, silver included. His scheme was flawed, given the psychology of man fiduciary, because the additional money he would put into circulation would have no gold coverage; it would be added to the stock that was already an "endless chain" of buckets dipping into our gold reserve; and Cleveland and his Secretary of the Treasury, Carlisle, can hardly be blamed for having none of it. Coxey, however, cared not a whit for psychological objections.

The quarry owner's ideas were in process of formation when he met Carl Browne in Chicago at the silver convention of 1893. The crank from Bloody Gulch flaunted his Mexican silver half-dollar buttons, and something in the Coxey who named his son "Legal Tender" responded to this theatrical streak. Browne had been a cartoonist, printer, editor, politician, rancher and labor agitator; he provided the demagogic touch that Coxey needed to dramatize his ideas. With Dennis Kearney, Browne had agitated against Chinese labor in San Francisco; he was a soap-boxer of the American breed, set apart from the socialist exhorter of the metropolitan areas by his circus appeal, his use of the telling Barnumism. Coxey invited him to spend the winter of '93-94 with him.

The subsequent marriage of true minds provided the nineties with their finest comic show. When he was in California, Browne had seen the marches of "industrial armies"—bands of itinerant laborers who made no bones about commandeering freight trains to go from one job to another. The idea took root in Coxey's mind. "Browne," he said, "we will send a petition to Washington with boots on."

The petition, of course, had no immediate effect, although Coxeyism, underneath all the hilarity it produced, stirred good souls to fear. Harry Thurston Peck, historian of the period, reported a thrill of horror at the "criminals and vicious characters" in Coxey's hordes, and repeated in his *Twenty Years of the Republic* the slander that "Coxey's prowling tramps" were responsible for "theft, rape and sometimes murder [that] marked the trail of this new *jacquerie*." Coxeyism was, as a matter of record, quite harmless, and the Coxey leaders were comically arrested upon their arrival in Washington from Ohio for treading on the White House lawn. The papers had played the march up; for every two sloggers in Coxey's ranks there was at least one reporter. Browne had imposed upon Coxey certain witless "theosophical" ideas, and the army marched under the banner of the "Commonweal of Christ."

The notion of a petition in boots, or a petition from the

brake beams and the blind baggage, took rapid hold in the West, among the laborers who were the forerunners, in spirit, of the I.W.W. Soon after Coxey's march, industrial armies had set out from Los Angeles, from San Francisco, from Montana and from the far Northwest. The host of Charles T. Kelly, with which the young Jack London marched for part of the distance, beat its way from San Francisco to Iowa, floated down the Missouri, and eventually wound up in depleted form in the national capital. Fry and Galvin's group roistered through Texas; General Hogan stole trains in Montana, and "Jumbo" Cantwell's legionnaires marched from the lumber camps of Washington and Oregon. In the East, armies that bore Marxian stigmata instead of the frontier stripes set out from Boston, Rhode Island and Connecticut. British observers trembled for the safety of the Republic as all these itinerant job-hunters approached Washington, but Coxey, Kelly, "Jumbo" Cantwell and the other Westerners, who were in the great majority, would have been extremely loath to proclaim Communism. Coxey was just a belated Jacksonian, a libertarian even as Sumner, one of the "have-less" folk who were struggling with the "have-mores" for a place in the beaming middle-class sun.

Nothing definite came out of the *beau geste* of Coxeyism; there were never more than between five hundred and a thousand industrial marchers in the environs of Washington at any one time. But Coxey's march dramatizes the hard times of the 1893 panic; and the results of the basic injustice of a system which bred "tramps and millionaires" can be glimpsed nowhere better than in a study of Coxeyism. And there was one portent in the marches of the industrial armies that spelled disaster for Eugene V. Debs. That was the practice, in the West, of granting injunctions against train stealing—enjoining laborers from theft of freight cars that were in the hands of Federal receivers of railway property. This might be laughed off as a bit of charming supererogation, to say the least, but it established a vicious precedent. Richard Olney, Cleveland's Bostonian Attorney General, was to blame for these injunctions, just as he was to blame for his acquiescence, in the summer of 1894, when a blanket injunction was issued against Debs and the American Railway Union. "Government by injunction" was in the making during the flutter of Coxeyism; it provided one of the great grievances that helped build up the socialist strength in the epoch of 1900-12.

BEHIND Coxeyism was a familiar down-spiral of depression. The panic of 1893 had officially commenced with the failure of the National Cordage Company in May of '93, just when all America was rejoicing in the symbol of her might, the Chicago World's Fair. The collapse of the cordage company was the immediate cause of the Stock Market panic, but earlier failures in London, which had reacted upon the American railroads which depended on foreign capital, had made the depression inevitable. In its western phases the resultant Coxeyism was an apt illustration of the newly enunciated Turner theorem: the frontier no longer provided a safety valve for the wanderer in Paul Bunyan's tracks, and this wanderer was compelled to turn east to Washington for help. The end of Coxeyism, so far as the public prints were concerned, came with the Pullman strike; the attention of the country was diverted by this, and Coxey lapsed into a silence of some thirty-seven years before he was again to bob up, in another period of stress, as mayor of Massillon, Ohio, and a candidate for President.

The Pullman strike broke out in May of 1894, after George Pullman had tried to reduce the wages of his workers without effecting a corresponding reduction in the rents charged in the company's model town. Debs's American Railway Union had won a wage dispute in April with James J. Hill of the Great Northern; it was feeling its oats. So, when Pullman refused to dicker with his employees who had joined the Debs union, the American Railway leaders were affronted. By June, Debs, young and idealistic, a man who couldn't be bought, had called a sympathetic strike of the whole brotherhood; the union refused to handle trains to which Pullman cars were attached. Lawlessness, whether provoked by the railroads, the police or the laboring men, broke out in Chicago; trains were burned; Richard Olney, fresh from his primary experiments in the use of the injunction, was listening to company lawyers who were informing him that the United States mails were being jeopardized, and forthwith an order went out to Federal authorities in Chicago to obtain an injunction against Debs and his board of strategy. The Attorney General's decision that the strike was in violation of the Sherman Anti-Trust Act which prohibited restraint of trade between the States was followed by a court decree. Then came the despatching of Federal troops to the Chicago area by Grover Cleveland as Debs violated the injunction by persisting in the strike. Altgeld, the Illinois Governor who had pardoned the living Haymarket anarchists, let out a characteristic roar. What right had Cleveland to interfere with States' rights? Altgeld had plenty of troops in the State militia to take care of violence. But in spite of Altgeld's remonstrance, the Federal troops remained from July 4 to July 20, and the strike was broken. Debs, found guilty of contempt, was packed off to the Woodstock Jail.

Here is an irony. When Debs went to jail he was a Populist sympathizer, an "old" American. But the government was about to give him leisure for an education; it was to make him a socialist. A hero to his class, Debs attracted worshipers from all points of the compass; Woodstock became a shrine. Victor Berger hurried down from Milwaukee, carrying under his arm a copy of *Das Kapital*. Debs read and pondered it; he read Kautsky and Edward Bellamy. The enforced schooling under government auspices did not immediately make him an orthodox Marxist, for, on his release, he threw his influence to Bryan. But when the Democrats went down to defeat in 1896, carrying with them the hosts of Populism who had joined them, Debs decided that the old parties were anathema. He gave up Bryan and devoted his energy to creating a socialist front for 1900.

As 1896 approached, the end of Populism was in sight. The silver "heresy" obscured all the other issues raised by the earlier Populist platforms. A campaign of fanned hate, with Bryan painted as a puppet in the hands of Altgeld, "the anarchist," and Debs, "the revolutionist," and with Mark Hanna savagely caricatured as "Dollar Mark," blurred all the social thinking done by the Populists. People trembled as Election Day approached; business was done on contingent terms, with promises hingeing on McKinley's success. Labor was intimidated; the small bank depositor feared for his savings. But, more important, the depression was reaching its state of balance at the bottom. A new method in metallurgy—the cyanide process for extracting gold cheaply from low-grade ores—was even then providing the expanded currency which Bryan was demanding; only it was in terms of gold, not silver. The Rand goldfields in South Africa and the Klondike deposits were shortly to end the famine and provide an even more "elastic" currency. Crop failures abroad increased the value of the American farmer's products, and the Populist demands seemed less urgent. But in spite of "Boy Bryan's defeat," valuable social thinking had been done, and young men's imaginations had been stirred. A La Follette in Wisconsin, a U'Ren in Oregon, a Cummins in Iowa, would remember the Populist years. The Progressives of 1900-12 would pick up the dropped planks of the Alliance political organizations, first in single states, then nationally. In the next decade, after an Indian Summer of Plutocracy, the unrest of the farm border would seep into the upper reaches of the middle class. But first would come a consolidation of business under McKinley to scare people who had resisted the revolt of the agrarians to the last inch in 1896. The middle class as a whole would see itself squeezed in the vise of trust-and-labor union. Then, and only then, would other sections of it march to war with its agrarian wing.

CHAPTER TWO

Windows on the New Century

☆

WILLIAM JENNINGS BRYAN may well have felt that the two Scotchmen on the Rand in South Africa, Forrest and MacArthur, who discovered the process for extracting gold cheaply from low-grade ores, had played a nasty trick on the silver cause. But Bryan was not forced to go without an issue for 1900, although it was not the precise issue he would have preferred. He had shown great ability at scenting out and dramatizing the grievances of rural America; if he had been able to combine this with a genuine appeal to the city proletariat, if he had been able to hold men like Debs in line, he might have achieved his fond dream of leading a righteous nation from the White House. As it was, he showed genuine insight in knowing when to subordinate even such a favorite of his as free silver. His course leading up to the campaign of 1900 was equivocal, and it is an open question to-day whether he deliberately went against his conscience in order to preserve an issue for that campaign. The pending treaty of Paris, which was officially to end the Spanish-American War, provided for the taking over of the Philippines. McKinley, after praying all night for guidance, as he later said, was for annexation; so were Lodge and Whitelaw Reid, owner of the New York *Tribune*. But an impressive body of public opinion, both Mugwump and Democratic, was chary of the prospective incursion into the colonial ways of Great Britain. From Texas came the magniloquent voice of Joe Bailey, calling for the preservation of the "old Republic." Down in Princeton Grover Cleveland spoke caustically from his retirement against annexation. Carl Schurz and Moorfield Storey, petulant Mugwumps, both of them, denounced the business of shepherding recalcitrant islanders who wished to be free. Bryan was chary of "imperialism," too, but there is at least a suspicion that he was not averse to playing politics with the situation to further his own public fortunes.

Whether with sophistry or from genuine conviction that the war must be ended at all costs, Bryan hastened to Washington to persuade his Democratic colleagues of the Senate to ratify the treaty with Spain, and allow the election of 1900 to decide our ultimate disposition of the Eastern islands. Not that he necessarily wanted imperialism to replace free silver as the issue for 1900; he was still chasing the sixteen-to-one phantom. But after the ratification, which Senator Hoar thought might have been prevented with a little oral aid from Bryan, the Commoner still continued to speak against retention of the islands. And in the convention of 1900, when he saw the way the wind was blowing on the silver issue, he accepted the situation which he had himself helped to create, and "anti-imperialism" was named as the foremost plank of the Democratic platform.

Thus, where free silver had been the "cowbird" of 1896 (to use Henry Demarest Lloyd's phrase), imperialism became the cowbird of 1900. Although he wished to preserve the Philippines from Spain, old Senator Hoar of Massachusetts, a Republican in the real sense of the word, lamented with some of his Democratic rivals the passing of traditional America. Others of his party, however, were vastly satisfied. Albert J. Beveridge, not yet a Progressive, not yet a historian with a true understanding of Lincoln, looked with immense, cocky and portentous satisfaction upon the scene as the new century opened. He glowed with the thought that Manifest Destiny, *our* Manifest Destiny, had crossed the Pacific with the acquisition of the Philippines; the twentieth century, he remarked, would be distinctively American. And Theodore Roosevelt and Henry Cabot Lodge, filled with the spirit of Mahan's navalism, purred with Beveridge. But up in Boston, William James, for once denying the implications of his pragmatic philosophy, was complaining that the United States was bolting the highway of its historic destination, and William Vaughn Moody was suffusing the fierce stanzas of his "Ode in Time of Hesitation" with the same complaint. Mark Twain, too, growled his hatred of the imperial mode. The "old" American lived on.

But the old American couldn't do much good. The election was run off; McKinley and the Rough Rider, Theodore Roosevelt, won all but four States outside the South. Debs, campaigning for the first time on the socialist ticket, polled some 95,000 votes. Imperialism being the paramount issue of the Democrats, the minor planks of their platform—those condemning monopoly and urging the direct election of Senators—were little heeded. In any case, the majority seemed content to string along with the advance agent of prosperity who had really made good on his 1896 prospectus; and the threat of Populism, with its sinister implications of government control of the railroads and banking, was laid away in a temporary shroud.

If the farmer was satisfied, Big Business was more so. And labor, by and large, was willing to gamble on the success of business. John Mitchell, President of the United Mine Workers, admitted that the wage earner had now reconciled himself to the fact that he must remain a wage worker until the end of his life; all the laborer asked for was a compensation commensurate with his work. Gompers and trade unionism were in the ascendancy; labor combinations in New York City and in Chicago were becoming a racket. Senator Hanna announced shortly that coöperation was henceforth to be the order of the day in the relations between business and the working man; and industrial leaders could offer the sign of the Full Dinner Pail to those who questioned Mr. Hanna's prophetic gift. There seemed some point to Mr. Hanna's prognostication when the anthracite coal strike of 1902, so pregnant with the possibility of disorder, was finally settled by arbitration.

At first Senator Hanna semed afraid of the "crazy man," Roosevelt, but the Progressivism of the Spanish War hero failed to come to any significant bloom during the first term. And before McKinley was shot, business had a President in the White House who was virtually a man sent from God. Even if Mark Hanna couldn't "shuffle and deal him like a deck of cards," the psychic bond between king-maker and king was too strong to be disrupted by either conscience or Constitution. The President's insincere protests about the trusts, for instance, were to be swallowed with large cupfuls of salt; they meant nothing; and James B. Dill, author of the New Jersey trust laws which enabled business to get around the intent of the Sherman Act, knew as much. Like others of his breed (and he proved to be a good prophet), James B. Dill believed that combination in the industrial field was inevitable; laws could not stop it. He, and E. H. Harriman, the railroad man, and Nelson Aldrich, Morgan's floor broker in the Senate, were perhaps the wisest realists of their day. As surely as Karl Marx himself, they had a thorough understanding of historic processes. For their brains, for their ability to guess right, they deserve a certain quality of admiration; in any case, they are more appealing than the Bryan who would permit quibbling to preserve an issue.

But these realists might have been equally perspicacious and fought on the other side. It was true enough, as James B. Dill said, that trusts were inevitable, that competition was the mother of combination, and that all a "sovereign" people could do was to bring combinations into social use. But the real thinking to be done was, and is, along the lines of social use; and the realists of the industrial world of 1900 were concerned not at all with any such thinking.

There were men, however, who tried to solve the problem as the nineteenth century merged into the twentieth. Their discontent took queer forms; it cut across many philosophical lines. Very often it made no sense at all except as pure protest. It looked back to Jefferson and Jackson; it looked across the ocean to the primitive communism of Tolstoi. It dallied with De Leonism, an intransigent brand of socialism that had gone its own fiery way when Debs and Victor Berger and Morris Hillquit commenced to think in terms of immediate objectives, such as shorter hours of work. It even looked forward to no government at all, following Kropotkin and the anarchists. Altogether, discontent at the opening of the new century made a crazy-quilt pattern.

And the largest, most vocal, element in this discontent had been schooled in the theories of the farm border of the nineties. As Professor Turner had suggested, we were a nation that was not only in one transitional stage, but in many simultaneous transitional stages. Class distinctions had not been drawn in hard and fast lines; because of this the prophets of discontent sounded a Babel of conflicting tongues.

But in spite of its lack of common objectives, the movement that was generated in the nineties, only to broaden and deepen under pressure of the business concentration of 1900, can at least be summed up as neo-democratic. Behind this movement were three American theorists of the nineteenth century, Henry George, Henry Demarest Lloyd and Edward Bellamy. There were, of course, as I have suggested, the foreign factors—Marxian socialism, brought to America by the German immigrants; the agitation of the anarchists, which had been domesticated in the New World by Johann Most, Alexander Berkman and Emma Goldman; but these importations from abroad merely gave minor twists to the forces running towards the La Follettian conception of social democracy. They failed, in themselves, to capture very much of the national imagination. Nor did the spectacle of the Fabian Society, founded in London in 1884, achieve anything more definite in the way of American influence than to open a few liberal minds to the programs offered, respectively, by Bryan, Roosevelt, La Follette and Wilson. The writings of Sidney and Beatrice Webb, of Graham Wallas, the Utopian novels of Wells, and the play-polemics of Shaw did help promote leagues for industrial democracy and agitation for the use of the Best Minds in politics, but the ground had been prepared for the English seed by the Populists of the nineties.

Henry George, however, did capture the imagination of an impressive group. His *Progress and Poverty,* published in 1879, offered a startling, deep-searching analysis of the processes of preëmption and exploitation under a system that was incongruously combining a conquest of the frontier with an industrial revolution. Given its definitions, this book seems to me a matter of incontrovertible logic. It became the Bible of an able and vociferous lot of men: Joseph Fels, the millionaire manufacturer of Fels Naphtha soap; Tom L. Johnson, the traction monopolist who became an enemy of the very process by which he had amassed his own fortune; Peter Witt, the Populist who came under the spell of Johnson; Brand Whitlock, humanitarian and artist; U'Ren, the shy Cornishman of Oregon, and many others. Out of it the Single Tax movement grew to dignified proportions in the stirring years before the World War. Even to-day the Single Tax has its adherents who cling to *Progress and Poverty* as the Christian Scientists cling to the canon of Mrs. Eddy.

Henry George was born in Philadelphia in 1839 of English and Scotch antecedents. Tiring of school at the age of 15, he shipped on a schooner bound for Melbourne and Calcutta. The conditions in British India were among the first examples of the results of landlordism to prey upon his fundamentally idealistic and religious mind; but the germ of *Progress and Poverty* may be traced more definitely to a conversation George had with an old miner aboard a schooner off the Pacific Coast. The miner was uneasy about the growing problem of Chinese labor. But what harm could it do, George asked, if the Chinese working men were herded off to the cheap diggings? "No harm now," said the miner, "but wages will not always be as high as they are to-day in California. As the country grows, as people come in, wages will go down, and some day or other white men will be glad to get those diggings the Chinamen are now working."

In his lifetime George was to see the California of the splendid idle forties transformed much as the miner had predicted. Ten years after the death of the evangel of the Single Tax, which occurred in October of 1897, California had notoriously become the worst labor State in the country. And before George's eyes, as he lived, was enacted the drama of the Southern Pacific in State politics—a drama that Frank Norris later packed into *The Octopus.* Before the completion of the first transcontinental railroad, when demand for space around the Oakland terminus ran high, George witnessed the skyrocketing of land values. All over California, wherever people congregated in the Eldorado of the forty-niners, land was being held out of use for speculative purposes, while the unfortunate late arrivals suffered from lack of ability to get a foothold on productive acreage. Putting two and two together, correlating the predictions of the old miner aboard the schooner with the glaring fact of the monopolization of land and natural resources that followed the free-for-all of forty-nine, George wrote a preliminary article on the land question.

George had had a good preliminary schooling (his father was a book publisher), but his real Alma Mater, so his son wrote, was the forecastle and the printing office. He first took up the trade of typesetter on his return from India. On a later trip West he became a prospector; he did farm work and itinerant manual labor; and he joined the printer's union. Returning East, in 1869, he set up a telegraph news bureau in New York for a struggling paper in San Francisco, but the bigger news monopolies forced him into bankruptcy. So Henry George took to walking the streets of New York, from aristocratic Murray Hill to the shabby East Side. It was the New York of Tweed's day, and of Jay Gould's, a New York in which, "...side by side with the palaces of the princely rich..." went a degradation, "a want and a shame, such as made the young man from the open West sick at heart."

The immense chasm that opened between rich and poor in New York confirmed the suspicions he had set forth in his preliminary article. So, back in San Francisco again, George commenced to gather material for *Progress and Poverty.* In 1877 he started work on it, and after a year and seven months of struggle, during which period he had often to pawn his own personal belongings, the book was finished. Publishers were not anxious to take the risk of issuing such a theoretical work; but finally D. Appleton undertook to market it on condition that George himself would pay for the plates. George agreed, and in January of 1880 the first trade edition was in the stalls—and *Progress and Poverty* commenced to outsell the most popular fiction of the day.

George brought considerable passion and insight to the writing of *Progress and Poverty;* so much was his heart in his work, as his son tells the story, that he wept upon its completion. As an economist, George was lucky to make his start with no inherited paraphernalia of classical terms; his eyesight was not blinded by the apologetics of the members of the Manchester School, with their rationalization of the industrial revolution. His work did not take the turn of *Das Kapital,* we may be sure, because of the American conditions out of which it grew; George did not despair of a competitive society. He had seen relatively happy times on the frontier, when there was room for everybody to compete. If you go to a new community, he wrote, where the Anglo-Saxon (that prince of competitors) is just commencing the race of progress, you will find an absence of wealth, but no beggars; no luxury, but no destitution. But as the community realizes the conditions which all civilized communities are striving for, poverty takes on a darker tone. This, George argued, is directly the result of progress. Hence George was at one with Rousseau and the philosophers of the Enlightenment in wishing to preserve primitive conditions.

Seeking for the all-inclusive formula—a "formula so broad as to admit of no exceptions"—that governed the relationship of poverty to progress, George found it in the Ricardian analysis of rent. Rent was equal to the difference in value between the wealth that could be produced on a given piece of ground, and the wealth that could be produced on land at the lowest level of subsistence. As land is improved, as its social value is augmented, owing to growth of cities, proximity of markets and so on, it naturally produces more, but rent, George noticed, tended to swallow up the whole gain, and the landlords pocketed what really should accrue to labor, on the one hand, and to the *entrepreneur,* on the other. Thus pauperization accompanies progress. To put it another way, the reason why, in spite of increased productive power on the worker's part, wages constantly tended toward a minimum which gave but a bare living, was that, with the increase in productive power, rent tended to an even greater increase, thus compelling a constant reduction of wages.

So George came to the conclusion that land should, through the medium of the Single Tax on social value, be forced down toward its "use" value. That done, George argued, both labor and capital would be able to find plenty to do; there would be no need for any disheartening talk about the class war, for there would be abundance for all who would work. The tax on the social value of land would make it highly unprofitable for the landlord to hold ground out of use; moreover, rent on unused ground would tend to a minimum solely because of new valuations pitched low to avoid the ravages of the tax assessor. Speculation in land values would at once disappear, and with this would go the inflation that leads to panics, depression and the eternal round of the business cycle. And, of course, the income derived from the land tax would immediately abolish the necessity for all other forms of taxation, whether on improvements or on productive labor.

One can hardly doubt the soundness of George within his orbit, for liberty, as soon as equal access to the land is denied, becomes, as the population mounts, merely the right to compete for employment at starvation wages or the right to cry for the dole. But George, in spite of his intelligent refutation of the one-sided Malthusian doctrine, in spite of his disposal of the classical theory that capital pays labor its wages, was hardly perspicacious all down the line. He put Malthus to rout by showing that *as population increases* human ingenuity finds ways to support it; he demonstrated that wages come out of the wealth created by labor itself. But he was a poor power philosopher; the problem of controls eluded him. He failed to see that a land-owning class, with its relation to the banking system which, in turn, is bound up with the mortgage system, is, to all intents and purposes, synonymous with the bourgeoisie itself. To make this bourgeoisie tractable, to take away its sources of revenue and investment and dividends, would entail *a whole revolution,* directed, to all practical purposes, against capitalism itself. In 1913, for instance, it would have involved separating Lee, Higginson and Company, and their Back Bay clientele, from the Calumet and Hecla copper mines on the upper peninsula of Michigan. Now just how could this have been done by appealing to the Democrats or the Republicans to tax away all land and monopoly values—to make land, mines and rights of way common property? The slush fund would at once have precluded any such demand. When the situation is thought through, doesn't George's minimizing of any class struggle seem like the act of the ostrich? And how would he, once his scheme was in operation, prevent large-scale bribery of boards of assessment?

George's philosophy fails in that it doesn't make its appeal in terms of the dialectical materialism that is the key to the power of regeneration. The Single Tax can't be dramatized to interest sufficient numbers of people. It is true that George offered, to the socialists of his time, the distant hope that all of the *values* of socialism might be achieved through the Single Tax, but he solved no problems of the mechanics of capturing power, of seizing the fulcrum that is the State, either through the ballot or otherwise, to bring about a desired result. The Single Tax remains poised as a vague expectation. For a time the theories of George were on the rise; Single Tax colonies—such as the one in Delaware that sheltered Upton Sinclair for a period—sprang up; but the demand for a solution by killing monopoly by fiscal prestidigitation is now disappearing. However intelligent and desirable it may be, the Single Tax offers little for marching men in the modern world to take hold of. Soviet Russia, more than any other single factor, has killed it—and the voice of Bolton Hall, crying out in 1932: "It is monopoly alone, not capitalists or capital, that George and his followers fight. And we will go on fighting till we have taken all the rents of the land created by the public, for public purposes, instead of taxes. We know what we want, and we know how to get it"—this voice sounds like the puffed plaint of a lost soul strayed out of the pre-war decade and calling with a querulous shrillness to a world that has forgotten Henry George and all his works. Even such a confirmed believer in the Single Tax diagnosis as Suzanne La Follette, when she came to revive the *Freeman* at the end of the twenties, left Henry George off the masthead of her magazine. She had come to realize, she wrote, that the Single Taxers knew everything but how to attain their paradise.

More obviously in the main stream of the neo-democratic movement than Henry George was Henry Demarest Lloyd, the father of all the muck-rakers that were to swarm over the social scene in the 1900's. Charles Edward Russell, one of the leaders in the campaign of exposure that gave the Rooseveltian decade its peculiar flavor, testifies to the pull Lloyd had upon him. "Lloyd," he said in 1912, "was the pioneer and leader of the great movement that has disillusioned Americans and probably saved them from an abominable industrial despotism. He planted the seed; his fortune, very unusual in such men, was to see the tilth in a thousand places and in ways of which he had not dreamed."

It was Lloyd who fired the opening gun in the attack upon the Standard Oil interests back in the days of the rebate wars. Russell was a student at St. Johnsbury Academy in Vermont when, in 1881, he picked up a copy of the *Atlantic Monthly* and started to read an article about oil. It was in that article that he got his first glimpse of the forces at work in America. The glimpse confirmed what was already a strong suspicion; Russell had been reared in an old-fashioned abolitionist family "whose opposition to the corporations was held to be the next great work after the destruction of slavery." His father had carried on a lifelong fight against the growing power for corruption of the railroads. But Lloyd's article really showed to Russell, for the first time, the distinct anatomy of the industrial structure. More important, it passed on to the young man who would later investigate the Beef Trust the technique of able, intelligent and factual muck-raking. It also set a pace that Ida Tarbell was to pick up in the days of McClure's campaign. When the *Atlantic* article was expanded into the book, *Wealth Against Commonwealth,* in 1894, it became, so Russell tells us, a great storehouse of information to which "numbers of able campaigners habitually resorted for their facts."

Lloyd came from a preacher's household; Calvinism was his daily pap when young. His mother wished him to become a minister, but although he had a strong moralistic bias, he thought in terms of this world almost exclusively. His commencement oration, delivered on his graduation from Columbia in 1867, was an adumbration of his life work, it being on the general theme of exploitation. "When the materials for soap making were found to be exhausted in England, and known to be abundant in Africa," he said with a precocious (for that time) emphasis on the materialistic conception of history, "then, when capital saw profit in African civilization, it invested largely in African missions; it paid such noble men as Livingstone to go forth and explore the country in the double character of missionaries and commercial agents, with a Bible in one hand and a contract for fat in the other."

Lloyd was brought up chiefly in New York City, and the influence of Henry Ward Beecher of Brooklyn's Plymouth Church on the young man was considerable. But it was the secular Beecher, who played his part in politics, that appealed to the young secular moralist. After taking his law degree at Columbia, Lloyd followed a course that commended itself to most of the young reformers of the day; he went in for the espousal of Free Trade. Soon he was assistant secretary of the newly formed American Free Trade League, of which William Cullen Bryant was President. He joined hands with the Schurzes, the Charles Francis Adamses, the Lyman Trumbulls and other "Liberal" Republicans in the fight on Grantism; but when Greeley was made the Liberal candidate in 1872, he refused to support him—Greeley was a protectionist. Meanwhile, the West beckoned; activity in the Free Trade League, in politics, in journalism, led him to the Chicago *Tribune* and to Horace White, another liberal of those Godkinian days. Chicago offered opportunity for work, for the city was in the throes of rebuilding its entire business district after the great fire of 1871.

Lloyd was a fit candidate, at that time, for the leadership of a Youth Movement. A young intellectual, with all that the term connotes, no literary activity seemed beyond him. His first job on the *Tribune* was that of literary editor. He reviewed *Middlemarch,* among other books; he founded the Chicago Literary Club, and the Illinois Free Trade League, and he was admitted to the Illinois bar. He had arrogance, astounding health and will. Writing to his brother, he said, with an egotism that at least argued a main direction, that he wanted power, but power "unpoisoned by the presence of obligation."

His fingers were in many pies; he helped Melville E. Stone in getting the Chicago *Daily News* going, and was even offered control of the *News.* In 1875 he became the financial editor of the *Tribune*—at a time when people, hard up for cash after the panic that had followed the collapse of Jay Cooke's Philadelphia banking house, were just beginning to realize that 1873 had demonetized silver. It was Henry's brother, Demarest, however, who, in this period, was the family's most promising muck-raker. Demarest had exposed the Erie Canal frauds while working for the New York *Tribune.*

Henry's money editorials in the Chicago *Tribune* were based on a belief that bimetallism was the soundest basis for money under a system that made a metal base a necessity. He hammered away at the issue, day in and day out. Later, the *Tribune,* along with William McKinley and others who had never been convinced "gold bugs," turned to the gold standard. Joseph Medill, owner of the *Tribune* in the nineties, was, as we have seen, the leading foe in the West of the Populists. But even the *Tribune,* in 1896, aided the silver forces, for John P. Altgeld, the Democratic Governor of Illinois, remembered the editorials written by Lloyd in the seventies, unearthed them from the files and employed them as campaign documents. "Nothing more prophetic was ever written," said Altgeld.

Relieved of financial writing in 1882, and transferred to the editorial page, Lloyd really commenced to get his eyes open. He had written his preliminary paper on the methods of the Standard Oil trust, but now he saw monopoly growing in every direction. He began to make a documentary study of the industrialization of a nation. Chicago was an excellent vantage point; the most radical city in the United States in the eighties, it offered a laboratory where currents could be studied more or less in the open. The Socialist Labor Party had grown to fair proportions there, and it was busy agitating for industrial justice to the worker. The interlocking events that were to lead to the Haymarket bomb tragedy of May 3, 1886, were already in process of unfolding their tragic sequence. This tragedy was to mean a great deal in Lloyd's development.

In the seventies and eighties the most blatant monopolies were, of course, the "uncommon" carriers, the railroads, and to these Lloyd devoted a special study. One of his first exposures was that of the treachery of the Land Grant Office in surrendering the public domain to privileged interests. In 1883 he anticipated the fiction of Frank Norris by writing two letters for the *Tribune* on "California Cornered," describing the political activities of the great railroad combination of the "Big Four" of the Pacific Coast, Huntington, Leland Stanford, Hopkins and Crocker, the men who had built the Central Pacific east to Salt Lake. Like the muck-rakers of the 1900's, Lloyd was not immediately attracted to either socialism or the Single Tax; they seemed at the time to be altogether too theoretical for use. He wanted to reform the social system which we then possessed, and toward that end he dug at its cancerous spots.

But he was verging on socialism in 1883 when, in an essay called "A New Magna Charta," which appeared in the *Tribune,* he wrote that "the unnatural principles of the competitive economy of John Stuart Mill will be as obsolete as the rules of war by which Cæsar slaughtered the fair-haired men, women and children of Germania."

His first important work—the article which sent premonitory thrills down the spine of the young Charles Edward Russell in a faraway Vermont town—was written in 1880. The *North American Review* would not touch it, but William Dean Howells, who was as fine a man as he was timid as a novelist, accepted it for the *Atlantic Monthly,* and the "Story of a Great Monopoly" went forth to its public. How the Standard Oil, through its control of the Pennsylvania, the New York Central, the Erie and the Baltimore and Ohio, made use of the rebating system to crush all rivals in the business of refining and selling oil, has become, since 1880, an old story—the classic example of how a monopoly is achieved. Ida Tarbell made it a household fable in the 1900's. But it was shocking news to the small business man of the eighties.

This preliminary tale of the Standard Oil practices marked the beginning of *Wealth Against Commonwealth,* the book of 1894 that became an arsenal for the muck-rakers. Other articles on combinations followed the *Atlantic* piece; Lloyd's *Lords of Industry,* published in 1884, initiated the trust discussion in this country, and even as late as 1888 it was used as fodder for the trust wrangling in an excited Congress that was looking toward the Sherman Anti-Trust Act of 1890.

Lloyd hoped, when writing these preliminary articles, to purge industry at the top, by inducing a moral reform in business men. But the Haymarket bomb outrage of 1886, an incident of labor's fight for the eight-hour day, turned him definitely to the ranks of the organized workers. The subsequent hanging of some of the anarchists who had gone to make speeches in the Haymarket Square, none of whom was ever actually connected with the throwing of the bomb, outraged Lloyd's moral susceptibilities, as it did those of William Dean Howells. He took the side of the more thoughtful men of America whose judgment has since been vindicated by conservative historians like James Truslow Adams, but in Chicago of the mid-eighties this meant social ostracism. His denunciation of the hangings meant denunciation for him; and the baying of the pack at the Knights of Labor, at the worker's cause in general, and at the eight-hour-day agitation in particular, caused Lloyd to confide to his notebooks "...the wages system must go." A pamphlet on "The New Conscience," written about the industrial situation, was read by Altgeld and others; Lloyd was beginning to have a profound effect on a few kindred minds, in spite of the hard looks, the contumely and the scorn of former friends.

Wealth Against Commonwealth is a book that has failed to live, in the way *Progress and Poverty* or *Das Kapital* have lived, because it is less an exposition of fundamental principles of economy than it is a reporter's book of facts. But as a book of facts it is daring and first-rate. Godkin sneered at it; John D. Archbold of the Standard Oil attacked it; but it was bolstered by all future investigation, notably by that of Ida Tarbell in her McClure articles. It was quarried, as Lloyd said, out of official records, "and it is a venture in realism in the world of realities." The sources were decisions of courts and of special tribunals like the Interstate Commerce Commission, the verdicts of juries in civil and criminal cases, reports of committees of State Legislatures and of Congress, and oath-sworn testimony corrected by rebuttal testimony and cross-examination.

Wealth Against Commonwealth makes better reading than Ida Tarbell's *History of the Standard Oil*. Lloyd had wit and verbal excellence; he had a trick of telling antithesis. As a wit he could write, "The Standard has done everything with the Pennsylvania Legislature except to refine it." The book opens with an adaptation of Rousseau's "Man is born free, but everywhere he is in chains." Lloyd's version of this, put into terms of economics, is "Nature is rich; but everywhere man, the heir of nature, is poor." The book attacked all "cornerers"—the syndicates, the trusts, the makers of pools. The majority, he said, cannot buy enough of anything, but the coal syndicate thinks there is too much coal, the iron syndicate that there is too much iron, and so on.

Lloyd and Henry George supplement each other at important points—both were agreed on the menace of monopoly. But Lloyd, the reporter, named his companies; and Lloyd, the thinker, went through Populism and into socialism, basing his confidence on the imminence of a coöperative commonwealth that would reorient a status economy in a modern world that is the product of a contract economy. Men, he argued, have become so intelligent, so responsible, and so coöperative that they can be entrusted in great numbers with the care of great properties owned by others—then why can't they be entrusted with their own State, with the mills, the mines and the stores owned in the interests of all?

To THIS question the novelist, Edward Bellamy, turned his attention in *Looking Backward: 2000-1887*. His answer was, "Men can be entrusted with their own State," and he proceeded to demonstrate the workings of an industrial Utopia in which the means of production were operated in the interests of all, with draughts upon the common stock available to any man who would work. The novel—"probably the outstanding American contribution to socialist literature," as a prominent historian of political thought has said—is really an American version of Étienne Cabet's *Voyage en Icarie*, published in Paris in 1847, just before the Revolution that unseated Louis Philippe. It is a dreary enough Utopia that Bellamy's novel paints, just as Cabet's Utopia was dreary enough. Both men believed in a regimented state; both believed in complete industrialization. What Cabet and Bellamy failed to see is that outlawry of the profit motive would inevitably mean less industrialization. But *Looking Backward*, in spite of its weakness in prognostication, meant a great deal in 1888, the year of its publication. The trusts that were frightening Lloyd, and the strikes that were frightening the entire middle class, made *Looking Backward* seem like an omen, and the Utopia described by Dr. Leete, a man of the year 2000, to a Mr. West, who had gone to sleep in 1887 under the touch of a hypnotic physician, emphasized by contrast the groanings of the industrial structure of the eighties.

Bellamy, a spiritual descendant of the great Bostonians of the days of Brook Farm, was a natural Utopian. When he was eighteen years old he had spent a year in Europe, and the troubles attendant upon the industrial transformation of eighteenth-century society into nineteenth impressed him with man's inhumanity to man. On his return to America he became a journalist, but this work did not satisfy him. Turning to novel writing, he produced *The Duke of Stockbridge,* a romance of the days of Shays's Rebellion, and *Looking Backward.* He continued his assault upon a profit economy in *Equality,* published in 1897.

Bellamy's society, as outlined in *Looking Backward,* bears some relation to the actuality of Soviet Russia. The epoch of the American trusts has ended in One Great Trust—a national syndicate, organized as one great business corporation. The labor problem disappears when the nation assumes the responsibilities of capital. An industrial army, regimented by universal draft, is divided into ten great departments, each of them having a chief. Money is unknown, but credit remains.

Bellamy's influence was, at first, very large. Over a third of a million copies of *Looking Backward* were sold within two years, and the book was translated into most of the European languages. Numerous Nationalist clubs were formed to further Bellamy's ideas of national socialism, and the success of his book moved the author to found the *New Nation,* a weekly. But the Nationalist clubs merged with the rising Populist Party in 1891, and Bellamy's influence ceased. Debs read him, but *Looking Backward* must have seemed pale to the prisoner in Woodstock when compared with Victor Berger's gift of *Das Kapital.* Daniel De Leon, most militant of American socialists, couldn't stomach the Christian passiveness of Bellamy's vision; he noted, with some accuracy, that Bellamy's work contained no social leverage, and so he returned to his own work as the American forerunner of Lenin. The influence of Henry George and Henry Demarest Lloyd on the agitators for social justice in the Rooseveltian decade is more ponderable than that of Bellamy.

WORKING with the intellectual tools forged for them by Henry George, a group of old-fashioned Americans, Jeffersonian in their tastes and predilections, marched forth in the nineties and the early years of this century to face down the hosts of predatory privilege. As Populism spent itself, and as prosperity commenced to hum after the Spanish-American War, the city radical came to the fore with his protests that "the system," however productive of wealth it might be, certainly did not diffuse its goods evenly throughout the population. Bryan had objected to urban wickedness, but to Frederic C. Howe, who had seen the worst sides of New York, Pittsburgh and Cleveland, the city was, in spite of slums, graft and special privilege, the shining "hope of Democracy." A dominant, growing municipal corruption seemed, as the new century opened, to call forth its dialectical opposite in a group of Reform mayors and their henchmen; and Reform spread, as a matter of necessity, to the State capitals. The urban reformers, diverse in personality though they were, had one thing in common: they were afraid of regimentation, of the party discipline of the socialists, of commitment to an articulated creed. Two of them, Clarence Darrow (who served in the Illinois Legislature) and Brand Whitlock (who became Mayor of Toledo), might be called philosophical anarchists, so suspicious were they (and still are) of the repressive instrumentality of the State. Henry George appealed to these men because the State, in *Progress and Poverty,* was reduced to a gang of tax collectors who were, periodically, to raid the landlords. The Single Tax doctrines, either swallowed whole or in part, provided gunpowder for some excellent mayors at the turn of the century—mayors in Detroit, in Toledo, in Cleveland and in Chicago. Good government in the American cities received enormous impetus from *Progress and Poverty.*

The predecessor of Whitlock as Mayor of Toledo was, perhaps, the first of the Henry George mayors. He was Samuel M. Jones, a sucker-rod manufacturer and factory owner, who believed, quite literally, in the Golden Rule and the Declaration of Independence. A noble-hearted Welshman, he became, among other things, a literal Tolstoyan anarchist. Nobody, he said, had a right to "rule" anybody else; the exception to this blanket dismissal of "rule" being, of course, the Golden

Rule, which was a matter of persuasion, not of blood and iron. This "Golden-Rule" Jones, as he came to be called, was a self-made man. He had been brought to America at the age of three, and had made his money as an oil pioneer and as a manufacturer of apparatus for oil wells. By going through the competitive mill he came to understand the processes of industrialism as well as either Tom Johnson of Cleveland or Altgeld of Illinois. Like Altgeld, he was at one time worth a half million dollars.

Jones became Mayor of Toledo in 1897, and held office until his death in 1904, when Brand Whitlock, his Single-Tax secretary, stepped into the breach. He had been elected by business men and the Republican boss, who expected him to help the street-railway and electric-lighting corporations to obtain a franchise. But Jones wouldn't go through with the promotion of graft. He turned against the Republican organization, and when the machine refused to renominate him he ran on his own ticket as plain Sam Jones. Without a party, without a committee, without contributions, he was elected anyway. And the business men who had originally supported him now turned to the cry, "Out with Jones, we want a business man for mayor"—this, in spite of the fact that Jones had been a business man all his life. Jones replied by quoting Whitman, Tolstoi and Jesus Christ. Brand Whitlock had brought Whitman into the sucker-rod manufacturer's life; henceforth, Walt's heady democracy was constantly on Jones's lips.

Jones had moral support in his fight on privilege, for not far away, in Detroit, another unusual mayor, Hazen S. Pingree, was promoting a fight for a three-cent trolley line for his city. Jones joined the battle by declaring for public ownership of Toledo's public utilities, even though Ohio State law prohibited any such ownership. The newspapers, the ministers even, answered by calling him "crazy." They were sure of his mental incapacity when he took away clubs from the policemen, when he preached sermons on "society" to the prostitutes and drunkards in his capacity of Magistrate in the Police Court.

Jones was the most picturesque of the whole group of disinterested figures who strove to bring fresh air into municipal politics thirty years ago. A big man, sandy-complexioned, with huge hands that showed he had worked hard in his day, he was a "reformer" the masses could trust. None of your kid-gloved "goo-goos" was Jones. Besides Whitman and Tolstoi, his heroes were Mazzini and William Morris. He even followed Morris in esthetic matters, compromising his position as a factory-owner by wearing an artist's dress: a cream-colored slouch hat and flowing necktie. However, his hair, clipped short, and his hypnotic eye, made him seem the practical man, for all that his eccentricities may have moved his enemies to shout "dreamer."

Jones didn't live to see the success of his program, but Whitlock, who followed him in office for four successive terms, did manage to obtain a new city charter providing for those darlings of the neo-democratic hopes—the initiative, the referendum, the recall and direct nominations.

The most prominent Henry George mayor of the pre-war decade came into office in Cleveland in 1901. He was Tom L. Johnson, fat and pleasant-faced, a reformer with a bubbling sense of humor, and a delight in battling at the drop of the hat. For ten years as mayor he carried on a resourceful, high-hearted, running fight against the Cleveland traction ring of Mark Hanna and Horace Andrews, and eventually got his desire—the three-cent fare—but only for a short period. He did not live to see Home Rule for the Ohio cities, but Newton D. Baker, one of his cabinet who became Mayor after his death, did. In Johnson's fight for a three-cent fare, Home Rule, municipal ownership and the Single Tax, there was enlisted a remarkable group. Besides Baker, who later rationalized himself out of the Johnson camp and became the paid attorney of the Van Sweringen brothers, there were Frederic C. Howe, who, like Baker, had sat at the feet of

Woodrow Wilson and Richard T. Ely at Johns Hopkins in the nineties; Peter Witt, a belligerent and vitriolic iron molder who had come from the Populist Party to join Johnson; and Harris R. Cooley, liberal clergyman. Johnson's personality held these discrete human particles together. And Johnson not only fought in Cleveland, he went to Chicago to help Mayor Dunne in his struggle there for the three-cent fare, even as he had fought for Henry George in the New York mayorality campaign of 1897. The spectacle of a rich man—for Johnson was rich—battling to rid the land of the sources of his own easy wealth was something that other rich men could not understand; a Chicago newspaper, thinking there was some nigger in the woodpile, called him "the fat casuist of Cleveland." But Johnson was in earnest.

He knew the methods of monopoly, for he had been a first-rate monopolist himself. Born in Kentucky, the son of an impoverished Confederate Army officer, he had come to maturity in the harsh atmosphere of the Gilded Age. He was a believer in privilege because he had never seen anything else; privilege was the way of the world. His training as a monopolist came when he was very young: when he was living in Virginia, just after Lee's surrender, he struck up a friendship with a conductor on a train that ran into Staunton, and the conductor gave him permission to sell papers on the train. Johnson got fifteen cents apiece for the Richmond and Petersburg papers, and twenty-five cents for the illustrated weeklies. For five weeks he held the monopoly; then, with a change in railroad management, went a change in the conductor, and Tom lost his graft. But the lesson remained.

When the Johnsons moved back to Kentucky, Tom entered the street-railway business, going to work for the du Ponts, friends of his father who had bought the Louisville franchise. He was successively bookkeeper, cashier and superintendent of this mule-power transportation system. His first sizable amount of money was made by the invention of a fare box, which netted him twenty to thirty thousand dollars.

This, too, was based on a monopoly right—the exclusive right to a patent. He used the money to buy, at the age of twenty-two, a majority interest in a street-railway franchise in Indianapolis, where he got his first insight into the connection between banking and monopoly. "The people's money," he wrote, "goes into the banks in the form of deposits. The banker uses this money to capitalize public service corporations which are operated for private profit instead of for the benefit of the people." But the connection between politics and monopoly still eluded him; it was not until he had gone into the traction business in Cleveland that he discovered, from Mark Hanna, the relation between political jobbery and the original granting of franchises.

Mark Hanna completed Johnson's education, but the young monopolist was still on the side of privilege. His own particular road to Damascus was the railroad between Indianapolis and Cleveland, and his conversion was much like Paul's, or Rousseau's; it came in a seemingly blinding flash. A train-butcher offered Johnson a book called *Social Problems,* by Henry George. Johnson thought it was about the "social evil," and said he wasn't interested. But the train-butcher persisted; he offered to return the half-dollar purchase price if Johnson did not like the book. Johnson read it, and decided he was in for a prolonged exploration. *Progress and Poverty* followed. He didn't want to believe the George doctrine, but its influence was too strong; it seemed to have no loopholes. Still fighting off his salvation, he took *Progress and Poverty* to his Cleveland lawyer, with a supplication: "You made a free trader out of me; now I want you to read this book and point out its errors to me to save me from becoming an advocate of the system of taxation it describes."

He also took the book to his Johnstown, Pennsylvania, partner in the business of manufacturing steel rails. Both the lawyer and the manufacturer wrestled with the book, made objections, read the book again, and ended by succumbing, along with Johnson. Johnson knew from his own experience that the basic facts of the book were right, and the conclusions, as George put them, were irresistible. To think, with Johnson, was to act; he sought out Henry George in Brooklyn. In 1886 he helped Father McGlynn, William McCabe, Louis F. Post and Daniel De Leon in the George campaign for Mayor of New York, and in 1897 he managed George's second campaign for the same office. The first fight resulted in a coalition between Tammany Hall and the County Democracy, who united on Abram S. Hewitt as a candidate to beat George and the young Republican nominee, Theodore Roosevelt. Hewitt won, although it is an old newspaper legend that George was counted out at the polls. In 1897 George died on the eve of the election. Meanwhile Johnson, at George's behest, had gone to Congress, had fought the high tariff men, had gotten George's "Protection or Free Trade" read into the Congressional Record, so that he might send it out to voters at governmental expense during the campaign of 1892, and had started a lifelong agitation for the Single Tax.

Johnson's greatest service to the neo-democratic movement was as Mayor of Cleveland, where, in Newton Baker's words, he "set new standards of city government" for the whole nation. Lincoln Steffens called Johnson "the best mayor of the best-governed city in America." As was the case with Jones in Toledo, Johnson found himself with pulpit and press and Chamber of Commerce arrayed against him. He got some help from E. W. Scripps's paper, the Cleveland *Press,* but the other journals knew their masters' voices, and the masters spoke for private ownership of public utilities and the five-cent fare.

The fight for the three-cent fare was carried on against all the odds which the American legal system can throw up. Injunction followed injunction; if ever there was a clear example of the use of the judiciary in maintaining the status quo, "government by injunction," it was in Cleveland in the early years of this century. Taxation presented another problem that was almost impossible of correction—but with the aid of Peter Witt's Tax School, which smelled out inequalities in the rates, and by means of a continuous, factual attack in both State and local campaigns, Johnson managed to bring Cleveland to a point where his followers were able to commence application of the Single Tax principles to the property of the entire city. Johnson was beaten for Mayor in 1909 just before his death, but the election of Baker, two years later, saved a good deal of the Johnson program—a program which, however, Baker was later to foreswear by his actions on his return to Cleveland after serving as Secretary of War under Wilson.

JONES and Johnson formed the spearhead of the municipal thrust in the Rooseveltian decade, but they were only the most famous of the purgers of cities. Municipal corruption in St. Louis was uncovered by Joseph W. Folk between 1900 and 1904. Judge Ben Lindsey, of the Denver Children's Court, fought boss rule in the Colorado capital. In Minneapolis Hovey C. Clarke uncovered the graft of the Ames ring when he was serving as foreman of the grand jury for the Summer of 1902. Mark Fagan, in Jersey City, tried to purge the local government of railroad and public service domination. Emil Seidel, a socialist, was elected Mayor of Milwaukee in 1910. And in New York, a "goo-goo," Seth Low, achieved election as Mayor in 1901. But the demand for better municipal government got its greatest impetus from an "act of God," when Galveston was overwhelmed in 1900 by a tidal wave which killed one-sixth of the population and destroyed a third of the property. The citizens, faced with the need for immediate action, put the burden of reconstruction in the hands of a commission of five. This commission form was made permanent in a new city charter of 1901. Houston, Texas, adopted the Galveston plan in 1905, so well did it work in the city of its birth, and government by city manager has been making slow headway ever since.

But city ownership, which Johnson advocated, and the three-cent fare have fought a losing fight. Even while Johnson was campaigning for municipal operation of traction lines, the theory of regulation of public utilities by commissions set up by the States was spreading over the country. The rising cost of living and labor was making the three-cent fare equivalent to a demand that trolleys be operated at a loss. The coming of the "jitney" bus, and, later, the large passenger bus, made even the five-cent fare too small to be profitable in many cities. And improvement in the transmission of electricity made local electric light plants too expensive; the problem of power control became State wide—a matter for State and national action, as it remains to this day.

WITH the fight on the public utility monopolies waged by the Henry George mayors went a persistent, organized and bold propaganda for the Single Tax, spread by such disciples as only George could attract. The Single Tax protagonists included Thomas G. Shearman of New York, Colonel Josiah C. Wedgwood, M.P., of London, Surgeon General W. C. Gorgas of the United States Army, Lawson Purdy of New York, Herbert Quick, the novelist, Frederic C. Howe, even Sun Yat-sen and Leo Tolstoi. The most indefatigable, earnest, unremitting Single Taxer of them all, however, was Joseph Fels, maker of Fels Naphtha Soap, a little twinkling man, as Steffens called him, who had an excess income of $250,000 a year which he could not use himself. Fels became interested in the land question by himself when he went to England from Philadelphia to organize a British branch of his soap industry. England being further advanced along the industrial road than the United States at the end of the nineteenth century, Fels could not help but observe the glut on the British labor market. He sought his own reason for this glut; it derived, he saw, from the process of taking land out of use to form the great estates. Return the land to the people, he said, and the labor glut would disappear, wages would rise, and prosperity would diffuse itself with some evenness throughout the island. This was Henry George, pure and simple, although Fels did not know it until later.

After a few experiments with colonies in England, with gardening the waste spaces in London for the benefit of the poor and at trying to persuade British liberals to take up his ideas (and Henry George's), Fels returned to America, with the notion of the Fels Fund Commission in mind. This Commission was organized in 1909, with Daniel Kiefer, "the most successful mendicant in America," as chairman, and with Frederic C. Howe, Lincoln Steffens, George A. Briggs and Jackson C. Ralston on the committee. Bolton Hall and Fels himself were advisers without votes. The Fels Fund sought to back men, not institutions. Besides centralizing the Single Tax efforts, and relieving advocates from the burden of collecting money, the Fels Fund made up the annual deficit of Louis Post's Single Tax magazine, *The Public,* published in Chicago. But the Fund, whether because of the World War or the psychological impossibility of getting a sufficient human force behind it, failed to accomplish much.

THE Single Tax has been called the only positive contribution made by an American toward solving the perhaps insoluble problem of economic democracy. As a matter of fact it was of eighteenth-century origin, a scheme of the French physiocrats headed by Quesnay and Turgot. But George gave it a new impress and a new force. When Quesnay "invented" the *impôt unique,* the fury of the industrial revolution had not broken upon the Continent, and when George came to similar conclusions, he, too, was thinking in terms of a non-industrialized community: California of the pioneers. A lingering afterglow of the great Age of the Enlightenment, the Single Tax was drenched, as George would have been the first to admit, in all the hopeful colors of the language of "natural rights." Making as it does a shrewd compromise between our traditional pioneer individualism and our vaunted equal opportunity for all, the Single Tax was well calculated to attract dynamic individuals who wished to preserve freedom of economic activity in a situation that was coming to defy freedom. Although George and Joseph Fels both insisted that all the benefits of socialism would flower in time from the success of the Single Tax, this eighteenth-century doctrine made its strongest bid for support among people who would sooner be caught stealing than be found with the Communist Manifesto of 1848 in their pockets.

The Single Tax is deceptively simple, deceptively perfect. On paper it hasn't a flaw; all its implications flow directly from George's own splendid definitions. But its definitions are —just definitions; one is not compelled to use George's geometry, for there are other axioms in an Einsteinian world. George, for example, failed to explore the whole question of the ownership of surplus value and whether or not creative brains are as much a "natural" resource as a gold mine or a prairie.

And George, as I have said, had no effective approach to the problem of power, a problem that must always remain central in any political and economic discussion. This objection must have seemed paramount to Clarence Darrow, one of the libertarians who was, at a certain stage, a believer in the Single Tax. In the end Darrow came to feel that its cocksureness, its insistence on "natural rights," were evidence of a Utopianism that could never be brought into relationship with the here-and-now. Socialism, he came to believe, was much more logical and profound—although, with his temperamental anarchic leanings, this Chicago lawyer who deserted corporation work to defend the underdog was never able to achieve more than passive interest in an organized Socialist Party. He fought for Debs in 1894, defending him on the "contempt" charge, and he was the attorney for "Big Bill" Haywood and the other members of the Western Federation of Miners in the Steunenberg trial at Boise in 1907, but that was his limit. Even a "logical and profound" socialism was not in accord with human psychology, in Darrow's ultimate belief. As for the doctrine of Henry George, it placed too small a value upon human selfishness (which cannot be said of Mr. Stalin); it was a hangover from the days when philosophers believed that nature was good, not indifferent, that only civilization corrupts.

And so the hard-boiled yet tender Darrow tossed the "Problem Solved" chapters of *Progress and Poverty* aside, and followed John Peter Altgeld in the political struggles that convulsed Chicago and Illinois as a whole in the nineties. Altgeld was like Darrow in his unwillingness to be deluded. He expected the worst; he was conscious of the fate of the Jeffersonian Democrat in a monopolistic age built on the Great Technology.

Altgeld was a pure democrat in his instincts, but the paradox in a world of monopoly seemed, to him, soluble only by making the government paternalistic—toward all the people. Here was the difference between Altgeld's definition of the duty of paternalism and McKinley's: McKinley believed in strong centralization for the benefit of traction magnates and manufacturers of Pullman cars. "McKinley has only one idea," said Altgeld, "and that idea wrong." As Governor of Illinois in the mid-nineties Altgeld was one of the few men in American history who has practiced democracy in office; because of this he was damned as few men have been damned. The story of the "Forgotten Eagle," as Vachel Lindsay has called him in a notable poem, is one of the saddest that can be told.

Altgeld is remembered to-day, if he is remembered at all, for two deeds that have been obscured by incredible misrepresentation and fog. The second of these was his embroilment with Cleveland over the Pullman strike. He first brought down upon his close-cropped, cowlicked head the virulent denunciation of Chicago and the United States by pardoning the three anarchists who had escaped the death penalty in connection with the Haymarket bomb explosion of May 3, 1886.

A group of laborers had gathered in Haymarket Square in Chicago on this May 3 to protest against the firing upon rioters of the day before by the police. The program of speeches, led by the Black (Anarchists) International had come to a peaceful conclusion, and the crowd was dispersing when, in opposition to the stated wishes of Mayor Carter Harrison, a cordon of police closed in upon the few remaining participants. Then the bomb exploded, killing one policeman and mortally wounding seven others. The police responded by firing into the crowd.

Eight of the leaders of the Black International were rounded up; the presiding trial judge decided that it was not necessary to prove their direct participation in the outrage; it was sufficient that their writings and speeches had "encouraged" violence. The jury found all eight guilty, condemning seven to death by hanging, and ordering life imprisonment for the eighth. On November 11, 1887, four of the convicted men were hanged. One, Louis Lingg, escaped the revenge of the State by blowing his head off with a percussion cap; two others had had their sentences commuted to life imprisonment. And that was how matters stood when Altgeld became Governor.

Altgeld took his own time about the pardons, in spite of the pressure brought by a few men like Darrow on behalf of the three remaining prisoners. He knew the depth of the feeling among the "corporation-minded" in Chicago about the bombing; he knew that pardon would mean ostracism for him, as sympathy for the anarchists had meant ostracism for Henry Demarest Lloyd a few years before. But, in his own deliberative way, he made sure the law was on his side and issued the pardons. Unfortunately, he included in his message a bitter attack upon the judge who had passed sentence on the anarchists. All the ugly passions of 1886 and

1887 were revived; the majority of the newspapers of the country were violent about Altgeld. It made not the slightest difference that the men he had pardoned were palpably not proven guilty. When Fielding, Schwab and Neebe walked out of jail, Altgeld had signed his own death warrant as Governor of Illinois. And when, during the Pullman strike of 1894, Cleveland sent troops to Chicago before any request from Altgeld had arrived at the White House, the protest from the Illinois Governor that the President had overstepped his constitutional rights brought forth nothing but enmity and sarcasm from the classes who wished to see the "Debs rebellion" quashed at any price, Constitution or no Constitution. The fact that Altgeld, as legal historians have since held, was the better judge of the law of the land made no difference at the time.

Altgeld was born in North Germany in 1847 of poor, uneducated and narrowly orthodox parents. His father was a plebeian, a wagon-maker. The family joined the great migration of '48 to America, but, like the father of Joseph Fels, for the sake of escaping poverty rather than for the idealistic acts and motives that had sent Carl Schurz to Wisconsin. The early life of Altgeld reminds one forcibly of Theodore Dreiser's midland childhood. There were the same parochial schools, the same crushing poverty. At thirteen Altgeld was working in the fields with a plow, and peddling farm produce; at fourteen he was "hiring out" as a farm hand to neighbors. His mother, like Dreiser's, was illiterate but kindly; his father, however, was both illiterate and mean—a stolid, tight old drill-master. The young John Peter knew what it was to feel the horsewhip on his back.

Yet he seems to have been a forgiving son, for he returned home often enough in his later life. His first trip into the world came when he was sixteen: he entered the Union Army as a substitute and saw some action in 1864. After the Civil War, back on the Ohio farm, he fell in love, but the affair turned out badly. Ten years later he returned from the West to marry the girl. In the meantime he had tramped the Middle States, worked with a railway grading crew, suffered a recurrence of fever contracted in wartime, and became a teacher in Missouri. Like Darrow, he used his teacher's job as a grubstake to support himself while he studied law. After admission to the Andrew County bar he went into politics, and the Granger movement, fusing with the Democrats, made him a State's attorney for his county. He had seen enough of human suffering by this time, and in consequence he hated his experience as prosecutor, but it gave him material for a book, *Our Penal Machinery and its Victims,* which had its formative effect in shaping the legal philosophy of the young Darrow, who read it in Ashtabula, Ohio.

In 1875 Altgeld came to Chicago. Marriage followed, and his law practice grew after a slow start. He foresaw that a fortune was to be made in real-estate deals, and he showed some skill at buying and selling lots to take advantage of the increasing social value of land. He even dabbled successfully in street-railway monopoly. But in spite of his making money out of the very thing that Henry George was about to condemn in *Progress and Poverty,* Altgeld was no ordinary child of the Gilded Age; his hard boyhood, his tramp experiences, his knowledge of the workings of the criminal law, had, with his temperament, preserved him from the insulation that usually accompanies success. Edgar Lee Masters remembers Altgeld's expression of sad thoughtfulness, his large, blue, gentle, understanding eyes, his habit of contemplatively picking his teeth as he meditated on the world's woes. Not precisely a prepossessing man, yet the very air about him, to Masters, seemed burdened with the intense power of an unusual personality.

Altgeld didn't like politics; he considered politicians mere Yes-Men, and would have used the phrase had he known it. Private individuals, he said, were the really influential people; "these are the men who mold public opinion and whose favor and support are sought by the politicians, and who, in the end, secure legislation and shape the policy of the country, using the office-holding classes as an instrument by which to carry out a purpose." Yet his feeling for the downtrodden led him to run for office when the Democrats urged him. In 1886, the year which saw Henry George running for mayor in New York and frightening Tammany into a compromise with the County Democracy, Altgeld was elected Judge in the Cook County Superior Court. The labor vote put him across. In 1890 he became Chief Justice of this court, but "sitting down" irked him, and he resigned a year later.

The election as Governor followed the resignation, and Altgeld became known as the "millionaire labor leader"—an exaggeration by half. It was soon to be a total exaggeration, for Altgeld's fortunes went down rapidly after he became Governor. A building, the panic of 1893, a refusal to be bribed and a grudge—all played their part in the eclipse of Altgeld as a moneyed man.

The building was the Unity Building, one of the first of the Chicago skyscrapers. With its frontage of eighty feet on Dearborn Street, it was the darling of Altgeld's heart. He had undertaken to finance its construction with the aid of an illiterate, but shrewd and crafty, banker, John R. Walsh. Sixteen stories high, and fireproof, it looked like an excellent investment to Altgeld. But when it was completed it was found to be out of plumb, owing to difficulties in the construction. Walsh wouldn't advance all the promised cash, so Altgeld had to borrow in small sums.

Even at that, Altgeld might have survived. But the panic of 1893 came, and at least half the Unity Building tenants were forced to vacate because they couldn't meet the rent. The tenants were mostly young radical lawyers who had moved in after the pardoning of the Haymarket victims had deprived Altgeld of his more wealthy and self-righteous clientele. Meanwhile, there was the interest on the mortgage to be met—and the mortgage was for more than $2,000,000.

Altgeld got through until 1895, but the noose was drawing tighter. It would be pulled sharp, eventually, by two men, Walsh and Charles T. Yerkes, the street-railway magnate who is the prototype of Dreiser's Frank Cowperwood of *The Financier* and *The Titan*. Walsh, Altgeld's main creditor, had a stake in the financial manipulations of Yerkes, and these birds of a feather were watching the Governor in the capitol at Springfield. Some of Yerkes's franchises were about to expire. The franchises, which had been limited by Illinois law to twenty years, Yerkes wished to extend for a much longer period.

Now Yerkes came from Philadelphia in a State made famous by Matthew Stanley Quay, the biggest "boss" of them all. Compliant legislatures in Pennsylvania were in the habit of granting franchises either "in perpetuity" or for ninety-nine years, and Yerkes hoped to ram his so-called "eternal monopoly bills," based on Harrisburg models, through the Legislature at Springfield. The politicians had been fixed by the Yerkes lobby, but Altgeld remained inscrutable, a final obstacle. What would the Governor do? If he let the bills pass he could have had all the money, all the time, he needed. The interest on the Unity Building bonds could be met. But Altgeld vetoed the bills.

And when, in 1896, the Unity Building defaulted on the bonds, Walsh, the tool of Yerkes, showed no mercy. Altgeld lost his fortune of a half million. He was a ruined man financially, as well as politically.

Altgeld was fifty-four years old at the time—too old to make a new start in business. His term of Governor drew to a close and he went back to Chicago. He had no heart for struggle. His friends worked on him; the poor and lowly came to see him. Eventually they persuaded him to run for Mayor of Chicago as an Independent, but his appeal was gone, and he lost. Six months before his death he became Clarence Darrow's law partner. The end came in March of 1902, from an attack of indigestion which overwhelmed him as he was making a speech at Joliet in behalf of the Boers of South

Africa. Two liberal clergymen refused to speak at his funeral, but Jane Addams of Hull House and Clarence Darrow substituted. And there beside the body Darrow rechristened the North German democrat who had defied Grover Cleveland and the Chicago mob hysteria—rechristened him John Pardon Altgeld.

ALTGELD alone, in the nineties, stood out as an example of the Progressive type of Governor. The abuse heaped upon his head is the common lot of the pioneer in social thought, yet not five years after his retirement from public office Progressive politics were stirring in more than one State capital, and more radical demands than ever Altgeld advocated were being accepted by majorities at the polls. Partly contemporaneous with Altgeld as a purifying force in State politics was William S. U'Ren, crusader for the "Oregon System." U'Ren was born in Wisconsin, of Cornish parents, and had spent his youth in his father's blacksmith shop and upon frontier farms. He studied law in Denver, and went to Oregon in search of both health and opportunity. A reading of Henry George's *Progress and Poverty* led him, like so many others, to political reform. U'Ren was behind the adoption of the Australian ballot in Oregon in 1891, the registration law of 1899, the initiative and referendum of 1902, the direct-primary law of 1904, the corrupt-practices act of 1908 and the recall of 1910. A self-effacing, quiet man, he held office only once, but his persistence in the work of voters' organizations made him a tremendous force in his State. He is alive to-day, serving on the consulting committee of the National Popular Government League which is fighting the power trust—the inheritor of the dubious mantle worn by the railroads and the street-railway systems thirty years ago.

Oregon, however, is far away. The Progressive movement in the States surrounding Altgeld's Illinois had to wait on the young sons of the Middle-West Populism of 1896.

La Follette led the way by becoming Governor of Wisconsin at about the time of Altgeld's death. In Missouri, Joseph Folk became Governor in 1904, after his fight on municipal corruption in St. Louis. Albert B. Cummins, a Progressive, was Governor of Iowa from 1902 to 1908. In the East, a reform agitation in the New Jersey State Republican Party, started by Everett Colby and George L. Record, was met by the Democrats, who elected Woodrow Wilson Governor in 1910. Charles Evans Hughes gave New York State two reform administrations after 1906, and even a Tammany Governor, William Sulzer, fought for a new primary system so hard that his party organization went back on him and obtained his impeachment and removal from office in 1913. In the Far West, Hiram Johnson was nominated as the Republican candidate for Governor of California in 1910 on the slogan, "The Southern Pacific Railroad must be kicked out of State politics," thus reorienting the fight of the eighties and nineties in the new century. Altgeld remains the spiritual forefather of all these men.

LONG before the collapse of the Progressives in 1912, Altgeld foresaw the doom of the neo-democratic movement. He sat in the Democratic convention of 1896, and smiled sadly at the demonstration for Bryan. He knew that applause is no substitute for action. And such moving spirits of the neo-democratic forces as lived on through the decade of the World War offer testimony to Altgeld's prophetic gifts. All of them—Brand Whitlock, Frederic C. Howe, Lincoln Steffens—described the same descending curve into baffled uncertainty. More than Ernest Hemingway's, they are the "lost generation." They had witnessed the same coiling of primitive democracy in "privilege"; they had seen the futile, or relatively futile, attempts of the Rooseveltian and Wilsonian party men to achieve social democracy; they had reflected on the irony that the automobile could do more to kill rule by traction rings than all the campaigning and speechmaking in the world; they had seen the usurpation by the great power companies of the dominating position once held by the railroads and electric trolley lines. What was the use? Corruption, as Lincoln Steffens later lamented, had won out.

Steffens has given us, in his autobiography, the most complete and candid confession of an attempt to understand a moving world from a point of view fixed by a past from which that world had already moved. And Frederic C. Howe, in his *Confessions of a Reformer,* offers similar testimony; his autobiography, published in 1925, reads like a model for Steffens. A third neo-democrat, Brand Whitlock, writing in 1913, set the pattern for both Howe and Steffens up to a point in his *Forty Years of It.* All three of these men had to admit their impotence in the face of events as the tumultuous after-war years carried the democratic world of their youth to the verge of dissolution.

When Steffens came home from Berlin, Heidelberg, the Sorbonne and the British Museum in 1892, it was to an America which neither he, nor any other member of his generation, had been trained to understand. The frontier, the great Way Out for the discontented, was just about closed, yet Steffens, the child of pioneers who had come to California by the Overland route and via the Isthmus of Panama, had been brought up to understand that a trust in Emersonian self-reliance, and a belief that simple Mosaic morality would solve all equations, was sufficient. A good man could always work up, if not in one place, then in another. Steffens's own father was a case in point; so was his mother, who had come out to California in the sixties to get married. At Heidelberg the young Lincoln Steffens had learned that there was no absolute basis for an ethics, but his studies had not weakened his emotional faith in the rules of the American game. He tells, with high good humor, of his first job-seeking. "The juvenile literature I had read as a boy, about lads who began at the bottom and worked up, had stuck." When he found no work he was amazed.

He finally landed on the New York *Evening Post* of "Larry" Godkin, and his true bent became manifest almost immediately. Evidently he was a great reporter from the start; it took him no time at all to become the *Evening Post* man in Wall Street during the panic of 1893. He tells us he didn't understand Wall Street when he was reporting the panic; he was too busy to see the implications of the facts. To him the financial structure was like the Sierra Nevada, an act of God. Moral financiers could make a moral stock market. And when the panic had subsided, and Wall Street was reorganizing the débris left by ninety-three, Steffens more or less carried the same simple notion about "good" men being sufficient into Police Headquarters where Dr. Parkhurst was just commencing to make a hullabaloo. There Steffens began to understand things, although his emotions still lagged behind his perceptions. He learned from Boss Croker, for example, that "bad" men were often no worse, *in effect,* than "good" men who depended on a "bad" system for their income. He discovered that "good" men were often the first to squeal when reform promised to be far-reaching enough to disturb that income. But the Lexow investigation was not compelling enough to disrupt Steffens's emotional pattern; it took years of muck-raking, in many cities and States, plus a futile attempt to apply the Golden Rule to labor-capital crises, plus a study of two revolutions, to bring him to the conclusion: "Good" men are helpless in a "bad" system; therefore, either change the system, or make a radical revision of our notions of Good and Evil. (In other words, either become a revolutionist or a cynic.) In Steffens's own words, the lesson of the life of a muck-raker was to be this:

"I had seen the Russian Revolution, the war, and this (Versailles) peace, and I was sure that it was useless—it was almost wrong—to fight for the right under our system.... Either we should all labor to change the foundation of society, as the Russians were doing, or go along with the resultant civilization we were part of, taking care only to save our minds by seeing it all straight and thinking about it clearly."

Seeing it straight means, to Steffens, admitting that corruption has become the norm in a democracy; that traditional morality, so far as economics and politics are concerned, is merely a veil behind which necessities impose themselves on men who act one way and talk for publication another. For behind the surface corruption, which is more or less constant, depending on the state of the public conscience, there is invariably the more subtle corruption that reaches to the heart of the "good" citizen through his pocket; one cleans up the noticeable, the blatant, graft only to find that a refinery or a public utilities company or some landlords are hurt—and the dividends of the "honest" citizen, who is also an investor, are cut down. Then the Seaburys, the William Travers Jeromes and the Gifford Pinchots drop the useless rôle of Canute as the tide of parabolic public opinion drifts in. Steffens saw it happen all too often in New York, where Big Bill Devery followed Roosevelt as the presiding genius of the Police Department, and where Seth Low, the "goo-goo" mayor, was followed by a Tammany mayor; in St. Louis, in Ohio, in Chicago and at Washington, where the idealism of Wilson, considerably battered at the close, was neatly balanced by the depredations of the Ohio gang.

The implications of Mr. Steffens's confession are that his generation tried valiantly, throughout the fifteen-year period of the quest for social justice, to understand plutocratic, industrial, monopolistic America by means of Jeffersonian, agrarian, individualistic shibboleths. It was like trying to stay the tides. The answer to trusts was "trust-busting"; the answer to corrupt government was "throw the rascals out"; the answer to a banking and business oligarchy of a few men was Woodrow Wilson's "New Freedom" for the small business man. For a time Steffens believed in all these answers, at least emotionally. He wrote as if he thought that simple honesty was, like patriotism, enough. And an aroused middle-class people, who read of "The Shame of the Cities" in *McClure's,* must have thought so, too, for out of the muck-raking, the exposure of corruption in the big cities and the States, and even in the rural districts of little Rhode Island, which maintained Nelson Aldrich in the United States Senate, came an enlargement, an expansion, of the program of the Populists into the Progressive Movement. Out of the muck-rakers' agitation, the belly-hunger of two decades, and the shocked attention of a democratic people that saw democracy foundering, came a few beneficial laws: Al Smith's factory legislation, and the like. But what has happened to the hopes of the Progressives? The War killed them, and Steffens knows it.

The prime value of Mr. Steffens's personal time-chart is that it throws open to us a laboratory in which a great many experiments have been carried out. We get, in Steffens's account, the "inside story" of the great push from below that crystallized so imperfectly in the Presidencies of Roosevelt and Wilson, a push that was killed many times over by the War, the Draft Act, the Versailles Peace, and the decadence that followed.

Steffens really knew he was trying to hold a lion by the tail back in his *McClure* days. One day Upton Sinclair came into the *McClure* office. "What you report," he said, "is enough to make a complete picture of the system, but you seem not to see it...." Steffens's answer was a description of what he saw, and it must have satisfied Sinclair, for he went out and said "that man sees it all right." But to make the point clear, Sinclair published an open letter to Steffens in a magazine. What Sinclair did not realize was that Steffens needed some time to adjust his imagination to the facts; one recovers from mental lesions slowly.

By now Steffens has recovered completely. But he has also recovered all too well; he has succumbed under successive inoculations of disillusions to the dangers of pragmatism, and is orally inclined to the theory that whatever is, is right—provided you think it is. This is a species of New Thought that enables him to sympathize with the Russian experiment at the same time that he sees a solution in Mussolini's coercive Merovingian state, where a Mayor of the Palace rules in the name of the King. It permits him to see the virtues in Lenin, the virtues in Henry Ford and the virtues in Herbert Hoover. He is full of vague hope—for the Seven-Hour Day and the Five-Day Week are just around the corner. He awaits them with an optimistic grin.

Frederic Howe, confessing his defeat in 1925, at least saved himself from jumping aboard the New Era bandwagon. He had not learned, he said, to pursue the truth to its ultimate lair—at bottom he was a moralist, not a realist or a scientist. He had not gotten rid of the classifications ground into him in his youth; he still believed, subconsciously, in "good" and "bad" people—the "good" folk being those of Anglo-Saxon stock, country-club membership and the amenities of Howe's own boyhood. At Johns Hopkins, from Richard T. Ely, Albert Shaw, Lord Bryce and Woodrow Wilson, he had learned that democracy must be "saved." The "best minds" could save it—minds like Ely's or Wilson's. But the War and the peace taught him, in the upper reaches of his consciousness, that only economic stabilization could build a stable—that is, a "saved"—world, and he came to realize that "liberals," such as himself, could do nothing to bring this about. And so he went to work, in 1921, for the railroad brotherhoods and the Plumb Plan in an effort to create a labor party. At last he was in one definite camp, and urging a group of men to follow its own interests—a euphemism, perhaps, for the Class War. He has not despaired of the ultimate success in America of a labor party—justice, he is now convinced, has never been given to people; they have had to take it for themselves.

If plotted on a graph, Howe's career of a "best mind" in politics to "save democracy" parallels Steffens's at all points. Born in Meadville, Pennsylvania, in the late sixties, a friend of Ida Tarbell, who comes from the same neighborhood, Howe had all of Miss Tarbell's early bias in favor of the small business man. His father, a manufacturer on a small scale, also had a furniture store. At Allegheny College, Howe learned nothing; he didn't question the sanctity of Matt Quay, the Republican boss of the State, for Quay went to church, and the big boss's lieutenants gave the young Howe railroad passes to Baltimore when Johns Hopkins succeeded Allegheny.

At Johns Hopkins, Woodrow Wilson stirred Howe emotionally, but Albert Shaw, with his lectures on city management, probably did more in a concrete way to point Howe's life. Socialism failed to interest the young student; Henry George's program seemed, at first, too "easy" a reform. Richard Ely taught him to be critical of the classical economics of Adam Smith, Ricardo and John Stuart Mill, and described an economic feudalism that was devouring the world of equal opportunity. But Ely's lectures served only to point the way back to a primitive democracy; so when Howe went to Cleveland he worked with Tom Johnson to kill, not control, monopoly of natural resources and rights of way. He finally came to accept the Single Tax.

Howe's first inkling of the impotence of law in the face of fundamental realities came, like Steffens's, in New York of the nineties. Jerry, the bar-keep, was his first realist—as James B. Dill, the trust creator, was Steffens's. Howe had been appointed captain of the assembly district that included Greenwich Village by Dr. Parkhurst. He was to spy on the saloons and the Raines Law hotels and report any violation of the rules. When he asked Jerry why the saloon didn't close on Sunday, he got a pat answer: "Because we have to pay $2,000 a year in taxes." "But if you can't observe the laws," said Howe, "you ought to go out of business." Well, the old-time Germans, Jerry told him, had done just that, but "they sold out to men who were willing to take a chance."

So that was the answer! There were always men to take chances. Legislation and taxation had made the saloon an evil by involving it in politics. Dr. Parkhurst immediately lost a crusader. In Cleveland, whither Howe took himself after a short unhappy interlude in Pittsburgh, evangelical reform left the young seeker cold. Tom Johnson managed to attract him because the Single Tax was an economic, not a moral, fight. But it was still a fight of the "best minds" against the powers of darkness who were running the world in the interests of the few. It was not until after Versailles that Howe came to realize that the liberal could not save the world; "he wanted to patch."

These liberal Americans—Steffens, Howe, Brand Whitlock—have all been tremendously afraid of doctrine, of commitment to party or program, even after they have been shown the feebleness of disembodied ideas. This is, of course, in the spirit of pragmatism, the dominant philosophy of the age; it runs all through William James; it is the key to Dewey's indecision, his refusal to formulate ends. Steffens became, at one time, a Single Taxer with no interest in Henry George; he became, later, a socialist with no interest in Karl Marx. He had no Pope. Brand Whitlock was even less interested than Steffens in doctrine; an artist, a lover of beauty, he could not, and cannot, abide a formula that may be quintessentialized in the phrase, "economic determinism." "I have gone through every political philosophy," he said after the War. "I can see nothing in socialism. The philosophy of Henry George of a free state in which the resources of the earth will be opened up to use is the only political philosophy that has ever commanded my adherence. But the world is not interested in such a simple reform. It wants too much government, too much regulation, too much policing. And it may never change."

THE extreme radicals of 1900 might say, were they disposed to speak to the Single Taxers and liberals from the grave or the armchairs of old age, "I told you so." Eugene V. Debs, in effect, said just that when he deserted Populism and Bryan to form his own Socialist Party with Hillquit and Berger. Daniel De Leon, the enemy of Debs and all other "opportunists," as he called them, was saying, "I told you so" soon after Henry George's defeat in the New York mayoralty campaign of 1886. The anarchists who carried on the tradition of Johann Most—Emma Goldman and Alexander Berkman—never had any faith in liberal meliorism. Berkman's futile *attentat,* when he shot and wounded Henry Clay Frick after the smash-up of the Amalgamated Iron Workers following the breaking by the Pinkertons of the Homestead strike of 1892, was his answer to meliorism, liberalism, even to parliamentary socialism.

Debs was, really, an advocate of parliamentary socialism—the American equivalent of Kier Hardie and the young Ramsay MacDonald of England, and Wilhelm Liebknecht of Germany. There was a good deal of "just folks" about him. A Hoosier, born in November, 1855, in Terre Haute, Indiana, he was the close friend of both James Whitcomb Riley and Eugene Field, two poets of the Valley of Democracy. Debs came of Alsatian stock. His nature was gentle, yet unbending; he was emotional and sensitive. Communists like Earl Browder dismiss him to-day as "more of a humanitarian than a socialist." Yet it cannot be said that Debs ever went back on his principles. At fifteen he went to work in the Vandalia car shops; at sixteen he was firing a locomotive on the road. To save his mother's peace of mind, he later quit railroading, and at nineteen he was clerking in a wholesale grocery. Yet his heart remained with the boys on the railroad. He refused a partnership in the wholesale grocery business, and also the general managership of the American Press Association, because, as he said, "There are too many things in business that I cannot tolerate. Business means grabbing for yourself." He joined the Brotherhood of Locomotive Firemen in 1875, and five years later became grand secretary-treasurer of the national organization.

Debs's first fliers in politics were taken as a Democrat. For the four-year period, 1879-83, he was city clerk of Terre Haute, and in 1885 he went to the Indiana Legislature. But he kept busy at his labor jobs throughout these formative years. He remained secretary-treasurer of the Firemen until 1892, and even continued to edit the organization magazine for two years after that. He helped to organize the national unions of the brakemen, carmen and switchmen. And in 1892 he gave up a $4,000-a-year salary to take a job at $900 a year to work for the American Railway Union.

This union grew mightily in its first months as an all-inclusive railway employees' organization, covering all the crafts in the industry, both skilled and unskilled. Inside of one year it had 465 lodges, with an approximate membership of 150,000. But it went to pieces when Cleveland broke the Pullman strike. Nevertheless, it performed its function in training Debs, who learned, through it, that his place was with the laboring classes as a whole, and not merely with the "Aristocracy of Labor." Bryan drew him off in 1896, but by 1900 he was working in his own direction. In 1904, as candidate, Debs got 402,400 votes—a great increase over 1900. In 1908 he polled 420,820, and in 1912, when the Socialist movement was at the height of its American power, he received 897,011 votes. Debs may have been, as Benjamin Stolberg says, the "end of Populism," and not a harbinger of the Revolution, but the "immediate demands" of the first Socialist platform were for "public ownership of all industries controlled by monopolies, trusts and combines," the "public ownership of the railroads, telegraphs, telephone, and all means of transportation, communication, water works, gas and electric plants, and all other public utilities," the nationalization of mines, the reduction of hours of labor and public works for the unemployed. For "immediate demands" they seem fairly revolutionary.

However, De Leon would have none of Debs. This domineering genius of the Socialist Labor Party was against all reformism, all sops. "The unconditional surrender of capitalism," he said, "is the battle-cry of the Proletarian Revolution."

De Leon was born on the island of Curaçoa, off the coast of Venezuela, in December, 1852. The son of a prosperous doctor, he received an excellent education in modern and ancient languages, mathematics, philosophy and history in Germany and Holland. After coming to America in the early seventies, he studied and won a prize lectureship in international law at Columbia University. His first experience with politics was in the Henry George campaign of 1886. Later he took up with the Bellamy nationalists, but a thorough study of Marx led him to believe that Bellamy's program had no point of attack. He joined the Socialist Labor Party in 1890, and maintained a position of supreme authority in the party until his death in 1914, fighting the "pure and simple" trade unionist followers of Gompers on the one hand, and the Debs "opportunists" on the other.

De Leon's fame to-day, outside of the ranks of his followers, must rest on his work as the forerunner of Lenin. Toward 1904 he was feeling his way to a final exposition of his ideas; he began, at that time, to regard the trade unions as the nuclei of the communal society, as the organizations which would take over the economic life after the revolution. Here is the germ of the Soviet system. Lenin said, after the Bolshevist success in 1918, that De Leon was the greatest of modern socialists—the only man who had added anything to socialist thought since Marx. "The American Daniel De Leon first formulated the idea of a Soviet Government, which grew up on his idea. Future society will be organized along Soviet lines.... Industrial unionism is the basic thing." Yet the germ of De Leon's system may be found in Edward Bellamy's novel, with its syndical arrangement of society.

The most bitter enemy of the American system of 1900 was Emma Goldman, who had seen her "pal," Berkman, go to jail for the shooting of Frick. A woman of an essentially "pure" nature, she defines anarchism in such a way as to make it seem the most intelligent and humane of creeds—until one bethinks oneself to remember that problems of organization, of means, of institutions for human concourse, are left in a delightfully vague region of the non-necessary. It is here that one is thrown, inevitably, back into the arms of either capitalism or socialism. Whatever violence there may be in the anarchist's creed, it must seem no more, and no less, reprehensible, than violence practiced on miners in the coal fields of Pennsylvania, and Harlan County, Kentucky, by the instruments of "law and order." And the anarchist sanction is fully as sensible as General Harbord's proclamation that war has a mystic sanction that lies beyond the bourne of intelligence either to dignify or condemn. Yet anarchism has gone its way into the past; the Emma Goldmans—atomic, incapable of organization towards definite ends—make no sense in a corporate world. If anarchism has any future, it is far beyond the horizon, and beyond the Communist horizon, once the state has "withered" away as a coercive instrumentality.

PROPHETS and soothsayers, haruspices and oracles—such must Henry George, Edward Bellamy, Daniel De Leon, Lincoln Steffens, Emma Goldman, have seemed to many in the years before the War. Yet there was one soothsayer, W. J. Ghent, who outshines them all. Ghent was a socialist, secretary to Victor Berger, and also at one time a secretary of the Rand School. But his vision was not of socialism. In *The Independent* for April 3, 1902, there appeared an essay on "The Next Step: A Benevolent Feudalism." This was later expanded into a book called *Our Benevolent Feudalism*. Ghent sorrowfully waved aside the Kropotkinian dream of a communistic "union of shop industry and agriculture," the hopes of the neo-Jeffersonian small farmer and small shop-keeper, and, finally, the Marxists, who were "too hopeful." And what does *Our Benevolent Feudalism* prophesy? Quite simply—the Fascist State.

CHAPTER THREE

Minority Report of the Novelists

☆

HENRY DEMAREST LLOYD might be offering his tentative and journalistic first objections to the processes of monopoly in the eighties; Henry George might be frightening the timid and the venal by combining with the socialists and the Knights of Labor in a political campaign; and a succession of strikes might be sending prophetic shivers down the spine of a Bellamy, but our novelists were slow to reflect the altering tempo of life in America. A sweet interregnum, a breathing-time, prevailed through the eighties as "local color," sired by Bret Harte, caught on in the magazines. This is wholly understandable, for, as a matter of fact, the forces making for industrial concentration seemed not to touch the average American who had had benefit of schooling. Minds change more slowly than facts; and, as William Allen White has pointed out, the influence of the American Sunday school persisted in shaping the writers of fiction even after Pittsburgh had become a staring reality. The American Tract Society, a Boston company, published Sunday-school fiction which was "taken out" by the literate young in virtually every Protestant community in the land. This fiction had one pattern—the pattern of Victorian melodrama, with virtue rewarded in earthly terms and vice firmly relegated to second place in the hierarchy by getting its material come-uppance. And as the winds of Darwin and Huxley began to blow, and as Robert Ingersoll began to pick flaws in the story of Saul's transmutation into Paul, the basic pattern for fiction gave way but slowly. Virtue was still virtue, vice still vice. America was still a pretty good place, and James Whitcomb Riley still saw the small town of Meredith Nicholson's *Valley of Democracy* in terms of Jacksonian neighborliness.

The rise of local color, however, indicated the first stirrings of the spirit of science in American literature. Deterministic theories of conduct were sifting in from a Europe that was restive with philosophical change. Old voluntaristic theories were disappearing under the abrading force that is stated at its most devastating in Haeckel; and as physics of the "billiard ball" type made Tennyson's lines about "one increasing purpose" sound a little silly, the European artists commenced to discover flux and chance taking the places formerly held by growth and teleology. In America, John Fiske, a youth who had been brought up on Emerson and Unitarian thought, became the prophet of Herbert Spencer, erecting the dogma of progress from simplicity to diversity, from lower to higher, into a divine law, but his fellow New Englanders, Henry and Brooks Adams, soon passed beyond this "picture-thinking" optimism of the Arnoldian "Power not ourselves that makes for righteousness" and were, respectively, embracing a jocular "conservative Christian anarchism" and "the law of civilization and decay." No sooner had Huxley popularized the term "agnostic" than it was seized upon by the brilliant Robert Ingersoll, who constituted himself the "bulldog of Darwin" for the North American continent. The Higher Criticism followed Ingersoll about, creating an atheist in every village, and agnostics by the dozens in colleges that had, only very recently, been the training grounds for the ministerial profession. And, as part of the picture of disintegration and reintegration, local color began to drive out consciously moralistic and teleological fiction.

The spirit of regionalism blows through the literature of local color, whether the author be Miss Jewett of the New England *Country of the Pointed Firs* or George W. Cable of old Creole Louisiana. And since regionalism is, at best, merely a matter of dress, and since local color springs from an interest in "writing," and not from any more deeply seated drive, the preoccupation seemed harmless, even where the "conditioning" of the American Tract Society remained in force. But a stronger realism than the verity of time and costume and landscape was in the offing as Zola's stories became a center of doctrinal disturbance in France. Striking upon an America that was not yet even fairly conscious of its tramps and millionaires "bred from the same womb," the terrible Zola seemed, to Thomas Bailey Aldrich, "a miasmatic breath blown from the slums," and to the comparatively young lawyer, Oliver Wendell Holmes, a teller of tales that were "improving, but dull."

The first person really to feel the shock and import of Zola's scientific and deterministic fiction was that delicate cultural seismograph, William Dean Howells. This child of the Ohio valley had two passions, if he can be said to have had passions; they were science and democracy, supposedly intertwined. Howells was in every sense a transitional figure. He had learned his writing trade in the Ohio newspaper offices of his father, and had achieved a first step into the world of the higher things when Lincoln, as a reward for a hack biography, appointed him to the Consul's job in Venice. But he lacked the frontier gusto and bumptiousness of his friend, Mark Twain, and he could not but eschew the life ardently espoused by another friend, Henry James, who fled to Europe because a world of form and contour awaited his sense of distinction in the older societies. The way between Twain and James was "only the whole of life"—realism, the petty life of the average law-abiding citizen made luminous by a subtle understanding. The swirl of forces of the Gilded Age failed to corrupt Howells, who retained some of the values of the Swedenborgian faith in which he had been bred. But the spirit of science, which followed the course of business enterprise across the continent, kept Howells from biting off the Brahmin credos with their echoes of Puritan theology. He lived in

Cambridge, but was not of Cambridge. His early science, however, came to him from literary sources. Sociology, as such, did not touch him until the eighties; then, with the crash of industrial conflict sounding about him, penetrating even to his Cambridge environment, he walked out into the strong glare of Karl Marx, willing, as was Wendell Phillips, to protest in behalf of the working class.

The growth of social consciousness in the fastidious Howells is a matter for applause. A gentle soul, abhorring violence and crudeness in all their forms, he spoke out bravely, as we have already seen, in behalf of the Haymarket anarchists in 1886. In a critique generally notable for its fairness, V. F. Calverton has twitted Howells for his rather naïve ideas about the power of the ballot in the hands of the workingman, but Ohio of the mid-century time was not the same school in which radicals of Chartist England, say, were introduced to the industrial conflict. Democracy was in Howells's bones; it was a religion with him; and faith in the common man as voter could not very well be eradicated by theorizing which carried no compulsion in terms of what he had seen.

Once in New York, beyond the pale of Charles Eliot Norton and the aged Lowell who so disappointed the young Hamlin Garland, come to Boston in search of gods, Howells's sympathies rapidly broadened and deepened. He had drawn, in faint strokes, a battle of social castes in his Boston story, *The Rise of Silas Lapham,* and in *A Hazard of New Fortunes,* his first picture of New York, the singular matter of a street-railway strike intruded into the pages. This novel, published in 1890, marked a definite turning point in the art of Howells. *The Quality of Mercy,* which followed in 1892, was more deeply interfused with social consciousness, for it treated of the results of a crime in which society itself was portrayed as the larger criminal. But *A Hazard of New Fortunes* remained, for Howells, "the most vital of my fictions." "We had passed," he wrote afterwards of the life which was reflected in this novel of the young nineties, "through a period of strong emotioning in the direction of humaner economics.... That shedding of blood which is for the remission of sins had been symbolized by the bombs and scaffolds of Chicago, and the hearts of those who felt this bound up with our rights, the slavery implicated in our liberty, were thrilling with griefs and hopes hitherto strange to the average American breast. Opportunely for me there was a great street-car strike in New York, and the story began to find its way to issues nobler and larger than those of the love affairs common to fiction." Compared to the treatment of labor troubles in Paul Leicester Ford's viscous *The Honourable Peter Stirling,* which was patterned roughly on the career of Altgeld's *bête noire,* Grover Cleveland, Howells's novel is, if not a child of *Das Kapital,* at least the fictional offspring of *Looking Backward,* which thrilled the author of *A Hazard of New Fortunes* in his Cambridge days.

From *A Hazard of New Fortunes* Howells passed on to definitely utopian fiction, following a popular craze for fictional utopias. He published *A Traveler from Altruria* in 1894, and *Through the Eye of a Needle* in 1907. The pattern of the first novel follows that of *Looking Backward* in its substructure of thought, for the Marxian law of concentration of the means of production through control of capital is followed to the Bellamy conclusion of the bloodless revolution by common acclamation and by means of the ballot. To continue the Bellamy parallel, *Through the Eye of a Needle* is, like the sequel to *Looking Backward,* called *Equality,* the detailing of a social order explored in the first book.

The utopianism and the mild, reticent industrial realism of Howells—with patience, kindliness and a twinkling, pungent irony informing the pages—were, however, growing old-fashioned even as they were frightening the good folk who were sorry to see their artist lost to "causes." Although Howells's mind was free and flexible, and his habit of thought candor itself (but temperate in expression), the Victorian realist was congenitally incapable of wringing the most from his drama. It has been noted, often enough, that his treatment of sex is hardly penetrating; he was chary of posing for himself problems that would offend sexual taboos; and his attitude toward *Crime and Punishment*—that the rackings and the tribulations of Dostoievski's harried souls would be untrue to the grain of American life, and hence beyond the powers of the local artist—is sufficient to date him in the age of Frank Norris, Stephen Crane and Theodore Dreiser. If we would keep abreast of the nineties and all they portended for the American dream, we must seek elsewhere than in the shapely books of Howells; we must look for the bitter and less tentative incidence in fiction of the two major phases of a larger process—the Populist clamor and protest from the farm border, and the concentration of capital that would, ultimately, make American investment banking the wonder, and then the goat, of the world. Squeezed between the farm revolt and the retort of a plutocracy nourished on the trustification of American industry, the really vital writers of the nineties were compelled to abandon, to some extent at least, both the voluntaristic theories of the Golden Day and the decorous surface realism of Howells. To Edgar Watson Howe, setting type in a Kansas town, and to Hamlin Garland, drinking milk at an oilcloth-covered table amid the hot buzz of flies, life was earnest in a way that Henry Wadsworth Longfellow never could have understood. And to Theodore Dreiser and Stephen Crane, slouching about the back streets of American cities that had grown too fast for justice, the drawing-room realism of Howells was impossible, since they had never known the proper setting. One and all, these writers were polarized, often unconsciously, by the historical materialisms of the moment. Their inability to escape their environment by way of the Door of Hope, the frontier, predisposed them to the deterministic philosophies that were already strongly intrenched in European thought. Howe, in his *The Story of a Country Town,* dragged in some eerie romance, but his book lives by virtue of its prefiguration of Lewis's *Main Street.* Garland was, himself, a born romantic, but the times were too much for him, and he throttled romance, in his early years of writing, because of the dictates of his class necessities. Even a person who was, by birth and training, above the economic battle—Frank Norris—found himself caught in a deterministic and sociological net; and the result of Norris's willing renunciation of his favorite, Robert Louis Stevenson, is our finest *collective* work of fiction, *The Octopus.*

PREVIOUS to the eighties, and well along toward the nineties, the average American didn't stop to look behind a certain version of the American West that was promoted by the artful advertising and adroit publicity of the railroads. These octopi, with their towering issues of stock upon which dividends had to be paid in order that still more capital could be drawn into the enterprises of spanning a nation with steel, underwrote campaigns for population, creating boom-town psychology, drumming up immigration and distributing glowing pamphlets and fake letters of recommendation. In the decade of the seventies the population of Nebraska virtually quadrupled; that of Kansas almost tripled its 364,399 of 1870. But the Great American Desert was not equal to the task of supporting the thousands who came. In 1887 there descended the droughts; but before that, in the town of Atchison, Kansas, a saturnine young man, Edgar Watson Howe, looked about him with at least one eye of a congenital realist and found life tasteless. His *The Story of a Country Town,* published in 1883—an exact contemporary, as Carl Van Doren has had the wit to point out, of Mark Twain's sun-shot *Life on the Mississippi*—was the first inkling, in fiction, that the Western country could be something other than glorious. Even Eggleston's story of the Hoosier schoolmaster, testimonial to a frontier poverty though it was, cannot be said to compete with *The Story of a Country Town.*

Ed Howe, still alive in 1932 as the "Sage of Potato Hill," was, at the time of the writing of *The Story of a Country*

Town, already the editor and proprietor of the Atchison *Daily Globe.* Frontier newspaper work was no cinch; it provided little leisure to indulge a taste for beautiful letters, and the tired quality of *The Story of a Country Town,* deriving from Howe's state of mind, is congruous to the picture of the general necessity of work in a pioneer community. Howe himself said of his story that "It was written entirely at night, after the writer had finished a hard day's work as editor and publisher of a small evening newspaper. I do not think a line of it was written while the sun was shining, but in almost every chapter there are recollections of the midnight bell.... A gentleman who once looked over a portion of the manuscript said his first impression was that it was the work of a tired man, and that the pen seemed to drag heavily in making the words. I fear this will be the verdict of the people...."

Carl Van Doren, probably Howe's most exhaustive critic, seems to me to fall into a misconception of the value of *The Story of a Country Town.* What lives for Van Doren are the stories of John Westlock, the passionate, though disciplined, prairie parson, and of Joe Erring, a "Kansas Othello" whose ambition was thwarted by a deficient education in human psychology. Westlock, a born trader, is held to a wife he has ceased to love by the religion of the period—hard, Calvinistic, dutiful; but eventually the strong man breaks the bonds for a moment, and runs off with a woman whom he soon deserts out of disgust for his own conduct. The stories of two ambitious men in the Kansas communities of Fairview and Twin Mounds move, in Van Doren's words, with "the cold tread and hard diction of a saga." The romantic elements of the novel—the mysterious mill of Damon Barker, the vicious horse of the dissipated Bragg, Westlock going forth in the storm to disappear forever—are surely dated, as Van Doren says, but when this critic goes on to proclaim the commentary on Fairview manners and morals dated, too, he underestimates the value of realism in a work that is only valuable for this very sane commentary. Indeed, what Van Doren especially prefers to the comment, the stories of Westlock's self-immolation and Joe Erring's failure at matrimony, are almost as antiquated as the strange things to be found in Barker's cellar. They have a Poe-esque flavor—Joe Erring's wife is a female version of the lunar breed of the lover of Ulalume, repining forever for a lost sweetheart; and Joe himself, with his sighing and his unreal philosophy of love, is a faraway plainsman's echo of the Byronic. One simply cannot swallow the story interest of Howe's novel. But the charge of dullness, leveled by Howe at Twin Mounds a full generation before it became a stock in trade of novelists of the Middle West, gives the book an historical interest. The commentary of Ned Westlock and little Biggs on the religion, the morals, the family skeletons and the general opportunities for eking out a living, of the jerry-built plain towns gives the book a modicum of preservative salt. It will live in American fiction as a document, not as a novel; one will return to it to realize the sad truth of a certain aspect of America's conquest of the West—the ignoble truth of the second generation, wandering between the worlds of the pioneer and Indian fighter, and of the amenities gradually introduced by the third generation at a later epoch.

Howe never repeated *The Story of a Country Town.* Exhausted by life, made a little surly by the attrition of the years in Atchison, he became a defender of the scrabbling order for which he had built up a good case of hatred in his novel. His defense took a Manichean turn which James Whitcomb Riley would certainly have been shocked to read. "Men hustling to do better than the competitors they hate have done more for the world," said Howe in *Plain People,* published in 1929, "than the great souls who dream of universal love." And on this philosophy of hatred the Sage of Potato Hill rests in an age that regards him a little quaint.

HOWE, with Octave Thanet and the Ignatius Donnelly of *Cæsar's Column,* was a faint chime announcing a mood of the

West that was fated to swell to impressive proportions. When Howe wrote his novel, the farmers' alliances were struggling upward, seeking to maintain a discipline that would make them effective in the political field. The movement grew slowly throughout the eighties, but when the hard times came at the decade's close the progress of organization was rapid, extending to the South of Tom Watson's Georgia, and enlisting the aid of an Eastern magazine publisher, B. O. Flower of the *Arena.* Under the banners of General James B. Weaver of Iowa, Ignatius Donnelly of Minnesota, Senator Peffer and Mary Ellen Lease of Kansas, the Populist forces marched into the national field, and commenced "raising hell," on the advice of Mrs. Lease, all over the country. For a literary pattern of the Populist revolt one must go to the pages of Hamlin Garland, to *Main Travelled Roads,* to *A Son of the Middle Border,* to *Rose of Dutcher's Cooly,* to *A Spoil of Office.* Here, and in the perfervid reporting in the pages of Flower's *Arena,* the pristine hues of Populism, and the economic realities that remained in back of the slogans of war, may be glimpsed at their most concentrated.

Garland was not the first to put the farmer into realistic fiction. Harold Frederic, who will live by his portrait of a cleric in *The Damnation of Theron Ware,* wrote *Seth's Brother's Wife* out of his hatred for the farm life of upper New York. There is no trace of the Jeffersonian crusader in Frederic, who escaped to London in the days of the *Yellow Book* by becoming the English correspondent of the New York *Times.* Joseph Kirkland, the son of a woman who had written vignettes of the Michigan frontier, put the land-hungry farmer into his *Zury, the Meanest Man in Spring County* in 1887. But the zeal of a Garland is not behind *Zury,* which closes on a note of softness and optimism.

Garland was lucky in his temperament—at least for a while. He has been, preëminently, an author of wax, soft to the imprint of any engraving tool of the times with which he had the fortune or the misfortune to come into contact.

Decidedly not a "source-man" himself, he acted as a literary broker for all sorts of social pressures and new ideas. And he had the good luck at first to run across superior minds—a luck that saved him, in his fermentative youth, from the banality of outlook that gradually usurped his character as he grew older in years. As a young man of twenty-three, sitting with his father and mother on the treeless plain at Ordway, South Dakota, the first of a number of opportune knocks came to his door. Hamlin Garland was, at this time (the year was 1884), a restless person; the dismal urgencies of life on a claim which he was holding down forty miles west of Ordway were wearing to the nerves of a young fellow with memories of the soft contours and clover of Iowa. So, when the Methodist minister, Bashford, brought a first breath of "culture" to the Ordway home, Hamlin was persuaded to try Boston as an antidote to the bleak winters and dragging summers of the Dakota plain. To combine two phrases of H. L. Mencken, the American peasant was set to clawing at the anthills at the foot of Parnassus.

And what a dogged clawing it was! With only a little money, which he had got by proving up and selling his claim, and armed with a number of useless letters of introduction from the Rev. Bashford, the young Garland reversed the marching orders of Horace Greeley ("Go West, young man, go West") and set out for the Boston of Holmes, of Lowell, of Howells and of Aldrich. Luckily for him again, he was not accepted into Brahmin society. The "city's intellectual life was low-toned and the pace of its citizens sedate," he wrote, although "an increasing material traffic thundered distractingly over granite cobbles." The bourdon of the streets, however, failed to disturb the late afternoon of the Genteel Tradition, whose high priests rejected the young man from the West. It was Garland's fortune to be compelled to fall back upon the resources of the Public Library, where heady documents from abroad might be obtained. And it was in the great hall of the library that an incipient crusader picked up his first flags and slogans.

Garland was, of course, brought up in the Jeffersonian creed of the floating West. The maxims of the Enlightenment were postulates with him, and, like his eighteenth-century brethren, he was at once "rational" and very much concerned with justice and the rights of man. A humorless person, idealistic and sentimental, he lacked the slightest tincture of irony or sardonic comprehension of the basic human lot. The power of self-criticism was beyond him. Hence, when he commenced to gobble up ideas, he seized upon anything that seemed either "rational" or calculated to improve the lot of the hapless victim of America's industrial expansion—the border farmer. That "rationalism" might lead one to the "chemisms" of Theodore Dreiser, given the assumptions of nineteenth-century science, did not cross his mind. "Veritism," a word which he encountered in Eugene Véron's *Esthetics* and in Max Nordau's *Conventional Lies,* pleased him because he had known the drab outlook of the Dakota prairie, and was coming to the conclusion that the older modes of literature were untrue to the facts. But, side by side with "veritism," Garland picked up the notion of the Single Tax, which Henry George was expounding and dramatizing. The truth of "veritism"—which, in terms of the West, meant land monopoly—must be altered in the interests of men who were born free and equal by the remedy proposed in *Progress and Poverty.* Thus easily did Garland reconcile the "scientific"—which a study of Herbert Spencer taught him to worship—with the class drives which were part of his fiber.

From 1884 to 1887 Garland was busy soaking up information. He steeped himself in the literature of the local-color school—Miss Wilkins, Sarah Orne Jewett, Cable, Thomas Nelson Page, Joel Chandler Harris, Bret Harte and Joaquin Miller. They seemed "scientific" writers—taking due cognizance of "place" and "time." Impressionism in painting also seemed part of this scientific renaissance. But the evolutionary theory that Herbert Spencer championed led upwards and onwards for the "scientific" Garland, and the ebullient young man sought to map this trend by writing a book tentatively called *The Evolution of American Ideals.* De Tocqueville and Whitman, Herbert Spencer and Henry George—all of them were buzzing busily in his head until, in 1887, he made a visit to the West.

The trip to the Dakota which he had thankfully left three years before marked the birth of Hamlin Garland, activist. It had been prepared for by contact with Joseph Kirkland, who urged upon him the career of the fiction writer. We need a real farmer in literature, Kirkland said, and Garland, always at his best when bucked up by other men, began experiments. On his trip to the West he had seen much to anger him, to stimulate him, to galvanize him. The farmers, in the midst of the depression, seemed "like flies in a pool of tar." On July fourth of his decisive year of 1887 we find Garland writing: "The dress of all the farmers I met seemed unkempt, miserable... George A's house showed rude comfort, but not a trace of beauty. Rag carpets, old gunny sacks on the floor. George and his family were eating their Sunday dinner of bread and milk. He was in his shirt sleeves with bare feet. The table was covered with blue oilcloth with vast pitchers of milk and dishes of pickles.... The irritable women dragged their tired and ugly bodies around, unlovely, characterless, finding comfort only in the gospels."

The spirit of this notation informs Garland's *Main Travelled Roads,* which was the product of the year of 1887. The words that sound ominously through the foreword to this volume are indicative of the tone of his early fiction—"ugliness," "endless drudgery," "loneliness," "the houses, bare as boxes," "the treeless plains," "the towns mere assemblages of flimsy wooden sheds," "an almost helpless and sterile poverty." A "dark mood was deepened into bitterness by my father's farm, where I found my mother imprisoned in a small cabin on the enormous sunburnt... plain." And the dark mood was vented in savage stories of enormous historical value, even if, esthetically, they leave much to be desired.

There is no hope in the best stories of *Main Travelled Roads,* although certain of the lighter tales make obeisance to the current demand for happy endings and the glorification of the pure country at the expense of the wicked city. The best tale in the volume is a fictional illustration of the Single Tax contention—that improvements on land should not be taxed. Obvious though it may be, with its drama crudely arranged, this story, "Under the Lion's Paw," tells with effective passion of a wanderer who took up a farm on shares. The wanderer and his wife and children put the farm into shape, build it up, improve it generally—and all because the owner, Butler, has promised to sell it to them when they have money with which to buy. When the time comes for the consummation of the deal, Butler charges for the improvements. The wanderer, Haskins, flies into a tantrum. "I'm kickin'," he says, "about payin' you twice f'r my own things—my own fences, my own kitchen, my own garden." But the villain, Butler, reminds him of the legal aspects of the case, and the unfortunate Haskins signs the deed and mortgage, paying a thousand dollars down and taking the mortgage at ten per cent on the rest. Another story, "The Return of a Private," which is obviously out of the life of Garland's own father, is a simple rendering of the emotions of a Civil War veteran upon his return to his Wisconsin farm. "His war with the South was over," says Garland, "and his fight, his daily running fight with nature and against the injustice of his fellowmen, was begun again."

Main Travelled Roads is not propaganda, in the opprobrious sense of the word. The propagandistic elements did not predominate in Garland's fiction until B. O. Flower of the *Arena* had taken the author in tow. Then, with Flower's money in his pocket and the command to help the Populist cause along by fiction and articles agreed to, Garland let his reformer's zeal get out of harness with the artist in him. A second trip to the West, in 1889, had turned him to Flower. During this visit to the paternal farm, Garland had seen his mother suffer a stroke of paralysis due to overwork and "the dreadful heat of the summer." He felt "like a sneak as I took my way to the train leaving my mother and sister on that bleak and sunburned plain."

The *Arena,* a thoroughly dull publication in retrospect, was the forerunner, in the nineties, of the muck-rake magazines of the following decade. Everything attracted Flower, from psychical research to laments for the "Woes of the New York Working Girl"; and a saccharine pseudo-Christian spirit often bathed the magazine in the light of the more oppressive Sunday schools of our youth. Articles on the "vulgar, brassy and intolerable" plutocracy of New York, in whose ranks one had to be "a great feeder" to be a great leader, dispensing "terrapin and canvas-back ducks, and rare brands of champagne, in lordly dining halls," jostled for space with more serious questions, such as: "Shall the United States Own the Railways?" Amid the clutter of the *Arena,* whose intellectual voltage was generally nil, Garland commenced plugging the Single Tax, writing on "The Alliance Wedge in Congress," and investigating the roots of Populism in the South, as well as in the West. A key to his thought, which shows how very far from socialism the militant youth from the Middle Border was, may be found in his "New Declaration of Rights," which appeared in the *Arena* for January, 1891. "We are individualists, mainly," he said of himself and his Single Tax friends, "let that be understood at the start. We stand unalterably opposed to the paternal idea in government. We believe in fewer laws and the juster interpretation thereof." And he amended Jefferson: "All men are born free and equal in opportunity, to live, to labor upon the earth and to enjoy the fruits of their own industry."

There is a drive in the *Arena* articles that is lost in the later books of reminiscence which Garland commenced to issue in fair profusion after 1912. But his *Arena* fiction—

A Spoil of Office and *Jason Edwards: An Average Man*—are pure social tracts. The lesson of the first novelette was summed up by the heroine, Ida Wilbur, in these words: "... thousands and millions of us must die on the road, I am afraid," but the Populist revolt must go on, for "the heart and center of this movement is a demand for justice, not for ourselves alone, but for the toiling poor wherever found." In *Jason Edwards* Garland gives a Single Tax answer to the question of why a Boston mechanic could not find independence by taking up land on the frontier.

After the Populist front was broken by the election of McKinley to office in 1896, Garland gradually withdrew from the lists of the agrarian crusaders. He was, on his own admission, "corrupted without realizing it," and one can see him going to pieces as flattery came from his new-found friends, Theodore Roosevelt and John Hay, among others. The world commenced to bewilder him as industrialism became aggrandized. Veritism, to a lover of Walt Whitman and Henry George, had ethical implications—one looked upon the world as it was, in order to know where to begin to effect a transformation in the direction of the heart's desire. But Garland forgot what he desired. In *Crumbling Idols,* which he published in 1894, the theory of Garland's own veritism is set forth. "The realist or veritist," he wrote, "is really an optimist, a dreamer. He sees life in terms of what it might be, as well as what it is; but he writes of what is, and, at his best, suggests what is to be by contrast." To such a realist, the naturalist's art seemed perverse. "What avail is this study of sad lives," asked Garland of Norris's *McTeague,* "for it does not even lead to a notion of social betterment." But "social betterment," in the fiction that sprang up in the wake of the Spanish-American War, was a matter of returning to the Victorian categories. Garland, insulated from the current of naturalism by his own insistence on ethical values, and loath to take the road of a Winston Churchill into good, clean, progressive fiction, let his latent romanticism come to a lush growth. He sought out the mountain West, far above the heat of the hated plains. In *Hesper* and *The Captain of the Grayhorse Troop,* for example, he proved a veritable Chateaubriand, making the "natural man" under God's open sky into the "good" man. And, while others stumbled into muckraking, the once militant Garland took the Telegraph Trail to Alaska, returning, in his imagination, to the life of an America which was all but dead. When he eventually traveled the back-trail from his *Saturday Evening Post* fiction (he even boasted that he had anticipated Zane Grey in some of his Western stories), it was to the field of reminiscence, to a chronicling of the lives of the Garlands and the McClintocks in *A Son of the Middle Border.* This book, with due allowance made for the softening of perspectives which age has brought to the once intransigent Populist crusader, is Garland's most valuable work—a real contribution to the social history of the American people as they take the road away from Thomas Jefferson.

GARLAND has been called a renegade by at least two American critics, C. Hartley Grattan and Granville Hicks. This is not wholly true; he never pretended to be more than an agrarian crusader, a Single Tax apostle and a Jeffersonian democrat at heart. His softening as an artist coincides almost exactly with the increase in the prosperity figures of the farming class with which he had cast his literary lot. The years of 1897 and 1898 saw crop failures in Europe, which created a market for the grain of the sons of the Middle Border. With the currency expanded in terms of the new-found gold, and with American wheat once more commanding a decent price in the world market, the energy-giving properties seemed kicked out of Populism. Even the closing of the frontier, which Turner had speculated upon in 1893, failed to cause an immediate end to the freeman's hope for a homestead. For, although it was true that land of prodigal quality was not to be had for the asking without going over the border into Canada, there were still 570,000,000 acres yet unclaimed in the United States, many of them of potential use for dry farming and for transformation by irrigation. As a matter of fact, for twenty years after 1898 the entries under the Homestead Act were larger than during the two preceding decades—especially so after the liberalization of the Homestead requirement, which enabled settlers to make property their own after three years instead of five. It is true, of course, that land cost more, but the rigors of the eighties had passed; new settlers had neighbors, better roads, improved marketing facilities. The succession of good crops, inaugurated in 1897 and 1898, continued on into the Rooseveltian decade, with values maintaining themselves in a way to please the farmer. In cold figures, the prices of agricultural products increased by nearly one-half between 1900 and 1910, and the value of farm property doubled within the decade. All this wave of well being proved, as 1931 has shown, to be a temporary phenomenon, but to a Garland who had never been particularly well-versed in the mysteries of economics, and who had never speculated on the approximate truth of the Marxian laws, it could hardly have seemed other than the beneficent workings of the Deity of an eighteenth-century rationalist's creation. Confused Garland was, but it is only common charity to regard him as a reflection of his time rather than a transforming force in it. He had had a hard youth; and as we watch him, in retrospect, taking his rather solemn pleasure in hiking through the tall timber or attempting to make of his adopted city, Chicago, a center of the arts, we can only reflect that his farmer friends, throughout these years, were glorying in gramophones, gossiping over that new mechanical toy, the telephone, buying automobiles, and sending their children to colleges where the greatness of American institutions was extolled without reference to European crop failures and the cyanide process for extracting gold cheaply from low-grade ores.

When he was a student at the University of California in the early nineties, the young Frank Norris contributed a story to the *Wave,* a San Francisco weekly. The tale was so horrifying to the literary taste of the time that a friend of Mr. Norris, senior, stopped him on the street one day and said: "If I had a son who wrote a story like that, I'd have him put out of the world in a lethal chamber." At least that is how Charles G. Norris, Frank's brother, recalls the anecdote. The wording, Charles intimates, may not be exact, but the sentiment at least testifies to the early formulation of purpose of the author of the terrible *McTeague* and the still more terrible *Vandover and the Brute.* Norris may have had his Stevenson side, and even his humorous side, but America's first really conscious naturalist meant to write of life in the raw, and he did write of life in the raw. His was a dedicated career, pursued relentlessly from the time he went East to Harvard to the time he slipped into the rôle of rather silly moralist in the final chapters of *The Pit.*

Unlike Garland, Norris had a brain that could see human beings in the whole perspective of economic law. Like Garland, he had a reverence for the new science of the late nineteenth century. And again like Garland, he was a realist who couldn't hold the pose; ethical values insisted upon intruding into his later fiction. A preternaturally earnest young man when it came to his art, he believed he had a mission to tell the exact truth, to treat of the plain people for the plain people, to see human beings in their relation to the mass, following them into the toils and gins set for them by the inexorable laws of nature. The novelist, he wrote, must "deal with elemental forces, motives that stir whole nations. These cannot be handled as abstractions [but] must be expressed by means of an analysis of the characters of the men and women who compose . . . society, and the two must be combined and manipulated to evolve the purpose—to find the value of *x*."

Zola was, of course, a god to the young Norris, who had encountered Naturalism after studying art in his 'teens in

Paris. "He was never," so his brother Charles recalls, "without a yellow paper-covered novel of Zola in his hand." *McTeague,* which he commenced while an undergraduate at Berkeley and at Harvard, taking five years to write it, is in the Zola tradition of *Nana; The Octopus,* a more ambitious work that achieves much only to collapse into a final specious ending, follows the broad-scale course of *La Débâcle.* These novels were matured slowly, seriously, the while Norris's Stevenson alter ego wrote romances—*Blix* and *Moran of the Lady Letty*—as a means of building himself up with the public. A third essay in undiluted grimness, *Vandover and the Brute,* was never finished; it was discovered, a "huge and terrible torso," as Parrington says, in an attic trunk after the San Francisco fire had destroyed more trunks than one. The romantic appearance of *Vandover* in 1914—incomplete, not entirely credible—in the book stores years after Norris's untimely death stands as a sort of symbol of the young author's life; he tried to compose a great trilogy of the wheat, commencing bravely in *The Octopus,* faltering at the close in the interests of an impossible poetic justice, and, in the sequel, *The Pit,* achieving nothing more than a movie scenario punctuated with some good descriptions. A novel supposedly to be called *The Wolf,* which was to have rounded off the trilogy by showing the effects and relief of a famine in a community in the Old World, was never written.

Norris's growth as an artist was a matter of continuous experiment along lines he had marked out for himself as an undergraduate at Berkeley and, later, while studying under a connoisseur of good writing, Professor Lewis E. Gates of Harvard. To gain a knowledge, as he thought, of men under elemental stress, he went as a newspaper correspondent to South Africa, and thence returned to San Francisco to engage in weekly journalism. The *Wave,* for which he wrote sketches, articles, stories and book reviews, was a railroad sheet whose main purpose was to combat the attacks on Collis P. Huntington and the Southern Pacific, but contact with the propitiatory forces of the industrial devil had no very observable effect on

Norris in *The Octopus*—unless it is to be found in the excuse given by the railroad president, Shelgrim, that if he were not head of "the Octopus," some one else would be there in his place, the laws of economic development under capitalism being what they are.

Norris's work in the *Wave* is tentative, but most of it finds a place in his mature books in altered, improved form. A story, "Judy's Service of Gold Plate," was later set into *McTeague* as part of the elaborate symbolism of greed which eventually undermines the character of Trina and drags the originally generous McTeague to a doom in the desert. Another tale, "Fantaisie Printanière," flashes the names of Trina and McTeague for the first time; in this story the hulking dim-witted giant brandishes those unforgettable hands that are already "as hard as wooden mallets."

Thomas Beer, in the most memorable phrases ever written about Norris, has spoken of the "immense common life" that swirls and eddies about the principal figures of *McTeague* and *Vandover*. The youth in love with broad forces, who saw life in terms of the ant-heap, spent the years of 1896 and 1897 practicing a trick which is employed lavishly in *The Octopus* to give the book a cosmic setting. This is the trick of piling detail on rhythmic detail, as in his report on the Santa Cruz carnival end: "And then, in that immense silence, when all the shrill staccato, trivial noises of the day were dumb, you heard again the prolonged low hum that rose from the city, even in its sleep, the voice of something individual, living a huge, strange life apart, raising a diapason of protest against shams and tinsels and things transient in that other strange carnival, that revel of masks and painted faces, the huge grim joke that runs its four-score years and ten. But that was not all.

"There was another voice, that of the sea; mysterious, insistent, and there through the night, under the low, red moon, the two voices of the sea and of the city talked to each other in that unknown language of their own; and the two voices mingling together filled all the night with an immense and prolonged wave of sound, the bourdon of an unseen organ—the vast and minor note of life."

In that passage Norris was practicing a trick that was to become the notable, although thoroughly specious, peroration of *The Octopus,* when he wrote, in terms of similar tonal swell, of how the wheat flowed out from California, in spite of grasping freight rates and the petty connivings of the economic man, to reach ultimately the starving populations of India. He was practicing the trick of piling detail on detail that makes his descriptions of the Chicago Board of Trade the saving grace of his cheapest novel, *The Pit.* He was playing with his fictional ground tone—the cosmic tone that sounds below and above and around all the Norris men and women.

The trick is, of course, more than a literary device; it is the key to the Norris philosophy. The broad-scale, collective novel should be, in Norris's own words, a work that "draws conclusions from a whole congeries of forces, social development, race impulses." Single men live by chance—it is only the cosmic that is perdurable. Individual lives are items of a "huge, grim joke"; and when America's first naturalist wrote of McTeague, the giant dentist, and his petite wife, Trina, it was to show how accident, complete and amoral accident, disposed of the pair. The novel is a study in blind determinism from the start, with gold calling the turn. McTeague was never a licensed dentist; he entered the profession by chance. Chance again intervenes when a lottery brings $5,000 into the lives of the couple. Trina holds on to the money with the intensity of a French peasant who has seen his father robbed; her miserliness in turn affects McTeague, who is inclined by nature to be generous, and who resents the stinginess which luck has brought into their married life together. The pair, given their tragic economic setting, help each other along in the process of disintegration—but neither is at fault; it is the universe that is at fault, the vast purposeless universe that gives men tiny brains and great bodies and marries them to women who act as the catalytic agents of human catastrophe.

McTeague represents Norris's sense of one phase of the industrial process that was transforming America—the phase that tossed men into slums, that made them dependent on forces beyond their single control, on laws, for instance, that required a dentist to have a token of his skill in the form of a diploma, even after years of practice had given him an empiric certificate of ability. But Norris not only understood this phase of the process; he had the imagination and the insight to go out from the city which had nourished him and reach an understanding of the theme that preoccupied Hamlin Garland—the theme of the farmer who had gotten out of balance in a national economy which was weighted to favor industry and the rich of the urban centers. It is the ability to encompass a grasp of the totality of the situation which distinguishes Norris from both Garland and the earlier Theodore Dreiser.

In *The Octopus,* an epic of the San Joaquin Valley, Norris became, quite emphatically, a muck-raker, a commentator in fictional form on the acts of the Southern Pacific Railroad which were so to arouse Charles Edward Russell in the next decade. In this vast drama of the growing of the wheat the novelist becomes, definitely, the moralist. In the pages of struggle there is no specific denunciation from the novelist's own mouth of the "octopus," Mr. Huntington's railroad that had raised and lowered rates at will, charging "all the traffic will bear." But Jehovah, as Thomas Beer has said, thunders at the close. He thunders when the villain of the piece, S. Behrman, a fat gentleman whose function in the story is that of forecloser of the farmers' mortgages, is tumbled, ridiculously, into the hold of a vessel, there to perish under a shower of the very wheat crop which he had hoped to sell in India for a fortune. The death is the crudest possible melodrama—a sudden panicky concession to all that Norris had fought in the fiction of his time. Throughout the book the railroad has been an economic necessity, called into existence by the laws of the unfolding universe, which care not what individuals perish. But Norris goes on from the sudden retribution of Behrman's death to comment on the railroad, and his comment springs from a quick dip into Matthew Arnold; the "wheat remains," and the moral law is upheld. "The larger view always and through all shams, all wickedness, discovers the truth that will, in the end, prevail, and all things, surely, inevitably, resistlessly, work together for good."

But what and whose "good" is another matter; the railroad has killed Vanamee's sheep; it has killed Buck Annixter, the leader of the San Joaquin ranchers who were fighting to hang on to their property; it has destroyed Magnus Derrick's honesty, making of an upright citizen a crude politician who countenances bribery on the theory that it is necessary to stoop morally to conquer an immoral monster. It has brought the country of the San Joaquin—which might stand as symbol of rural America from the Georgia cotton acres to the fruit ranches of the Northwest—under the domination of the city money-changers, and has sounded the knell of Jefferson and the triumph of Hamilton. And all this that famine might be prevented in India!

The scene of the nineties is in *The Octopus* in a variety of illuminating ways. Caraher, the anarchist whose "cure" for the iniquities of the railroad is a piece of lead pipe stuffed with dynamite, is brought West from the city orbit of Johann Most. Presley, the poet, is obviously patterned on the Edwin Markham of "The Man With the Hoe"; and Presley's poem carries out over the country as "The Man With the Hoe" carried over the country, following upon publication in a San Francisco newspaper. The lethargy of the people as a whole in a land of growing "trusts" is noted. And the underlying economic philosophy—a philosophy which Norris does not develop in so many cold words of his own—is Populist. Norris's sympathies, made plain by the death of Behrman, the middleman, are obviously with the ranchers who are the shippers of grain. He was no Marxian novelist—although his novel, as I have said, is our finest *collective* work of fiction.

It is collective where Dos Passos's *1919,* for example, is individualistic. For it shows a *group* of people, and how they make common cause to bear up under economic forces beyond their joint control; it portrays them largely in their group relationship to society. The Marxian Dos Passos, on the other hand, takes his individuals as single symbols of a decaying society, and he follows them as individuals; they nowhere work together, collectively, for a group end. But the question of the collective versus the individualistic novel is, at best, an academic question; the novel is something to be used by social philosophers, not something to be written definitely to support a philosophy. It matters not whether Norris favored one group as against another in his work; what does matter is that Norris, by and large, was an honest novelist and a perceptive one, a novelist who could see America whole. "I never truckled," he wrote, "I never took off the hat to Fashion, and held it out for pennies. I told them the truth. They liked it or they didn't like it. What had that to do with me? I told them the truth." In the light of the close of *The Pit,* where the moralist once more intrudes to spoil a theme which is, ostensibly, that of the marketing of the grain, and its effect on the marketers, these words may seem overbrave, but they have a large measure of truth. That they could have been written with any appositeness at all in the nineties, given the prevalent taste in fiction, is a matter for national congratulation.

FRANK NORRIS was an educated man—and perhaps that was his trouble. He had been brought up in Chicago and on the Pacific Coast, within the orbit of the ascendant middle class. Quite naturally, he shared the prejudices, the unconscious morality, the values, of his own sort, no matter how much he might strive to forget all he had swallowed in his childhood. The closing scenes of *The Pit,* when the big, bold, masculine wheat-market manipulator, Curtis Jadwin, runs off with his New England wife, Laura, to commence their mutual regeneration under the ægis of the Golden Rule, are indicative of the leaven that was always working under the surface in Norris. Indeed, the fate of Norris bolsters somewhat a generalization that might be made to the effect that it is a handicap to be cast forth into the world with a decent upbringing and a formal education *in a time of pronounced social change.* It was Rousseau, an uneducated man by formal standards, who had the intelligence to sense the fate of the old régime in eighteenth-century France. In America, it was Theodore Dreiser, badly taught, self-trained, and without benefit of the usual middle-class family upbringing, who had the acumen to comprehend an American type of the eighties and nineties that was crying for admittance to the novel.

Dreiser was born in 1871, at Terre Haute, Indiana, in the Hoosier country that has stood, more than any other environment, for the neighborliness of democracy. But certain chances preserved the young Dreiser from the fate of Booth Tarkington, Meredith Nicholson and James Whitcomb Riley. Like Altgeld, he had a loving and ignorant mother, and a hard, bigoted father. The beauty of country America, to which he was by no means insensible, was not related to any Jeffersonian tradition in the young Dreiser's mind, for his schooling was of a meager sort, such as could be picked up in the narrow German Catholic parochial institutions which his father insisted that he attend. Hating his father's mentality, which seemed to him of a piece with the paternal inability to hold a position long enough to support a family with any decency, Dreiser carried over his disgust for the "mentally weak" parent to the Catholic discipline. His early phobias kept him from absorbing the usual social stereotypes of the period; the moral, Protestant discipline of the midlands did not touch him; and when he went to Chicago after a youth spent in the poorer quarters of Terre Haute, Sullivan, Evansville and Warsaw, Indiana, it was with an inquiring eye chained to no psychological necessity to see things in "normal" terms.

Luck was with Dreiser. To a Howells, trained in the early democracy of pre-Civil War Ohio, the "promoter," the "captain of industry," could hardly seem as significant, say, as a nice, normal middle-class family such as the Kentons. To a Tarkington, raised in the atmosphere that is quintessentialized for us by Meredith Nicholson, the "promoter" and the "captain of industry" could only seem to be chasing the American dream in his own way. Such inequities as might result from building up a power company, say, at the expense of the consumer would come out right in the wash; excess profits would be utilized to subsidize invention, to endow colleges, to beautify cities, and so on. But to Dreiser, with no tradition to maintain either by protest or by closing the eyes, the "promoter," the "captain of industry," the master of capital, could be glimpsed in colors of the America that was emerging. Dreiser did not understand the American great of the eighties and nineties in terms of any dialectical materialism, or of any historic process—he could not think the situation through with his meager native equipment. But his knowledge of the financial manipulator, his tastes and desires, was exhaustive.

Dreiser's Cowperwood books—built up on an adaptation of the career of Charles T. Yerkes, the Chicago traction manipulator who crossed swords with Governor Altgeld in the nineties and lost—were not published until 1912 and after. But they belong, actually, to the nineties, to the period in which their author was wandering muzzily and disconsolately about the streets of Chicago, St. Louis, Pittsburgh, New York and Toledo. *Sister Carrie* and *Jennie Gerhardt* preceded them in point of time, the first book having been recommended to Doubleday, Page and Company by Frank Norris at the century's turn, only to be relegated to the cellar because it offended the taste of an epoch that was lapping up Winston Churchill's romances. But more than either of Dreiser's full-length portraits of two lower-class American girls thrown on their own, the Cowperwood books, *The Financier* and *The Titan,* are of the era of an ascendant and thoroughly raffish plutocracy. Called "a trilogy of desire," the Cowperwood series will eventually be rounded off with a third panel, *The Stoic,* which will transport an eager (although aging) American appetite to London, to mastery of the tube system, and to a nonplussed end as desire fails in its reach.

Frank Algernon Cowperwood, whose motto is "I satisfy myself," is a projection, not only of Charles T. Yerkes, but of Dreiser himself. For the burden of Dreiser's autobiographical writings, *Dawn* and *Newspaper Days,* is a burden of desire—of a formless wish for power, of dreams of fair young women, of a wish for a carriage, for a life in Bohemia, for the money to dine in lobster palaces. Balzac, whom Dreiser read in Pittsburgh of the Homestead strike and the Carnegie fortune, appealed to Cowperwood's creator because he had spread upon paper a vast Paris in which ambition might be gratified. Over and over again, in his autobiographical books, Dreiser repeats his certainly far from spiritual dreams of youth, of love, of money, of art.

They are dreams out of the gilded pages of *Munsey's Magazine* of the nineties, in which photographs of the homes of the rich are used to illustrate sycophantic articles about the great American fortunes. But they are also true to the actual imaginations of the great of a parvenu society. Cowperwood, with his cold skill at gambling, his understanding of the mechanisms of pyramiding and profit-taking, his sensual love for many women, his lavish and eclectic art gallery, his Fifth Avenue magnifico's palace, may seem fantastic on first acquaintance, but he is no Hearstian supplement caricature, as a flipping of the leaves of Barron's notes will prove to the satisfaction of any doubter. J. P. Morgan himself was "magnificent" in the Yerkesian way, with his love for young ladies, his cornering of the *objet d'art* market wherever possible, and his passion for imperial Rome. Nelson Aldrich, who was Providence's street-railway magnate as well as United States Senator from Rhode Island, had a love for luxurious rare rugs; Frick blindly amassed money and pictures; the Pittsburghers, made rich by the creation of the United States Steel Corporation, went in for an orgy of spending that would have seemed obscene even to Cowperwood; John W. Gates made gambling and manipulation a career. An architect obviously patterned after Stanford White builds Cowperwood's New York home in the White style—which was one phase of our spiritual "pillage of the past," even as Richard Hunt's imitation of Loire valley châteaux on Fifth Avenue was another. By any test of comparison, Cowperwood is the real thing.

Dreiser, in fact, was not clever enough to fake; and where he obviously fails, as in the erotic passages which he is unable to expand in terms of inner truth, we can easily assume that he is guessing and eliding. He cannot fool us. He could never have entered the society of the Dinosaur Age by the methods of an Ivy Lee; he simply had to tell the truth in terms of raw gobs of visual fact because he was too clumsy, too insensitive to subtlety (which, by the way, is a word he enviously loves to parade) to get by with the methods of flattery and cozening. Because of this congenital inability to lie, Dreiser, even though he may have once desired to create fictional trade goods in order to become rich, has turned out a figure in Cowperwood that is realistically true to the imagination of emerging plutocratic America, the America of Joseph Benson Foraker and Boies Penrose, as contrasted with the moribund "Old Republic" of Senator Hoar and Carl Schurz.

Back of the remarkable Cowperwood books, which come trailing clouds of the glory of monopolistic America, is a fact which Henry George made a foundation of his Single Tax doctrine: that one way to prevent economic misery is to restrain men from making personal fortunes out of public franchises, whose increment belongs to the people who make them possible. When Cowperwood was a boy, watching a lobster devour a squid in a tank—a struggle that brought home to the youth the law of the survival of the fittest—"the little bob-tailed street cars" of America, as Brand Whitlock calls them, were "teetering and twinkling" along the rails of the small American communities of the time. They were drawn by mules and by broken-down horses; to drag a street car was "the most cruel, degrading and ignoble fate that could befall a horse." There was some money in this early stage of street-railway transportation, and Cowperwood saw how the game of franchise-grabbing was worked in his early career as a broker and financier in the Philadelphia of Jay Cooke's age. There was money in the second underground cable stage. But when electricity came in as a motive power, the street-car business entered a third phase; in Whitlock's words, "it ushered in at once the greatest era of speculation in franchises and social values, watered stocks and bonds. The era of exploitation came upon us, and out of these privileges to conduct public utilities, i.e., privileges to absorb social values, enormous fortunes were made, with all the evils that come with a vulgar, newly rich plutocracy. To keep, extend and renew these privileges, they must have their lawyers, and their newspapers to mislead and debauch the public mind; they must go into politics, organize and control the machines of both parties, bribe councilmen and legislators and jurors, and even have judges on the bench subservient to their will, so that the laws of the state and the grants of the municipality might be construed in their favor ..."

Whitlock, four times Mayor of Toledo, understood the situation; Dreiser dug below to discover the type in control of the situation. The Cowperwood series, which enters exhaustively into street-railway manipulation in Chicago, has been likened, by Stuart Sherman, to "a club sandwich composed of slices of business, alternating with erotic episodes," and untrue, as a whole, to life on the *human* level. But no one ever claimed that Cowperwood represented the human race at its finest flowering; he simply *was,* and Dreiser, by grace of environment and lack of education in the so-called humanities, was just the man to uncover him. The Cowperwood series cannot be waved out of existence on moral grounds, any more than an earthquake can be conjured away by admonishing the earth to obey the inner check. What can be fairly urged against Dreiser is that he did not fully understand the social significance of Cowperwood; he did not see him in a larger picture, either from a Populist viewpoint or from the Marxian position. Cowperwood's labor philosophy is that of McKinley or Nelson Aldrich: "I have at least eighteen thousand stockholders who want a decent run for their money, and I propose to give it to them. Aren't other men getting rich? Aren't other corporations earning ten and twelve per cent? Why shouldn't I? Is Chicago any the worse? *Don't I employ twenty thousand men and pay them well?"* This last statement is not analyzed for its fundamental speciousness by Dreiser, who, as Clifton Fadiman says, is merely content to throw a bone to the proletariat now and again in the Cowperwood series. When Dreiser offers his own comment on Cowperwood's career, as he frequently does, it is only to marvel and wonder at the spectacle of a strong man bucking the *mores,* flaunting public opinion in the matter of sex life, getting away with amoral predaciousness for a time, going to jail solely because other crooks succeed in putting him there, coming out and making the world his oyster once more, going up in a proud arc, coming down when chance disposes and, generally, acting under the "chemic" compulsions of a science learned from Huxley and verified by Pittsburgh. Men divide into the lions and the lambs; there is no meaning to "good" and "bad."

But Dreiser, even as Hamlin Garland and Frank Norris, couldn't hold the amoral pose. Years after he had written *The Financier* and *The Titan* he came to understand the position of Cowperwood in historic sequence; and in *Tragic America,* with the same fumbling and tenacious earnestness which informs his novels, he has sought to equate the figure of Yerkes to the grinding of the faces of the poor, and the mulcting of the consumer, in the America of the rise of the industrial overlords and the centralization of credit. *Tragic America* may be a crude job, but at least it is evidence of a will to get to the bottom of life in the stony wilderness of the economic man. "Let no one underestimate the need of pity," wrote Dreiser in *The Financier*. In *Tragic America* the pity that has all along been in Dreiser at last comes out of the brooding stage. He begins to talk about "equity." In the "trilogy of desire" the many prove stronger than the one, whether the spectacle has any "meaning" or not; in *Tragic America* Dreiser recognizes the possibility that the many may prove stronger than the few in terms at least approximating the Marxian dialectic.

THE sharpest commentator of the nineties was a man who never considered his age, so far as his fiction went, in economic terms—in fact, he once seriously told Gustavus Myers never to attack the upper crust. This person who couldn't see the economic application of his own fiction was Stephen Crane, an atomic person who instinctively rejected all the values of his society. Hamlin Garland, who helped him to get a start, has made the apparently incomprehensible statement that he couldn't see Crane developing "as Booth Tarkington has developed." But the judgment has its queer truth; Crane couldn't think in terms of the general, while Tarkington has worked out the implications of a philosophy in a number of related novels. (The objection to Tarkington is that his hierarchy of values is a low one.) Crane was, of course, the best of his generation so far as sheer *writing* went. But architectonics were beyond him. He could, in *The Red Badge of Courage,* make a startling single statement that heroism is not all it may seem, and, incidentally, evince a good psychological insight into the motives of men under stress. He could, as in *Maggie,* play ironically upon the whole notion of Christian charity in a world whose virtue is a matter of totem and taboo. And he could, as in *The Blue Hotel,* show that "every sin is the result of a collaboration." Crane was excellent at refutation. But refutation does not make a literature of grand conceptual outline, of philosophic breadth; it is simply the art of the paragrapher in fiction form. Crane was capable of brilliant single statement; he was not capable of synthesis. The seeds of development were not in him; and perhaps it is fortunate for his young reputation that he died before he commenced to repeat himself. In any case, Crane stands as symbol of America's literary luck as the decade of muck drew nigh. For Garland went soft as the irritants which caused him to function were removed; and Norris died. Dreiser, unable to get *Sister Carrie* before the public, and forced to scrabble for a living in Grub Street by editing magazines to suit the popular taste, went underground for ten years. Ed Howe produced nothing. And naturalism, with its exemplars gone or silent, was drowned in a flood of cheap romance, and then in a second flood of "problem" fiction whose chief claim to distinction is that it never even properly posed any problem to begin with. The nineties, in their way, had a few literary titans; at least they had a few men with large, if incomplete, vision. But the decade that followed was a decade of inconclusive ferment, whose contribution to imaginative literature would not come until after 1912. It was a decade of underground work in the arts—important in many ways, but a desert stretch in the totality of American literature.

CHAPTER FOUR

The Muck-rake Pack

☆

W. J. GHENT'S prognosis of a benevolent feudalism was not, it must be admitted, an act of pure divination. For in March of 1901, after J. Pierpont Morgan had created the United States Steel Corporation, the newspapers—or such of them as had not set out to bask in the sun of Empire, Bigness and Industrial and Imperial Might—were filled with gloomy forebodings of a corporate feudalism, whether beneficent or no. And the other side of the feudal shield was Communism, or so more than one editorial writer thought; Arthur Brisbane, the son of a socialist of Greeley and Brook Farm days, feared, for example, that the epoch of great trusts in the offing would inevitably call forth its counter-principle of a "labor trust more dangerous and aggressive than any other."

Whatever the future might hold, however, the symbolism of United States Steel—fifty per cent Morgan ingenuity, and fifty per cent water—was fairly obvious. It meant the beginning of the end of competition in another basic industry. Previous to March 3, 1901, the Carnegie Steel Company—a vertical trust, controlling its own product from the Lake Superior ore bed to the salesman's order book—had been preëminent in steel; Carnegie had become a byword for ruthless and brilliant competition. The "little Scotch pirate" did not approve of the industrial pools that formed only to break up with the dishonesty of constituent members; he scorned the Morgan "community of interests." His competitors felt this attitude whenever there were hard times—although, for the consumer, the Carnegie tactics were vastly preferable to the methods by which Rockefeller had stabilized the oil industry and, incidentally, obtained control of ninety-five per cent of the product.

Carnegie, in 1900, wanted to retire. For thirty years he had nourished a dream; he wanted to be both Mæcenas to the arts and Lord Bountiful to organized charity. "The man who dies rich," he said, with a touch of the characteristic Carnegie disingenuousness, "dies disgraced." But before a career of ostentatious and fully publicized giving could be undertaken as a diversion for old age, Carnegie must dispose of his steel works. And he wanted them in safe hands.

There was one man in America who could consolidate steel, and he was J. Pierpont Morgan. But Morgan was loath to act, even though Elbert H. Gary had urged upon him the desirability of stabilized steel. He certainly never would have acted at Carnegie's direct invitation, for bouncing, twinkling Andy, the "little white-haired Scotch devil" of Tom Scott's affection, was the type of person which the gruff, powerful Morgan could not stomach. Carnegie, however, had guile sufficient to the task. He literally bluffed Morgan into purchasing the Carnegie works and merging them with nine other corporations to form the greatest trust in the world.

Pierpontifex Maximus, as he was known behind his back, had just achieved a fair measure of stability in the railroad world after ten years of work, taking the bankrupt lines of the early nineties and putting them on a relatively non-competitive basis. His National Tube Works, which had bought much of its material from the Carnegie concern, proposed to erect additional blast furnaces and steel works. To Carnegie, this seemed unfriendly. So, in retaliation, the Scotchman threatened to "establish an extensive pipe-and-tube manufacturing plant, representing an investment of $12,000,000," which would have meant a steel war, involving Morgan's interests. But Morgan failed to respond to the retaliatory threat. Carnegie countered by playing his trump card: he circulated the rumor that he was planning his own railroad lines in Pennsylvania to compete with roads under the Morgan domination from Pittsburgh to the seaboard. Morgan became uneasy as stocks began to fluctuate. And then Carnegie, the guileful, sent the man with the tongue of honey, Charles M. Schwab, to New York. Coupled with Schwab's suave representations, the threat of unsettling the railroad situation—which might have entailed a disastrous renewal of the rate-wars of Jay Gould's day—brought Morgan to the bait; he decided to "do something about this fellow Carnegie." The result was the purchase of the Carnegie Steel Company, and the subsequent capitalization of United States Steel at $1,403,450,000. Carnegie was paid off, largely, in bonds; he said he took the total bond issue of the new corporation—$303,450,000—instead of stocks because the stock was not water alone, but air. Carnegie was right about the water and air, but Morgan's version of the deal also had its truth: he had paid the Scotchman off in bonds, he said, because he wished him forever out of steel in any active way—Morgan had had enough of "Carnegie cattle work along the border."

Carnegie could now achieve his wish to die poor. And consolidation in American industry was relieved of its greatest threat: the Carnegie competitive methods. The consolidation of steel was a culmination, in a way, of a movement that had been going on ever since the Civil War, only to be interrupted periodically by panic, such as that of '93. Trust-forming, which had been outlawed supposedly by the Sherman Act of 1890, had picked up again after the panic of the early nineties by use of the holding-company device, a method made possible by the wording of the Sherman Law and the easy attitude of New Jersey and Delaware, both of which went into the business of selling industrial indulgences and absolution. By 1898 the United States had ceased to be a "commodity" country, and had become a manufacturing and exporting nation. Cheap raw materials, a plethora of foodstuffs, a constant supply of immigrant labor, the high tariff—made even higher by the Dingley bill of 1897—and an expanding market—all of these happy factors combined to increase manufactures eleven-fold in value between 1850 and 1900. Population and the value of agricultural products, in the meantime, had increased only three-fold; hence it was not unnatural that the balance of political power had shifted from the rural to the urban districts.

The Spanish-American War had stayed, for a moment, the apprehension of trusts and monopolies, an apprehension that had characterized the late eighties and early nineties. But the consolidation of steel revived the bogey of corporate wealth. And the little fellow, the small business man, the "forgotten man" of that day and generation, if he chose to look at the statistics soon after the new century had opened, might well have feared for his future. In 1899 the Amalgamated Copper Company and the American Smelting and Refining Company had been formed. The American Sugar Refining Company, a trust of the 1891 vintage, had escaped the teeth of the Sherman Act by a fortunate Supreme Court decision which said, in effect, that control of ninety-five per cent of a product did not constitute a monopoly in restraint of trade. The Standard Oil had been reorganized under the Jersey laws in 1899; the Consolidated Tobacco Company was formed in 1901; the International Mercantile Marine in 1902. In 1904, there were, according to John Moody's figures, 318 industrial trusts representing mergers of practically 5,300 plants and a capitalization exceeding seven billions. By 1914 companies doing an annual business ranging from over a hundred thousand to a million dollars, and the class above a million dollars, employed more than three-fourths of the wage earners and made more than four-fifths (in value) of the products of a nation.

The movement toward consolidation had gone on in the railroad world, as well as in the industrial, with the result that, by 1900, nearly all of the high-grade mileage was controlled by six groups: the Vanderbilts (who dominated the New York Central and the Northeast, excepting New England); the Pennsylvania system; the Morgan-Hill combination in the

Northwest; the Gould-Rockefeller lines in the far Southwest, with connections to the Atlantic seaboard; the Harriman lines (Union and Southern Pacifics and the Illinois Central); and the Moore group (the Rock Island and other lines leading into Chicago). The Rockefeller and the Morgan interests were heavily invested in the independent New Haven road, and the Vanderbilt and Rockefeller groups had large blocks of stock in the Delaware and Hudson. A "trustification of money," as the Pujo investigation of thirteen years later would reveal, had made all this consolidation possible.

More fundamental to it, in a philosophical sense, was the Great Technology made possible by the development of the scientific method, the Baconian outlook. And even as business consolidation was coming to its flourishing peak, the methods of the Great Technology were making their impact felt in the world of the American magazine, with results that would cause the plutocratic masters of the industrial centralization to shiver—for a brief moment.

In the beginning, however, the genius of the American cheap magazine was Frank A. Munsey, as money-bound a man as any captain of industry or promoter who ever trod the corner at Wall and Broad Streets. This curious country boy from Maine, who chose literature, of all things, as a stepping-stone to wealth, had come into a magazine world that, at the beginning of the nineties, was strangely out of touch with the realities of American life. The magazines were neither published and sold by modern methods, nor were their contents at all in tune with life as the American knew it. Until 1890, the "big four" were the literary magazines—the *Atlantic, Scribner's, Harper's* and the *Century,* which sold at twenty-five to thirty-five cents a copy. *Harper's* was edited by Henry Mills Alden, with George W. Curtis and, later, William Dean Howells, in the Editor's Easy Chair. *Scribner's* was looked after by Edward L. Burlingame, who made it an illustrated literary magazine, like *Harper's,* but with more attention paid to art and to the special department of wood engraving. The *Century,* under Richard Watson Gilder, was, perhaps, even more "literary" than *Scribner's* or *Harper's.* The *Atlantic Monthly,* which had published Lloyd's attack on the Standard Oil and the rebate system, had more diversity of appeal than the three others, and was edited by greater men, commencing with James Russell Lowell and continuing through the tenure of William Dean Howells. But, one and all, they were citadels of the "genteel tradition," survivors out of the world of the scholar gentleman.

Into this tepid arena, at the beginning of the nineties, plunged Frank A. Munsey, with his belief in Ford methods—"big volume and small margins." Munsey was to the modern magazine, in America, what E. W. Scripps was to the newspaper: the father of literary mass production. Innovations in the printing art had made a cheap magazine possible by 1891, the year of the founding of *Munsey's* in its twenty-five-cent incarnation. Glazed paper made from woodpulp—a cheaper medium than rag-paper—and the invention of the photo-engraving process had combined to reduce the mechanical costs. American advertising was already on the rise. But the wholesalers—consisting of the American News Company of New York, with its forty or fifty branches throughout the country—stood, a monopoly, in the way of the pioneer.

Before Munsey's adventure, S. S. McClure had launched his *McClure's* at fifteen cents in 1893. John Brisben Walker, who had founded the *Cosmopolitan* in 1886, cut his magazine to twelve-and-one-half cents a copy, but was soon back to fifteen. But it is doubtful if either of these competitors would have been able to maintain their fifteen-cent front if Munsey had not come along, in 1893, with a ten-cent magazine, the first in the country, to dramatize the change.

The middlemen—those who bought, perforce, from the American News Company—refused from the start to handle *Munsey's* at the stipulated wholesaler's price of seven cents a magazine. And the refusal was almost fatal. Munsey had no printing plant of his own, no electro-typing establishment, no bindery. His capital, as he said, was all on "the wrong side of the ledger." But he held out for the seven-cent price. A vicious trade war resulted, and Munsey, oddly enough for a timid man, won the scrap; by 1899, his investment was worth $5,000,000, his monthly circulation had reached 650,000. With his Down-East shrewdness, the triumphant editor—in an article called "The Making and Marketing of *Munsey's* Magazine," published in *Munsey's* for December, 1899—pointed out that articles, fiction, engraving and pictures cost no more for an edition of a million copies than for one of a thousand.

Munsey's admiration was not for the quality of his articles, fiction, engraving and pictures, most of which were of a low grade; his praise was all for bigness. "If all the paper used in these four [Munsey] magazines every month," he wrote, "were made into a ribbon as wide as the magazine itself, it would cover a distance of 22,916 miles, or go nearly around the world." Or if it were made into "the ticker in a stockbroker's office, it would cover 366,644 miles, or go around the world nearly fifteen times." There speaks the authentic voice of the Boy Broker.

But a better man than Munsey was in the field made safe by the survival of a ten-cent magazine; he was S. S. McClure, the greatest magazine genius America has produced, an Antrim Irishman, blond, ebullient, enthusiastic, forever on the wing, seeking ideas and authors to carry them out, the man who brought Kipling's *Kim* to America and who became, himself, a character in two novels, Robert Louis Stevenson's *The Wrecker* and Howells's *A Hazard of New Fortunes.* During the nineties the superior caliber of McClure was not immediately apparent. As the new century opened, however, McClure was feeling his way toward a dynamic social conception of the uses of a cheap magazine. The biggest fact of American life was—the business consolidation. McClure knew it in his bones. He had sent some one to the Armour Institute of Technology, which had been established in Chicago at the time of the World's Fair, to write it up, and the author had included in his article some material about Mr. Armour and the packing industry. This gave McClure a lead: he decided to have articles written definitely about the most important American businesses. It was suggested in the McClure offices that the methods of handling and distribution of the Standard Oil Company would be of interest, so McClure planned a series on oil to begin in February of 1897. The talk about trusts, started by Henry Demarest Lloyd, had become general, McClure noted, but he had no bias either for or against them at the time.

There happened to be, on the *McClure's* staff, a motherly young woman who had once taught Sunday school in Frederic C. Howe's home in the oil regions of Northwestern Pennsylvania—Miss Ida M. Tarbell. She had already demonstrated her ability at historical research in the period of the French Revolution, and had recently written a popular life of Lincoln. McClure put her on the job of looking into the Standard Oil—a job that was to take five years of study before she had completely mastered and checked up on all the material for the famous *History of the Standard Oil Company.* Three years of research were put in before the first chapter was printed in *McClure's* for November of 1902.

This was hardly muck-raking in cold blood, however. Miss Tarbell, who was credited, later, whether slanderously or not, with having an animus against the Rockefellers because of the ruin of her own relatives in the early years of the oil business, merely saw with the logic of her background the little fellow as the noble fellow; the Standard Oil, through no preconceived plan in McClure's mind, became, again, the "Anaconda, hideous in his deformity," as it had been in Lloyd's *Wealth Against Commonwealth.* But events conspired to make one series of haphazardly muck-raking articles the beginning of a campaign.

The business consolidation that stared McClure in the face at the end of the nineties had not been attained by wholly extra-political means. An invisible government had passed over the country coextensive and coeval with its westward expansion. Laws were enacted in the interests of business. As William Allen White humorously remarked: "It was just as easy to see the railroad's side as it was to see the other side, so the mass of Federal decisions for years favored the railroads." And the railroads were the foundation of the structure. The wholly legal "corruption" of the courts—we may assume that no money was passed—was merely the capstone of what Lincoln Steffens, McClure's greatest muck-raker, was shortly to baptize "the System."

Out in Cleveland, as Ida Tarbell's first article was about to appear, Tom L. Johnson was already fighting a System that had corrupted the city government in the interests of maintaining a traction monopoly, keeping carfares up, and paying a high dividend upon heavily watered stock. Miss Tarbell suggested to McClure that an article on certain admirable aspects of the city government of Cleveland would be worth while. A "constructive" person, Miss Tarbell. So Steffens, who had just joined Ray Stannard Baker and Miss Tarbell on the McClure staff, went West with no definite idea in mind, but with a hazy notion that copy, either by himself or others, awaited him. While on his trip some one told him of corruption in St. Louis, where a certain Joseph W. Folk, circuit attorney, was fighting a ring of boodlers. The result was, after some investigation, a joint article in *McClure's* for October, 1902, written by Claude H. Wetmore, a St. Louis reporter, and Steffens himself, called "Tweed Days in St. Louis." It was the first muck-rake article—having beaten Ida Tarbell's first piece on the Standard Oil to the newsstands by a month. Thus was S. S. McClure involved in muck-raking.

AND then came the yelping of the muck-rake pack. The dogs let loose, they swarmed all over the land, doing some harm, but an incalculable amount of good in the way of educating the American people to realities. Muck-raking, indeed, provided the basis for the entire movement toward Social Democracy that came to its head in the first Wilson Administration. This movement, it is true, grew out of Populism, and was aided by the spread of socialism, but it never could have gone very far without the incessant din in the American cheap magazines during the Roosevelt and Taft Administrations. McClure, having genius, shaped it at the start into educational channels. He had always had a passion for education, and the muckraking he undertook to foster was always documented, sane, "proved" to the last fact. And he was thorough; not one article would he have on an aspect of the growth of American industrialism, with its political concomitants, but would grow into a series, exposing the anatomy entire. An Englishman, William Archer, comparing the flaccid cheap magazine of London with our own, was moved to remark that "the historian of the future may determine how much of the 'uplift' that distinguished the Roosevelt Administration was due to the influence of the McClure type of magazine; we cannot, at this distance of time, see things quite in proportion; but it seems to me certain that Mr. McClure both paved the way for President Roosevelt and potently furthered the movement with which his name will always be identified."

The yelps of the pack grew louder, bolder. The *History of the Standard Oil Company* continued on through 1903. Steffens, excited by what he had found in St. Louis, pursued corruption to Minneapolis, to Cleveland, to Cincinnati, to Chicago, to Philadelphia, to New York—writing a series that grew into a handbook of American city government as it was at the beginning of the century and, indeed, is to-day. Steffens's articles were later gathered into a book, *The Shame of the Cities.* A second series on the shame of the States—called *Enemies of the Republic* in *McClure's* and *The Struggle for Self-Government* in book form—followed from Steffens's pen. Ray Stannard Baker commenced to explore the labor problem, finding graft even in labor organizations, but more duplicity among the employers. *Everybody's Magazine* picked up the challenge, commencing with Thomas W. Lawson's *Frenzied Finance* (1905), and printing Charles Edward Russell's exposures of the beef trust in the same year. Samuel Hopkins Adams investigated the patent-medicine situation—or racket, as we would call it to-day—in *Collier's,* spreading some horrible stories throughout 1905. And in the same year Ray Stannard Baker, in *McClure's,* started *The Railroads on Trial,* a series that would run on into 1906, when the debates in Congress were leading up to the Hepburn Rate Bill, which would put at least one or two teeth into the Interstate Commerce Commission.

Other notable additions to the "literature of protest" there were, too. Burton J. Hendrick told the story of Life Insurance in 1906 to a *McClure's* audience that had been very much excited by the insurance investigation conducted by Charles Evans Hughes in 1905. David Graham Phillips, the reporter and novelist, wrote a blistering, peppery, and sometimes inaccurate series called "The Treason of the Senate" for the *Cosmopolitan* in 1906. His facts were assembled for him by Gustavus Myers, according to Isaac Marcosson, but it is questionable that he used them as Myers himself would have used them. The *Cosmopolitan* having been bought by Hearst, it commenced, with Phillips's articles to give muck-raking the tone of the yellow journals. But Phillips's series was, in the main, justified, as Steffens's work was already there to prove. The campaign went on, following McClure's lead, on the one hand, and Hearst's on the other. Russell traced the connection in California between the Southern Pacific (*The Octopus*) and the State government for Hampton's in 1910, the very year that Hiram Johnson, Republican nominee for Governor, decided that the railroad "must be kicked out of politics." Judge Ben Lindsey of the Denver Children's Court wrote on criminal law and juvenile delinquency for *Everybody's* in 1909, with Lary Ritchie, now Hoover's Man Friday, doing some of the investi gations for the series. And *McClure's,* seeking to discover the connection between the "System" and prostitution, carried a number of articles by George Kibbe Turner on the "social evil" and allied vice in 1909. The underworld came in for a lurid series by Alfred Henry Lewis, called "The Apaches of New York," which rocketed through *Pearson's Magazine* in 1911-12. Even the *Saturday Evening Post,* in these years, had some of the stigmata of the muck-raking magazine.

Up to 1906 the movement had not been known as "muck-raking." It was, as conducted by S. S. McClure, simple sociology —fact-finding, with no specific "cures" urged, and with moral indignation subdued to the necessity of sticking to the record. How careful McClure was may be gleaned from his autobiography. He paid a high price for good reporting, and depended on his own staff writers. Steffens, for example, averaged four articles a year—and each article cost McClure about $2,000. Ida Tarbell's series on the Standard Oil averaged three a year for five years—and for each installment McClure was out of pocket $4,000.

McClure sought to present a whole picture of society. William Archer, writing with amazement in the British *Fortnightly Review* for May, 1910, told his countrymen of the McClure type of "richly documented, soberly worded study in contemporary history"—"thorough" and "understatement," he said, were the two preëminent McClure words. And if *McClure's* turned up plenty of corruption, why, corruption was the dominant fact of American life at the time. "...Defiance or evasion of the law, social selfishness, and a denial of the fundamental rights of man were everywhere to be detected," wrote Harry Thurston Peck in 1905. "Yet far more significant than all these things was the fact, made clear by a thousand evidences, that the heart of the nation at its core was sound; that there still existed the capacity for strong indignation which springs from righteousness that every evil raised up swift avengers; and that all the blots upon the escutcheon of the Republic failed utterly to dim its brightness."

Hopeful Harry Thurston Peck! Yet it cannot be said that McClure, in his efforts to acquaint Americans with their own

System, did not do his best to release the springs of indignation in the electorate. He, more than any one else, made Americans aware of a new conception of sin—the conception explored by Edward Alsworth Ross of the University of Wisconsin in his *Sin and Society: An Analysis of Latter-Day Iniquity,* published in 1907. "Modern sin," Ross wrote, "is not superficially repulsive." "Unlike the old-time villain, the latter-day malefactor does not wear a slouch hat and a comforter, breathe forth curses and an odor of gin, go about his nefarious work with clenched teeth and an evil scowl. . . . The modern high-power dealer of woe wears immaculate linen, carries a silk hat and a lighted cigar, sins with a calm countenance and a serene soul, leagues or months from the evil he causes. Upon his gentlemanly presence the eventual blood and tears do not obtrude themselves."

Ross made a list of the iniquities exposed by the muck-rakers. Because the hurt of the modern sinner passes "into that vague mass, the 'public,' and is there lost to view . . . it does not take a Borgia to knead 'chalk and alum and plaster' into the loaf. . . . The purveyor of spurious life-preservers need not be a Cain. The owner of rotten tenement houses, whose 'pull' enables him to ignore the orders of the health department, foredooms babies, it is true, but for all that he is no Herod. [And] when the catastrophe does come, the sinner salves his conscience by blasphemously calling it an 'accident' or an 'Act of God.' "

But people are sentimental, Ross observed, and "bastinado wrongdoing not according to its harmfulness, but according to the infamy that has come to attach to it . . . they chastise the old authentic sins, but spare the new. They do not see that boodling is treason, that blackmail is piracy, that embezzlement is theft, that speculation is gambling, that tax-dodging is larceny, that railroad discrimination is treachery, that the factory labor of children is slavery, that deleterious adulteration is murder. It has not come home to them that the fraudulent promoter 'devours widows' houses,' that the monopolist 'grinds the faces of the poor,' that mercenary editors ... 'put bitter for sweet and sweet for bitter.' The cloven hoof hides in patent leather; and to-day, as in Hosea's time, the people 'are destroyed through lack of knowledge.'"

Lincoln Steffens was the first to supply the people of the Rooseveltian decade with protective knowledge. The text-books on American government were woefully deficient in teaching home truths to students of American government, municipal, state and national, and not even James Bryce suspected the worst. "Where," asked William Allen White, the Kansas editor with practical political experience, in a review of *The Shame of the Cities,* "where in the constitution are the functions of the boss described? Where in the constitution are the relations between the local corporation attorney and the people described? Where in the constitution does the chairman of the State Central Committee of the dominant party get his authority to sell legislative indulgences to corporations that contribute to his campaign fund? Where in the constitution may one find how the thing we call capital gets into government at all?"

Steffens gave factual answers to White's rhetorical, though pertinent, list of the Constitution's deficiencies. There is no need to detail the facts here; there is need to sketch the whole picture, the anatomy of municipal, state and national government as Steffens uncovered it. "'Big business,'" he discovered, "was, and still is, the current name of the devil, the root of all evil, political and economic." But "'Big Business'... is a blind phrase, useless; it leads nowhere." It is true that, in back of political corruption, were the railroads, banks, public service corporations, and so on, all of whom stayed in politics, after they had got what they wanted, merely to protect the water in their stocks, so that they might earn the more on the actual investment without raising a hue and cry among the populace. The railroads and public service corporations were, of course, "big," but there were, too, saloons, gambling and bawdy houses, which were small. Even as Henry George had discovered, Steffens learned that what these big and little businesses had in common was not size, but the need of privileges—what La Follette came to call "Special Privilege." They needed franchises and special legislation, which required legislative corruption; they needed protective tariffs and interpretations of the law in their own interests; they needed "pull" with judges, prosecutors and the police.

Privilege, then, was the root of all the evil—to "throw the rascals out" and to put into office "good" men merely caused the "good" men to do "bad" things, for "privilege" still remained—the "good" men had to choose between parties clamoring for this "privilege." The very act of choice connoted "pressure" and "corruption" in some one's eyes. Society, said Steffens, was paradoxical in its system of rewards and punishments. It taught the ideal of success, set up the temptation of power and riches to men and nations, and then *punished the losers,* letting the winners in the race, the successful, the rich, go. "What we ought to do," Steffens concluded, "is to let the losers of the race go, and take down the prizes we offer to the winners."

While Steffens was uncovering "political corruption"—which is, as he proved, merely a hypocritical and long-winded phrase for "politics"—Ida Tarbell was showing that business was "bad" in itself; that, to succeed, a business man had to eat up, crush, scotch, trample out his rival for materials, credit and markets. And Ray Stannard Baker was describing the corruption of labor unions by contractors in the building business who, in turn, got their jobs and opportunities through political pressure. In a notable article, published in *McClure's* for September, 1903, Baker demonstrated how "Capital and Labor Hunt Together" in Chicago, whose citizens were made the victims "of the new industrial conspiracy." This article does much to clear up the question of how far back in Chicago life the racketeer's pedigree goes; "Al" Capone, it shows, is merely one human milestone along an old, old road.

On investigation, Baker discovered a merger of the interests of the Chicago Coal Teamsters' Union and the Coal Team

Owners' Association. Together they had monopolized the coal business of the city. Independent operators, men who owned their own teams and wagons and oftentimes the coal, had banded together, and gone to the Teamsters' Union. "We will," they said, offering an olive branch, "hire no scabs if you, in turn, will haul no coal for outsiders." Labor accepted the terms. "This sort of monopoly," Baker wrote, "is new to our American life"—after "cracking each other," the forces of capital and labor were getting together to crack the public, keeping prices and wages up together. And when natural gas offered competition, the monopoly took care of that by refusing to haul any more coal to Marshall Field and Company, to the Auditorium Hotel, and so on, until an agreement had been signed by the consumers to use no more natural gas for five years.

The coal combination, Baker found, was but one among many—others being The Milk Dealers' Association working hand in glove with the Milk Drivers' Union, and the Sheet Metal Contractors' Association teaming up with the Amalgamated Sheet Metal Workers' Union. Whenever "peaceful" threats failed, these capital-labor combinations in restraint of trade resorted to terrorization—sluggers were brought in, and even murder resulted. It was here that the gangster as an adjunct to business, as a force for "stabilization," got his real start.

In New York, whither Baker pursued his inquiries, the startling discovery was made that the building trades were using the labor boss as their new tool, and a situation similar to that in Chicago had developed. In San Francisco, labor grew so strong, after 1901, that it owned the town. The labor unions elected their own mayor, got a grip on the city, and drove the scab out. Then followed a labor monopoly of business—with the capitalists taken into partnership. Working on the Chicago principle, wages were put up twenty-five per cent, and prices from fifty to one hundred per cent. The distance of San Francisco from the Eastern labor market made all this possible.

Baker went on from his labor explorations, which included a study of the Western Federation of Miners, most militant, idealistic and disciplined of labor organizations, to a comprehensive report of the iniquity of the railroads—with particular emphasis on the rebate evil, forced by the Standard Oil seeking a favorable rate on refined oil, by the Carnegie Steel Company, by the beef trust and by the fruit industry. "Control the rate, and you control the railroad," was his formulation of the reason for the rebate. Chicago packers, he found, underpaid the cattle raisers, and overcharged the meat consumers, by means of the trust which had been built up on the rebate. The packers, he wrote, were "traitors to the principles of democracy." The methods of the beef trust of Armour, Swift and the rest—suddenly dramatized for the country in 1906 by the appearance of Upton Sinclair's *The Jungle*—were documented by Charles Edward Russell, in his *The Greatest Trust in the World,* which was serialized in *Everybody's* in 1905. "The men who operate [this trust]" said Russell, with the extenuation of the nascent socialist, "are very good men" as the world goes, but are caught by the system and "driven along by an economic evolution beyond their knowledge or control."

The picture of society painted by the muck-rakers was amazingly complete, although the fiction purveyed by McClure and other editors of the time was feeble, dilatory and false to the life in the surrounding articles. But realism in fiction would come later. McClure himself was not content to halt at money corruption—his complaint with Steffens was that *The Shame of the Cities* and *Enemies of the Republic* stopped short with the financial aspects. And so, when McClure was informed by the Boston *Evening Transcript* that Americans were a moral people, and lived just as well under corrupt government as not, he set out to determine the truth of this ukase. The *Transcript* was routed by the facts McClure turned up. Taking the period of our most rapid expansion, McClure found that in the years between 1881 and 1895 murder in the United States had increased six times as rapidly as the population, and was thirty times as frequent per million inhabitants as in the countries of Northern Europe. George Kibbe Turner, an addition to the *McClure* staff, was turned loose on Chicago, to uncover the human waste that was the concomitant of the System which Steffens had portrayed in terms of the waste of dollars and cents. Turner's article on the relation between municipal government and the exploitation of women led to a famous Vice Commission's Report on Chicago, and Archer, the English critic of the muck-raking magazines, was duly impressed with the "amazing picture of organized, police-protected vice and crime—a picture every line of which was evidently the result of patient, penetrating investigation and intimate personal knowledge."

OTHERS were not moved by the Olympian patience of the notable staff of *McClure's.* Sensationalism, the raucous note, the blood-hound bell, the combined methods of the stock promoter and the yellow journalist, entered the muck-rake arena with the publication by *Everybody's* of *Frenzied Finance,* by Thomas W. Lawson of Boston. Taking over Lincoln Steffens's phrase, "the System," Lawson, a stock-market operator of the most flagrant gambling stripe, applied it to the methods of Big Business, the bankers and the State Street and Wall Street brokers. Lawson was used to the grand manner—or the gambler's simulation of the grand manner. He dedicated his story—the "inside" story of the Amalgamated Copper Company—with a rhetorical flourish to "Penitence and Punishment," but it was plain, from both his past and later behavior, that neither penitence nor punishment concerned this ebullient soul. Lawson's very method of getting his series before the public smacked of his methods as the President of Trinity Copper—he was the "promoter" in literature, even as he was the promoter in stock-rigging and the advertisement of his curious estate at "Dreamwold." *Everybody's,* at the time, was an obscure magazine, not yet one of the ornaments of the literature of protest. To its owners Lawson came, asking no recompense for his series, but demanding only that the magazine spend $50,000 or more in advertising his financial peep-show. By his own account, Lawson added $250,000 more for publicity purposes, and the circulation of *Everybody's* responded at once, mounting, within a year, from 150,000 to more than 750,000. Crowds jostled and clamored each month for the latest installment of the series. "The System," as explained by Lawson, "is a process or a device for the incubation of wealth from the people's savings in the banks, trust and insurance companies, and the public funds." Lawson's characterizations of the beneficiaries of "the System"—of J. E. O. Addicks of Delaware, of Widener and Elkins of Philadelphia and public utilities fame, of H. H. Rogers and William Rockefeller of the Standard Oil, of James Stillman of the National City Bank, of F. Augustus Heinze, copper man of Montana, and of James R. Keene, the horse-racing broker whom Morgan had used to "make a market" for the newly incorporated United States Steel—all these were vivid, touched with the malice that makes for edge. As such, they made ridiculous Lawson's protest that he took no issue with men; "it is with a principle I am concerned."

The story of the Amalgamated was the story of racketeering in copper stocks, of foisting large quantities of water upon an always gullible public. There was truth, plenty of it, in what Lawson had to tell, as Barron's published journals were later to reveal, but Lawson's singular concern for the moral fiber of the community was unconvincing; and the skepticism of the newspapers was borne out, in 1908, when Lawson, disgusted, as he said, with the "saffron-blooded apes" of the public, went back to his first love, stock speculation.

Even as the methods of frenzied financiers were under process of exposure in the pages of *Everybody's,* the literature of protest, of exposure, was not yet known as "muck-raking." The first mistake, the signal that the top of the movement had been reached and deterioration had set in, was yet to be made; but it was not long in coming. William Randolph Hearst, it was, who made the slip—who brought odium upon the muck-rakers, all of them, whether good or bad. While the Hepburn Railway Rate Bill was being debated in a recalcitrant Senate, with a public fed upon Ray Stannard Baker's *The Railroads on Trial* watching the fate of the legislation with eager eyes, Hearst announced that his *Cosmopolitan* would initiate a number of exposures that would be "the most vascular and virile" thus far printed. The Hearst bill of particulars contained a sneer at *McClure's* and its staff—"well-meaning and amazingly industrious persons writing without inspiration" who had succeeded only in piling up "indiscriminate masses of arid facts."

What Hearst had in mind, for the *Cosmopolitan,* was a series of articles called "The Treason of the Senate," by David Graham Phillips, a former Pulitzer employee and a novelist of some repute. This was a logical move, since the Senate, next to the Supreme Court, was the most important cog in the machinery of the "politics of acquisition and enjoyment." Phillips, however, was not the best man in the world for the job—Steffens, who had written on "the boss of the Senate," Nelson Aldrich of Rhode Island, would have turned out far more reliable stuff. But Steffens, of course, was a dealer in "arid facts," trained by Godkin of the *Post,* not Pulitzer of the *World;* while Phillips, on the other hand, had a vigorous supply of the best Hearstian epithets. His series commenced in the March issue of the *Cosmopolitan* and continued for nine months—running under the epigraph from the Constitution: "Treason against the United States shall consist only in levying war against them, or in adhering to their enemies, giving them aid and comfort." "The Senate," he wrote, "is the eager, resourceful, indefatigable agent of interests as hostile to the American people as any invading army could be, and vastly more dangerous: interests that manipulate the prosperity produced by all, so that it heaps up riches for the few; interests whose growth and power can only mean the degradation of the people, of the educated into sycophants, of the masses toward serfdom."

Corruption being the attempt to serve two opposed masters, the Senators, Phillips said, came within the definition of the word. They were elected by the people, whom they nominally represented, but they served the "interests." The first to be brought upon the carpet by Phillips was Chauncey Mitchell Depew, the "Vanderbilt-New York Central" Senator. Then followed the chastisements of Aldrich of Rhode Island, whose daughter had become the wife of John D. Rockefeller, Jr., and whose very good friend was J. Pierpont Morgan. Aldrich, a Hamiltonian with expensive tastes, was the "right arm of the 'interests' "; Arthur Pue Gorman, Democrat of Maryland, was the "left." Other members of the "merger" of Democrats and Republicans for betraying the people to the "interests" were Spooner of Wisconsin, Bailey of Texas, Elkins of West Virginia, "Fire Alarm" Foraker of Ohio, stipendiary of the Standard Oil, Lodge of Massachusetts, "the familiar coarse type of machine politician, disguised by the robes of the 'Gentleman Scholar,' " Allison of Iowa, master of compromise and Aldrich's chief spreader of salve, and so on.

The series stirred much interest, and brought forth a general reviling of Phillips from the ranks of the unco' guid, although men there were to back up the charge that the United States Senate had become the "Rich Man's Club" and the American "House of Lords." Phillips was embittered by the attacks, and refused to write any more articles, but, as Charles Edward Russell wrote to Cornelius C. Regier of the University of Iowa (author of an excellent unpublished thesis on "The Era of Muckrakers"), "in two years... it was a common remark that he had purified the Senate."

It was the thoroughly justified attack on "poor old Chauncey Depew" that constituted the slip which brought the term "muck-raker" upon the *littérateurs* of exposure, and it was Theodore Roosevelt, who thought Norris's *The Octopus* and Sinclair's *The Jungle* overdrawn, who was responsible for tarring the whole school—from Ray Stannard Baker and Lincoln Steffens, the scholars of the movement, to Phillips and Lawson, the dealers in pyrotechnics. At a private dinner of the Gridiron Club, on March 17, 1906, Roosevelt took as his text a passage from Bunyan's *Pilgrim's Progress* "...the Man with the Muck-rake, the man who could look no way but downward with the muck-rake in his hand; who was offered a celestial crown for his muck-rake but who would neither look up nor regard the crown he was offered but continued to rake to himself the filth of the floor." The speech was not reported, for it is the Gridiron Club's rule to preserve strict privacy of expressed opinion, but gossip of the characterization spread nonetheless. So Roosevelt, with his instinctive recognition of the moment to strike, decided to get the speech "reported in full." At an engagement which he had to dedicate the cornerstone of the House of Representatives Office Building, on April 14, 1906, he balanced an attack on Big Business with an attack on the "lunatic fringe" of the magazine writers. The fact that it was aimed only at the lunatic fringe was, however, quickly forgotten. The word "muck-raker" was seized upon by a public that had acquired a taste for the Roosevelt epithets. The President had forever fixed a name to a generation, a decade, a school of writers. Whatever T. R.'s sins may have been (and we shall come to them), he at least had the virtue of picturesque and salty speech. Steffens, Tarbell and Baker, Phillips, Lawson and Russell—they had to like the term, for it would follow them for the rest of their lives.

AFTER Roosevelt's denunciation, muck-raking trickled out. Charles Edward Russell, one of the most earnest men who ever wrote a paragraph, accepted the designation blithely, and continued to expose rottenness wherever he found it. In 1912 he was still hammering away at the railroads, at special privilege. But he couldn't "go it alone," with no support, so he had joined the Socialist Party. Baker, after helping La Follette write his autobiography, turned to his essays in contentment, which he published under the name of David Grayson. Steffens became interested in a Christian socialism, in the application of the Golden Rule to industry, and in revolutions. Miss Tarbell became a Yes Woman for the Judge Garys and Owen D. Youngs—the critical sense gone. And muck-raking degenerated in style and acumen—done, where it was done, sporadically. The sweeping, documented, balanced surveys which McClure had paid thousands of dollars to assemble gave way to the single article, which shed a little light on one spot, but put no wrong in its historical setting. "Meaning" had gone out of muck-raking.

Why did "The Magazines Soft Pedal"? Russell sought to tell the public in *Pearson's* for February, 1914. It was the advertising departments of magazines that had put a damper on the muck-raking spirit. The department stores had easily held two ends of the garrotte around the newspapers' necks, he said, quoting La Follette's argument of 1912, but the magazines were more difficult to subdue. A combination among manufacturers, and bank control, however, led to "undue" influence, and the magazines sold out. *Everybody's,* he said, lost seven pages of advertising in an issue when his series on the beef trust was running—and the advertisements which disappeared were of hams, preserved meats, soap, patent cleansers and fertilizers, and railroads. Whole pages went glimmering when Russell commenced writing about the tobacco trust—which was nominally dissolved by the Supreme Court in Taft's Administration. Mournfully, writing as one in at the death, Russell listed the defunct muck-raking magazines—*Hampton's,* the old *Arena, Success,* the *National Post, Human Life,* the *Twentieth Century. McClure's* became a pretty-pretty magazine, a purveyor of cheap fiction; the *American,* which had been remade by Steffens and Miss Tarbell into a muck-raking organ for a short interlude, turned into its present incarnation. But more potent than the advertiser's garrotte—and the garrotte played its part, we may be sure, whether openly or through the growth of a new "community of interest" in the magazine field—was the indifference of a public that still allowed itself to be destroyed through lack of knowledge; the public that thought the Rooseveltian and Wilsonian reforms were bringing in the millennium, instead of driving the methods of a rapacious industry underground and clearing a path for the new magniloquence of "service."

WHAT did the muck-rakers accomplish? On the theory that it takes a lot of running by the human animal to remain in the same place, a great deal. The Hepburn Act, which will come in for its analysis later, was one triumph in the muck-rakers' list; the labor legislation of the Wilson terms undoubtedly owed much to the magazine agitation. The direct election of United States Senators may have been aided by Phillips. The pure food laws harked back to Sinclair's *The Jungle,* a muck-rake novel. The Bureau of Corporations, and the anti-trust activities, feeble though they were in promoting competition and preventing monopoly, rested on the work of inquisitive magazine writers who continued the social thinking of the Populists. But the muck-rakers could do nothing to keep down the rising cost of living, which was the most conspicuous phenomenon to the average man in the years just before the War. They could do nothing to iron out the business cycle, which is a more important aspect of life under a machine civilization than all the graft in the world. They could do nothing, ultimately, to right any of the fundamental wrongs—and perhaps the public was wiser than it knew in growing tired of the good old sport of exposing those who "do us good and plenty."

The English critic, William Archer, hit upon the weakness of the muck-rake magazines in 1910. "The logical weakness of their position," he wrote, "lies in an insufficient thinking-out of the fundamental ideas on which their crusade is based. They do not see that most of the evils they attack are inevitable results of the national creed of individualism. They lack either the insight or the courage to admit that some form of collectivism is the only permanent check upon the enslavement of the people by the most amazing plutocracy the world has ever seen." McClure himself, intelligent though he was, could only find a remedy for the ills his reporters had turned up in the commission form of government. I wonder what he would have had to say in 1931 when Cleveland abandoned the city manager plan because it had fallen into the hands of the "old gang," the machine?

As WAS usually the case in the decade of muck, it was Mr. Dooley who had the last word. "Th' noise ye hear," he told his friend Hennessy, "is not th' first gun iv a rivolution. It's on'y th' people iv th' United States batin' a carpet. What were those shots? That's th' housekeeper killin' a couple iv cockroaches with a Hotchkiss gun. Who is that yellin'? That's our ol' frind High Finance bein' compelled to take his annual bath."

CHAPTER FIVE

Blighting the Plum Tree

☆

THE beating of carpets, the sniping with the Hotchkiss gun and the annual laving of our old friend, High Finance, broke in upon an American literary public that had, only recently, been fed fat upon Stevenson, Sienkiewicz, the Graustark romance of George Barr McCutcheon, Richard Harding Davis's *Soldiers of Fortune,* F. Marion Crawford, James Lane Allen, the Robert W. Chambers of *Cardigan,* Winston Churchill's *Richard Carvel* and *The Crisis,* and the library-bred Virginia romances of Mary Johnston. The alteration of taste, from the soft to the surly, was so abrupt that it defies any easy answer from the mob psychologist. It was as if the American public, after downing one last glass of syrup, had cried out in a spasm for a regimen of tannin, lemon juice and brandy. The taste for romance has been correlated with the Spanish-American War fervor, and the vote which swept the hero of San Juan, Theodore Roosevelt, into the Governor's chair at Albany. But 1902—the very year in which Ida Tarbell and Lincoln Steffens commenced the muck-raker's anatomy of the American Leviathan—saw the evaporation of the desire for novels that out-Thackerayed Thackeray and out-Scotted Scott. A primary disturbance in the McKinley "New Era" had manifested itself when Harriman, backed by Jacob Schiff of Kuhn-Loeb, and Morgan suddenly, as it seemed, commenced battling for Northern Pacific stock, actually sending the price per share to $1,000 in the Spring of 1901. But the resultant unsettled condition in the market did not drag us into panic; crops remained good, and a bumper production of wheat, which sold at high prices in Europe, saved us from the usual aftermath of greedy speculation. However, for those who could read the signs, the activities of the titans seeking to control the industries and the credit structure of the satisfied plutocracy portended overextension, a drying-up of purchasing power at the bottom and a reversion to the times of the early nineties.

The muck-rakers seemed instinctively to scent this, although—as we have seen in the case of S. S. McClure—they were not consciously aware of the way the wind was about to blow. The magazine movement was foreshadowed, ever so faintly, in the fiction of 1902 and 1903. Francis Churchill Williams had written his *J. Devlin, Boss,* in 1901. Out in Toledo Brand Whitlock was putting the finishing touches on his *The Thirteenth District,* which warned the public of 1902 that politics were not all they should be in a democracy. The career of Richard Croker was put between novel boards, in ungainly but energetic fashion, by Alfred Henry Lewis, whose *The Boss,* published early in 1903, contained a recognition of facts that it would take Lincoln Steffens several years to discover for himself and the *McClure's* public. *The Spoilsman,* by Elliott Flower, written around public utility politics in Chicago, was another product of 1903. Fiction, coevally with the staff of *McClure's,* had learned again the connection between "the interests" and political manipulation—and the American political novel, which had lapsed into desuetude with the coming of McKinley, perked up as the public, suddenly scuttling from enchanted sweets, turned to contemplate the terrible shame of the cities.

Poor though it is in quality, and feeble in underlying thought, the political novel of the Rooseveltian decade is very important to one who would understand the tone and color of the years of the muck-raker. In his *Those Earnest Victorians* Esmé Wingfield-Stratford performed an autopsy upon the popular fiction of the mid-nineteenth century in order to arrive at a real comprehension of the values of the mass. The popular fiction of an age is, perhaps, the only key to contemporaneity, as Wingfield-Stratford has shown. It is certainly true of the decade of muck. Where, for example, can we arrive at a more conclusive knowledge of the ethical bias, the lack of comprehension, the inability to think in terms of human power divisions, of the men who marched to Armageddon with Roosevelt in 1912 than in the political novels of Winston Churchill? Where can we conclusively discover the ferment of a decade, heady and undirected, if not in the works of David Graham Phillips? Where is the inability to think a situation through that was a characteristic of the years of the strenuous life better exemplified than in the political fiction of Booth Tarkington? The works of these men, superficial as they are, give one the key to a decade as nothing else can.

The political novel is, of course, a branch of the "problem" novel—and Whitlock, Phillips, Churchill, Tarkington and Lincoln Steffens, all of whom essayed to put political problems into fiction, were either forerunners or contemporaries of the brood of "problem" novelists who swarmed over the land in the years before the World War. Whitlock, Phillips, Tarkington and Churchill, in fact, wrote some problem novels that were not political. But while the muck-rake era was at its palmiest they ran with the pack. For about four years—or until the Taft interlude brought a more conservative tone to national politics—the political novel flourished, educating people who hadn't the inclination or the ability to follow the more precise exposures of the magazine writers in the sinister implications of boss rule, the connection between Big Business and the "slush fund," and the general necessity of "turning the rascals out" and electing "good" men to office. Only gradually did it dawn on writers that in concentrating on politics they were neglecting economics, which were more fundamental and hence better subject for fictional inquiry.

The political novel of the decade of muck had at least a relatively honorable ancestry in the preceding century. Disraeli is commonly given credit for inventing the *genre;* George Eliot's *Felix Holt* is political, in a sense. Both Trollope and George Meredith experimented in the field, and in America we had our pioneers in the Henry Adams of *Democracy* and the Samuel Clemens and the Charles Dudley Warner of *The Gilded Age.* In the nineties Hamlin Garland, as we have seen, put the Populist revolt into *A Spoil of Office,* with dubious success. Paul Leicester Ford's *The Honourable Peter Stirling,* published in 1894, is chiefly interesting to-day for its incidental exploitation of the strike issue—it reveals the popular revulsion in the nineties against the dreaded bogey of anarchism, and it gently but firmly upheld the American rentier of that day in his decision to outlaw the class war. Stirling is a "boss," but a good one; and the "armchair" reformer of the Curtis type is used in the Ford novel as a foil to prove the necessity and the practicability of the Stirlings of this world. Unfortunately, Peter Stirling is even more of a paragon than the Snivel Service agitators, and quite incredible, to boot. Grover Cleveland was an honorable man, but he was never as faultless as Peter Stirling, his egregious shadow in fiction.

In both *The Gilded Age* and *Democracy* the American inability to press an issue to its ultimates—the main inability that characterized the political fiction of the 1900's—was to be seen. Twain drew two memorable portraits in *The Gilded Age,* the lovable Colonel Sellers, and the despicable Senator Dillworthy, who was modeled on the notorious Senator Pomeroy of Kansas. But the fact that both Colonel Sellers and Dillworthy represented but two phases of the same ugly thing never seems to have crossed Twain's mind. He could not see that speculation in land was more of a burden to the people of a nation than graft at the national capital—was, indeed, a superior form of graft in itself. The lesson of Henry George never seems to have struck Mark Twain, the child of the frontier, or his co-partner in the writing of *The Gilded Age,* Charles Dudley Warner, the gentle essayist of Hartford, Conn.

Democracy, the product of Henry Adams's sojourn in

Washington during the corrupt Grant régime, lacks the *brio* of *The Gilded Age,* which achieves satiric distinction, even if it doesn't attain to distinction of thought. The political novelists of the 1900's might well have taken *Democracy* for their model, for all they did to improve on it. This novel is, as Parrington has said, the fictional work of the "kid-gloved" reformer. It is the vulgarity of democracy which Adams objects to—nothing else. His Senator Ratcliffe, loosely patterned on the reputation of James G. Blaine, is corrupt—that is, he arranges a subsidy for a shipping company in return for a sum, which goes to pay campaign expenses. But the business that must needs persuade politicians, by bribery if necessary, to think the "correct" way is not satirized. A bit of Civil Service reform, a corrupt practices act, and more New Englanders with a conscience in office—such are Adams's inferred nostrums for the situation. There is not a speck of consciousness in *Democracy* of the underlying economic struggle that makes graft inevitable—and hardly as important as changing the bases of the struggle. What if Ratcliffe did take a little money for the subsidy? The purchasing power of the nation probably remained the same in the face of this particular form of double-dealing. If he had arranged for the subsidy by conviction, and refused so much as a penny, the wrong would still exist so far as the ultimate consumer was concerned. The unequal division of the national wealth between the industrial East and the agrarian West, which was the outstanding economic fact of the Gilded Age and after, did not concern the heir to the mantle of the Adamses who were, preëminently, "good" citizens. Of what account, to Henry, were the implications of anything so vulgar as an industrial revolution when the moral certainties of a charming though powerless woman, Mrs. Lightfoot Lee, were about to be sapped by the forceful Senator Ratcliffe? None at all—but an older Henry Adams, grown philosophical, would one day deny the thesis of his novel in *Mont Saint Michel and Chartres* and the famous *Education.* In these books the fact of the dynamo would seem more important than a little graft—a word, by the way, that didn't exist until Josiah Flynt, the hobo writer, made it current in the nineties.

AMERICAN writers, so it would appear, are incapable of learning from their forerunners' mistakes. Certainly the Gertrude Atherton who tried her hand at the political novel in *Senator North*, in 1899, might have profited by knowledge. Her book promised much at the start—but it descended midway to the level of a "society" novel, and the public which loves a lord bought up twenty-two editions in three years. In *Senator North* the Populists of the West invariably appear as wild men; the Hamiltonians, America's *manqué* aristocrats, are the heroes. But Mrs. Atherton's solitary incursion into political fiction is scarcely important, save as an index of taste. The real muck-rake article, which shared the shortcomings in intelligence and the inability fully to diagnose that characterized the novels of Henry Adams and Mark Twain, did not make important definitive appearance until Alfred Henry Lewis's *The Boss* roiled the waters of the era of the Full Dinner Pail. Lewis was of a divided mind; he had a real admiration for Andrew Jackson, whom he put into a highly spiced biography for a later muck-rake public, but he also admired clever chicane when he saw it, and "the boss" was that most rare of all birds, a good realist. Lewis took the Steffens path out of his perplexity; he put all the blame on the "system," and demonstrated, before Steffens had gotten around to it, that "good" men were as bad as the "bad" men when their dividends were threatened. At the end of his novel he quotes an estimate of his "boss" that sounds suspiciously like William Allen White's analysis of Richard Croker—the "troglodyte" survival in American politics. The estimate is an insult or a compliment—depending upon whether one condemns the man or the "system." But however Lewis's hypothetical journalist intended it, the public which bought the political fiction of the Progressive era gave its answer: More honesty. And this answer, however much individuals like Lewis might protest that the "system" had every one caught, carried with it the implication that the individual was to blame. For if the answer is really "honesty," then the "system" can be reformed by the individual making the answer. Else there is no reply short of the Marxian formula —and this the Progressives were not prepared to admit.

WINSTON CHURCHILL was certainly not prepared to admit that common honesty wouldn't do. "A peculiar ethical rapture," says Waldo Frank, "has earned the name American." This *sui generis* state of moral transport which Mr. Frank had in mind informs the work of Churchill from start to finish. Like Garland and Norris, Churchill came out of the West, from St. Louis specifically, to write fiction and to join what has now become known as the "uplift." More than either Garland or Norris, he had the moral New England bias. If the inner history of the effect of the "scientific" liberalizing of Protestantism upon the American writer could be traced, Mr. Churchill would doubtless offer a fit subject for inquiry. Unfortunately, we can only assume that he transferred a Messianic zeal, a will to save the world, to fiction because the church, in his day, no longer offered a fit career for the ethical American. The church had ceased to lead when the colleges liberalized their curricula to pass beyond the stage where they prepared only for the ministry; from that time on we find the church on the defensive, giving ground here and there, probably a force making for a genteel liberalism, but certainly not a generating force. Clergymen like Dr. Washington Gladden, who denounced Rockefeller, had a following, but they took their cue from the muck-rakers.

Churchill, however, made the novel his pulpit. This Westerner of New England stock, always ardently the patriot, was educated at the Naval Academy in Annapolis, where he had the opportunity to study a tradition and absorb a mood. The result of his enlivening contact with the stately old homes of Annapolis, plus a study of the Cavalier tradition in early America, was a decision to embody the critical periods of the history of the United States in the type of fiction that was, at the moment, extremely popular. Once Midshipman Churchill had resigned from the Navy he married into a wealthy St. Louis family, thereby assuring himself of the leisure to pursue the underlying documentation for *Richard Carvel,* which he published in 1899. This story of the birth of the Republic is modeled, more or less, upon the wide Victorian pattern of Thackeray's *The Virginians* and *Henry Esmond,* and, like *The Crisis* of 1901 and *The Crossing* of 1904, it makes fictional use of the historical theme of Bancroft and other standard historians—that America is the product of "the movement of the divine power which gives unity to the universe and order and connection to events." With its set pictures of life in colonial Maryland and Virginia, and its romantic use of the figures of John Paul Jones and Charles Fox, *Richard Carvel* struck the errant fancy of a public that had been keyed up to heroic desires by the victories at San Juan Hill and Manila Bay; and *The Crisis,* a tale of divided loyalties in the Border State of Missouri in the Civil War, continued the popularity of America's newest romantic novelist. So well did Churchill catch on, in fact, that late in 1901 it was estimated that *Richard Carvel* had sold 420,000 copies, and *The Crisis* 320,000. But the tide of romance would swiftly run out; *The Crossing,* which reached the public in 1904, was an anti-climax; and Churchill found himself taking stock of his position of popular novelist thrown suddenly into a decade whose popular clamor was for muck.

Luckily for the chances of his continued public favor, he had moved to New Hampshire, to the town of Cornish, where the political situation of a locality commenced to interest him. His home at Harlarkenden Hall soon became the center of intense political activity. Roosevelt, who was then about to enter on a term in the White House by virtue of his own magnetic appeal to the voters, had abrogated the "gentlemen's agreement" with Aldrich, Platt and the Old Guard to carry on the McKinley policies, and had promised his constituency a strenuous four years in Washington. The trust-buster excited Churchill's ethical imagination; here, indeed, was a David come to hurl the stone at the Goliath of greed. One reformer touched off another. As Roosevelt started hammering at the railroads, Churchill began writing fiction built around political themes in general, and the diabolical railroads in particular, always with the Populist, or "Progressive" bias. And not only did he turn to political fiction, he actually entered public life, as Booth Tarkington did out in Indiana. Material for the novels that would display the wicked machinations of the railroads of New Hampshire was literally thrown at him during a period in which he served as representative from Cornish in the New Hampshire State Legislature (incidentally, the largest State Legislature in the United States). And more material came his way when he stumped for the nomination for Governor—a nomination he narrowly missed receiving. Stanley Johnson is authority for the statement that Mr. Churchill would have been nominated had the intervening machinery of a convention not kept the rank and file of the party from expressing its true wishes, but of how many potential candidates cannot this be said? However, Mr. Churchill took his defeat in good grace. He continued the attempt at "purification" of his State Republican machine, organizing the "goo-goo" element of the party into a Lincoln Club, and helping to create a majority for the Progressive Governor Bass, who rose to the crest with the Bull Moose surge.

One would hardly be justified in excavating the political novels of Mr. Churchill were it not for the fact that the very temper of the Rooseveltian decade, as the average "good" citizen helped create that temper, is to be found in *Coniston* (1906) and *Mr. Crewe's Career* (1908). Like Bryan, like La Follette, like Roosevelt, Churchill had a theoretical preference for the little fellow—for the small business man and farmer who had become uneasy in the shadow of the trusts.

And like the political leaders of the era, Churchill was quick to identify his cause with morality in general. He voiced the opinions held by most of the "old" American stock that was articulate at the time, basing his political convictions on a few simple and as yet uncontested axioms: the Republic was founded by wholly disinterested men with the common welfare at heart; the Constitution was the embodiment of disinterested political wisdom, and was therefore as safe as Gibraltar if we could only get back to it; and the way to get back to it was to elect honest, disinterested men to public office. But the Churchill (and Rooseveltian) formula was based on the wholly unrealistic supposition that the United States of 1904 was a nation of single individual interests held in leash by individual consciences that somehow worked freely in the sight of a just God. Unknown to Churchill, this was a primitive agrarian answer to a misunderstood and almost wholly corporate situation. Churchill did not realize that only equals can meet as equals. He was still living, intellectually and emotionally, in a day of open land, of physiocratic principles, when every man could become his own untrammeled master on a few acres of his own cultivation. He thought there was still a possibility of government based more or less on a delegation of authority by equal and honest individual integers. Simple morality, for him, was enough. And, of course, if his diagnosis had had any validity, his answers would have been sound. It is comparatively easy for a man on a farm, provided his acres add up to a going concern and are unmortgaged, to give an uninfluenced individual answer; he has nothing to fear, and can say, "Get thee behind me, Satan," without loss of slumber and the certainty of pressure from the credit market. But obviously it is not so simple to put the tempter aside when one's bread and butter are in the balance; and it is notoriously impossible to persuade the electorate to disturb even very corrupt business conditions when such roiling of the economic waters means a cutting down of income, and the old story of the woes of the business cycle. But Mr.

Churchill was no Steffens, to ponder a situation before making up his mind. As novelist and repository of the Progressive conscience, he did not think the matter through to its economic base before planning his fictional campaign in his study. What he did was to stencil the pat agrarian answer in a situation in which each man was dependent on a complex of forces beyond individual control; he spoke fervently in terms of a lost society of equal integers. And of course the answer wouldn't wash. And, by the same token, his political fiction wouldn't wash; its drama comes to no fruitful issue.

Mr. Churchill, we may say if we wish to give him all benefit of the doubt, was half-right, and he spoke the half-truths that are more difficult to nail than outright falsehood. At the front of *Coniston* he quotes from James Russell Lowell, the nineteenth-century Goo-goo (Good Government apostle): "We have been compelled to see what was weak in democracy as well as what was strong. We have begun obscurely to recognize that things do not go of themselves, and that popular government is not in itself a panacea, is no better than any other form except as the virtue and wisdom of the people make it so, and that when men undertake to do their own kingship, they enter upon the dangers and responsibilities as well as the privileges of the function. Above all, it looks as if we were on the way to be persuaded that no government can be carried on by declamation." But virtue is, as virtue can, and wisdom—short of suicide—is as wisdom is not too frightened to be. The matter narrowed down, as Churchill could not see, to the "virtue" and "wisdom," not of the "people," but of those who had, by one reason or another, the power to rule; and their very power was based on a striving for pecuniary ends that denied all the values which Mr. Churchill held most sacred. An unexploited continent had enabled a certain type of person—the predatory Cowperwood type, whom Veblen had analyzed and Dreiser was to paint—to achieve power for the grasping, whether in railroads, oil or the preemption of power sites; and a pioneer psychology had led to the popular exaltation of this type. But Mr. Churchill was naïve enough, as was his whole Progressive generation, to suppose that most people, poor in this world's goods, would still have the simple guts to deny themselves the easiest path (as it seemed) to a portion of the goods—which was the path of coming to terms with those who had the power. By exercise of the vote—an exercise totally divorced from class organization along the lines of industrial unionism to back up the threat of the vote—Mr. Churchill argued that the plain people could turn the rascals out and elect honest men, even though they might starve in a chaotic interlude before things were working once more. And this in blithe ignorance of the fact that a fast-growing part of the electorate was composed of stockholders and those who depended on stockholders. Mr. Churchill was, in his novels, virtually proposing that those in power should magnanimously vote themselves out of power. He could see, perhaps, that government was a reflex of a conflict of interests, to be determined by pressure, but he saw the pressing interests as individual. He provided no methods for the plain people to take over control by organizing, along economic lines antecedent to politics, for a heavy *group* pressure. And his candidates who were to offer themselves as saviors of the plain people whom Lincoln loved always came, miraculously, from the upper classes as paragons of self-sacrificing purity, good-breeding and disinterested intelligence.

The two political novels, *Coniston* and *Mr. Crewe's Career,* dramatize the impotence of Mr. Churchill's answer. From the point of view of good fiction, this might have been made an esthetic virtue: good fiction is more often than not made out of impotence in the face of overwhelming odds, provided the impotence go down to defeat with full realization of its lot, or with the author's ironic realization of the circumstances. But Mr. Churchill ends each novel on a fraudulently hopeful note. He dedicates *Mr. Crewe's Career* to the men who "in every State of the Union are engaged in the struggle for purer politics," but the struggle in his pages never converges on an active issue. Frederick Tabor Cooper long ago put his finger on the fatal dichotomy in the Churchill political novels when he said: "He uses . . . a double theme; first, the big, basic idea underlying some national or ethical crisis; and, secondly, a specific human story standing out vividly in the central focus with the larger, wider theme serving as background. Where his stories fail to achieve the epic magnitude is in lacking that essential symbolic relationship between the greater and the lesser theme." In other words, identification on the part of his heroes and heroines with the Progressive forces could lead them to no leverage by which they might attempt to alter conditions; they could only take it out in talk, and remain functionally aloof. How true this is, not only of the Churchill figures, but of the hosts that expected a social revolution to spring from the march to Armageddon in 1912! The dichotomy of *Coniston* and *Mr. Crewe's Career* is symbolic of a Progressive incapacity to do more than talk—and then patch, once the plutocratic opposition has made certain it could circumvent the intention of the patching process.

The pages of *Coniston* and *Mr. Crewe's Career* are sweetened with miraculous changes of heart on the part of Mr. Churchill's somehow fundamentally Christian villains; and the sense of miracle robs the novels of all internal consistency. Once "reform" has entered in, there is no further coming to grips with politics as they are; divine grace must therefore be invoked. The message of the novels is, to put it brutally, "a little child shall lead them"—although in each case the "little child" has no means of taking hold in the political sphere and altering a single thing. There may be individual adhesions to "honesty"—but they can only be made permanent by a Jethro Bass getting out of politics, or an Austen Vane remaining out of politics. The dirty work in the arena still goes on to the swelling music of admonitions from the unco' guid.

Nevertheless, in spite of the lack of issue and the sickly flavor of Christian passivity, the novels of *Coniston* and *Mr.*

Crewe's Career are highly interesting from the standpoint of being a good anatomy—in fact the best we have—of boss and corporation rule in America from Jacksonian days to, roughly, 1910. That they would be more interesting if the fiction had been left out is beside the point for the present purposes. Mr. Churchill planned the two novels to give a sort of panorama of national destiny from the days of the Jacksonian revolution to the days of Roosevelt, and he succeeds in making them good panorama. *Mr. Crewe's Career* was even good muck-raking, good pamphleteering, for it made the people of New Hampshire aware of a statute, on the books since 1889, by which the Attorney General of the State was compelled to proceed against the railroads for violating a legal obligation for more than twenty years.

The origin of the "boss" is set forth, with convincing detail, in *Coniston,* which commences in the middle of the 1830's. The Era of the First Six Presidents has gone by, Good Feeling and all, and the hordes of Jackson have, quite pragmatically, walked off with the spoils. And in the town of Coniston the tanner's son, Jethro Bass—whom Mr. Churchill modeled on an actual boss, one Ruel Durkee of Cornish—has been mulling things over. Coniston is still something of a New England theocratic village, with the economic, political and religious leaders of the community coming from one and the same class. But Bass, a shrewd Yankee of plebeian stock, breaks the ranks. In Mr. Churchill's over-nice opinion, he debases the ideal of American government. By buying up mortgages among the farmers, by doing a favor here and there, by cultivating the main chance of power, he manages to dominate the Jacksonian overturn in New Hampshire. Though patently admiring some qualities in his boss, Mr. Churchill thinks his methods quite reprehensible. But, by any law of human gratitude, are they so reprehensible? Jethro is fair toward his henchmen; he forgets to foreclose mortgages; and he is always disposed—for a vote—to let the interest go over. If the theocracy had been similarly willing to forget in an emergency, it would never have lost its power. And as for the vulgarity of Jethro Bass, his unwillingness to accept his "lot"—well, all the "best people" have to get a start sometime.

In spite of the stern but hopeless opposition of the old-time theocracy, Jethro Bass goes on to more power. He extends his influence to other reaches of the State, and by 1860 he and his lieutenants and retainers are in a position to dominate the nascent Republican Party, to which they naturally turn when the slavery issue forces a liquidation of the Democracy of New Hampshire. Mr. Churchill's eye is clear in the matter of recording, in brilliantly concrete terms, the growth of the old-time New England boss after the Civil War; and for general confirmation of the picture we have only to look up the New England coast from New York to little Rhode Island, where, after Appomattox, a certain General Brayton acquired control of the country districts and made a later compact with Nelson Aldrich to share power between them.

The important legislation of New Hampshire is, in the early Grant régime, in the hands of Bass. But the railroads, which have reached the stage where consolidation is imminent, make things difficult for a boss who has built himself up on the power of the mortgage. Even as the bands of steel are binding a continent, Crédit Mobilier scandal or no Crédit Mobilier scandal, these bands are similarly binding New England. At first there were little roads by the dozen. Then there entered cutthroat competition as road paralleled road. Trades are now in order; combinations must come. And Bass, although his rule is threatened for the first time since the Jacksonian overturn, holds the key to the situation because of his power in the rural districts and especially in the wooded North Country. The farmers of New England, even as the farmers of La Follette's West, are afraid of combination. To force compliance in the legislature which the agrarians dominate through the "rotten borough" system, the railroads must make peace with Jethro Bass—and the peace will cost money. The political set-up provides no material for a Sophocles, as we shall see, but it might have provided fodder for an anatomy of pure chicane in the American manner. Mr. Churchill, however, is too "moral" to submit to the limitations; he must bring in a Christian conversion and a gift-book romance. It so happens that Jethro Bass, in the long dead past, had loved Cynthia Ware, the daughter of the Coniston minister; and he has since become the guardian of a second Cynthia, child of the first. Two stories, one of political manipulation and one of redemption of the old boss through love, run parallel, converging abruptly and speciously at the end. The interior struggle of the boss is never more than indicated. And the result leaves politics where it was; Jethro Bass, as he himself realizes, may get out and become "moral" to please the young Cynthia, but another Bass will take his place. The convert to righteousness can only become Christian in Mr. Churchill's rapidly disintegrating book by accepting non-instrumental character. Where, in such a preachment, is there an answer to the question posed by James Russell Lowell and quoted at the commencement of the narrative? Why has Mr. Churchill written his book? We do not know. What started as a serious study of the curve of bossism ends as a popular romance, and the whole issue is left in the air. What is more, Jethro Bass is forced, in the interest of the love story, to sell out at the very close in a really despicable manner that is not all in character. It does not seem despicable to Mr. Churchill, who puts the incident forward as evidence of sterling worth. Briefly, Jethro's ward, the second Cynthia, wants to marry Bob Worthington, son of Isaac D. Worthington, the railroad president who is for consolidation. Jethro has gotten out of politics as the result of his conversion, but when he learns that Isaac D., in his wrath, has attempted to keep Cynthia from Bob, the old boss gathers his forces, takes the "throne room" in the Pelican Hotel at the State capital, and proceeds to go after the consolidation bill. With the fate of the legislation once in his pocket, Jethro forces Isaac D. to withdraw his objections to Cynthia. Does this ring true to the boss type? Men like Jethro

Bass have their own morality; they don't let their friends down that easily. The god of love comes too easily from the machine.

Mr. Crewe's Career exemplifies the same faults, and the single virtue, of *Coniston.* Time has passed; Jethro has long gone to his rest among the granite hills; and men of his stripe have ceased to rule over units any larger than the village. The single boss has given way to the Feudal System; a railroad, Isaac Worthington's creation, now rules the New England State, as the Boston and Maine once actually ruled New Hampshire. Its attorney, Hilary Vane, New England lawyer of talent and descendant of the old moral stock, occupies the "throne room" at the capital, much as J. Henry Roraback in Connecticut has occupied an important room at the Allyn House in Hartford when railroad and light and power legislation has been at stake. Vane dictates to the committees, seeing to it that the "right" men get the right jobs. The voters of the State are virtually disfranchised; they vote for the Republican candidate whom the railroad approves. Mr. Churchill is again on firm ground in his anatomy of corruption; we have actual records of the very sort of situation he is describing, as one may discover by reading the history of the Southern Pacific of Collis P. Huntington in California. And there is a theoretical justification for the railroad methods; as Steffens has pointed out, a railroad often *had* to corrupt a State in the latter half of the nineteenth century to maintain its existence. Mr. Churchill puts this justification into the mouth of his railroad president; the corporation had to go into politics to defend itself from "the blackmail politicians of the State Legislatures." "Study the question on both sides," says President Flint, "study the question from the point of view of men who are honestly [sic] trying, in the face of tremendous difficulties, to protect innocent stockholders as well as conduct a corporation in the interests of the people at large, and for their general prosperity. . . ."

Of course, the railroad in question does not conduct the corporation in the interests of the people at large. But Mr.

Churchill is not content to expose the methods of his railroad; he must pattern *Mr. Crewe's Career* on the formula of *Coniston*. Mr. Crewe, the amateur in politics, the rich man who thinks he can employ his leisure by serving his countrymen in the approved British fashion, gets himself sent to the State Legislature. He is somewhat mortified to discover that he must first deal with Job Braden, a village descendant of the school of Jethro Bass, but he goes through with the trade and reaches the legislative chambers. There he can do nothing; the "interests" are entrenched. And it is to a non-political figure that Mr. Churchill is forced to turn for an ideal—to Austen Vane, the son of Hilary Vane. Austen is, supposedly, a Rooseveltian figure, but purer than T. R., since he has no votes to win in a primary. He goes against his father, by taking, in his capacity of lawyer, a case against the railroad. The daughter of old Flint, the railroad president, learns of the case, and she and Austen fall in love. The rest is a matter of persuading Hilary to get out of the dirty work of political manipulation, and a few speeches delivered at Mr. Flint. There is no problem, for Austen won't run for Governor. The son of Hilary Vane likes to dwell on "the fancy of the springing of a generation of ideals from a generation of commerce which boded so well for the Republic...." But lesser people still have to eat. And when John Curtis Underwood, Mr. Churchill's most flamboyant fugleman, remarks that the people are "ready to realize that the movement that Austen Vane represents has come to stay; and there is no doubt whatever about their intention to stay with it..." we can only smile with the superior, if saddened, wisdom of 1932.

Mr. Churchill, in common with others of his generation, went on from the political novel to the economic problem novel, at first showing an increasing desire to escape the limitations of this sordid planet. *The Inside of the Cup,* which was published in 1913, was an attempt to carry out what Upton Sinclair would call "a lovers' quarrel" with the church—a "setting-forth of a personal view of religion." Christianity, so Churchill argued, must be severed from business connections and re-fashioned in a primitive democratic mold. In this he was repeating, almost word for word, the earliest Protestant objections to the Holy Church of the powerful of Europe; he was taking the path of the Plymouth Brethren, the early Methodists, the Quakers, et cetera, all over again. *A Far Country,* which followed in 1915, was a Christian criticism in fiction of the profit motive. A "Banker Personality," created in the image of J. Pierpont Morgan, presides behind the scenes in this novel—"...the American principle personified, the supreme individual assertion of the conviction that government should remain...in the background, while the efficient acquired the supremacy that was theirs by natural right...." Morgan represents, in Churchill's opening eyes, "the crowning achievement of the unity that fused Christianity with those acquisitive dispositions said to be inherent in humanity. In him the Lion and the Lamb, the Eagle and the Dove, dwelt together in amity and power." *The Dwelling Place of Light* (1917) was in the same vein, but more realistic—perhaps the best of the Churchill novels in its unity of tone. This novel was born of the Lawrence strike, when the Industrial Workers of the World were attempting to organize the Eastern mills in the name of the Syndicalist revolution. Churchill's sympathies are with the Syndicalists. The conflict in this novel is not turned crudely into an opportunity for moral propaganda; but for all that, the psychology of sex is still beyond the author. Since *The Dwelling Place of Light,* a brave last effort to keep in tune with more candid times, Mr. Churchill has lived in silence—and wisely, for the type of novel he is equipped by early training to write sounds ludicrous to those who have had any contact at all with modern psychology, or with fiction since French naturalism and the psychological romance fathered by Stendhal have spread their influence wide to the four horizons.

IF WINSTON CHURCHILL most adequately displays the inchoate quality of the Progressive mind, with its abrupt skitterings to the cover of a dead supernatural authority that makes for righteousness, David Graham Phillips exemplifies in fullest fictional form the strenuosity of the movement. John Curtis Underwood, the Progressive contribution to literary criticism, has called Phillips "the Roosevelt of American literature"—which might well have frightened T. R., whose unkind cut of *The Plum Tree* is recorded in the letters to Owen Wister. But Underwood is correct, although his comparison need not be taken as the compliment which *Literature and Insurgency,* Underwood's book of criticism, intended. Phillips, like the President, "thought in his hips." The fact that "reform" was in the air was sufficient to make him a muck-raker. Granville Hicks, in the only sensible critique of the man that has ever been written, has remarked upon Phillips's acute sensitivity to whatever happened to be the journalism of the moment. Some of the earliest Phillips novels sought to ride the tide of favor for the Graustark romance; *The Master Rogue,* the author's earliest foray in fictional muck-raking, came in 1903, soon after Steffens and Tarbell had touched off the campaign of exposure in *McClure's.* By 1907, as the muck-rake force was trickling out into its decadence, Phillips made a lightning change to what Mr. Hicks has called, with a tinge of irony, "constructive criticism" in *The Second Generation*—a novel in which Phillips, like the Austen Vane of *Mr. Crewe's Career,* muses upon "the fancy of the springing of a generation of ideals from a generation of commerce which boded so well for the Republic. . . ." A taste for a forthright treatment of the sex problem, which *Sister Carrie* had failed to elicit at the beginning of the 1900's, was, as the Rooseveltian decade ran toward its close, commencing to pervade the sanctums of the popular magazines, and here, too, Phillips showed his uncanny skill at diagnosing the latent desires of the novel-reading public. A play, *The Worth of a Woman,* produced in February of 1908, prefigured the trend that Robert W. Chambers would ultimately reduce to its lowest terms in *The Restless Sex. Old Wives for New,* a novel based on the play, followed; and Phillips's subsequent career, leading up to *Susan Lenox: Her Fall and Rise,* is in the new vein whose exploitation coincided with the early rise of Greenwich Village, the domestication of Freud in America, the fanfaronade for the "new woman" of Inez Milholland's suffragist fancy, and the opening of Mabel Dodge's salon.

The intrinsic value of Phillips's excursions into sexual debate is dubious, although it has been said with some show of plausibility that he did valuable work as a pioneer in creating an *ambiance* for the Dreiser of *Jennie Gerhardt* and *The "Genius"* and the Sherwood Anderson of Winesburg's ingrown romance. Yet it is possible—Frank Harris to the contrary—that too much credit can be lavished upon Phillips for any pioneer work in sexual candor; after all, Shaw and Wells, even Brieux, had more to do with breaking down American taboos in the pre-War decade; and the "sensational" aspects of Phillips's work probably insulated him from fructifying contact with American writers who were, at the time, working in secret upon novels and stories of high seriousness in which sexual clarity and honesty would be the dominant characteristic. But as a political novelist, Phillips is more important. Drop him from the history of the novel of sexual candor, and the contour of that history remains unchanged; since the crumbling of the Puritan morality, Susan Lenoxes have become commonplaces, and would have become commonplaces without Phillips's most serious novel. But drop Phillips from the history of political fiction, and an element is permanently gone. Although both he and Churchill are alike in their belief in "honest" men, and though both of them look back to a mythical day at the dawn of the American Republic when citizens were somehow not moved by economic interests, Phillips, with the impetuosity of a Roosevelt, attempted in *The Plum Tree* a far more grandiose theme than the corruption of a single New England State. The Harvey Saylor who shakes the plum tree after the manner of Matt Quay of Pennsylvania is a President-maker, nothing less—the brains and power of the majority party. It is as if Phillips wished to expose the entire system at one swoop, to make it simpler thereby for a blanket decapitation by the Progressive forces. Phillips is, of course, far less circumstantial than Churchill, for all his reportorial training and ability. He is not in possession of Churchill's detail, which came straight from an immersion in political campaigning and party maneuvers in a legislature. But in novels like *The Plum Tree* (and *Light-Fingered Gentry,* which made fictional capital of the insurance scandals that had put Charles Evans Hughes in the Governor's chair at Albany) there is a quality of strenuosity that is not in Churchill, who, after all, loved peace and amplitude and Christian meditation. It is the strenuosity of the Charles Edward Russell type of reformer, forever straining to scent out some new abuse to flay in the public prints. Churchill, one can charitably say, followed his logic from muzzy premises, but he at least had a logic. Phillips, on the other hand, caught up a sense of grievance from the air and built fictions hurriedly upon it. His output for ten years is some twenty novels, each on an average of 100,000 words in length. He was the catch-as-catch-can journalist, working against time to get spot news across. He rode a movement, like Churchill, and when it was subsiding he hastened to find another bandwagon. For Churchill, however, the end of the Bull Moose stampede meant the end of worldly hopes; there was nothing left but a retreat to the kingdom of heaven that is within.

Phillips, in summation, was a first-rate crusading newspaperman in an age that made much both of its more flashy reporters and its great sensational journalistic proprietors—Pulitzer, Hearst, Scripps. As a young man the future star reporter and feature writer lived in Madison, Indiana, where his father was a banker. Two years at De Pauw, and two years at Princeton, comprised his formal college education, which he supplemented by private tutoring in languages and much reading in his father's library. At college he had met Marshall Halstead, son of the more famous Murat of the Cincinnati *Commercial Gazette,* and through this connection he managed, after some difficulty, to get a job on the rival Cincinnati *Times-Star.* Within a few months he had convinced Halstead that he was worth adding to the staff of the *Commercial Gazette* at twice the salary he had received on the *Times-Star.* "Halstead told me," said the city editor of the *Times-Star,* "that I had done remarkably well in training the young man. As a matter of fact he did not need any training; he was a born reporter."

Three years after his Cincinnati début Phillips was in New York, where he went to work for the *Sun,* most literary of New York papers. Later he became the London correspondent of the New York *World,* with which paper he was identified in one capacity or another for nine years—or until he had resigned to spend all his time on fiction and magazine work. Charles Edward Russell, Pulitzer's city editor, recognized the ability of the young man, and Pulitzer himself, in 1897, thought well enough of him to transfer him to the editorial department. But when Phillips wrote his first, and somewhat autobiographical, novel, *The Great God Success,* which he published under a pseudonym, it made Pulitzer uneasy. Pulitzer considered his bright young man was using time which should be devoted to the paper—and besides, there was the suspicion that Phillips had made Pulitzer the villain of the story. The end of Phillips's days as a daily newspaper writer was in sight, and 1902 found him free-lancing, commencing his career in the Grub Street open market with a series of acidulous articles on journalism for the *Saturday Evening Post.*

Phillips impressed certain of his contemporaries—Beveridge, Isaac Marcosson—but he did it by pointing the finger of scorn at what they already knew to be in for a slating. He persuaded by his contemporaneity, and when his news value had gone, he went with it. Frank Harris, who edited the American *Pearson's Magazine,* a muck-raking organ, for a time, considered him the best American novelist, thinking his understanding of women particularly good. John Curtis Underwood praised him with superlative gestures; the upholders of the *status quo,* on the other hand, leaped at his throat for his articles on "The Treason of the Senate." Both praise and blame were as hectic as the themes of the Phillips books. In 1910 the zealous critic of the selfishness of the average American woman received a number of ominous letters to which he paid no attention. On January 23, 1911, he was shot by a young musician, Fitzhugh Goldsborough, who had considered his family insulted in one of the Phillips novels. The assassination, which had been plotted for several months, was a two-day newspaper sensation in the best Phillips manner. After that came *Susan Lenox,* and a number of posthumous novels that were feeble stuff for the train-butchers, as Mencken has said. The rest has been largely posthumous silence.

The Plum Tree, Phillips's major adventure in political fiction, came in 1905. He had skirted the political theme before in *The Cost,* in which the somewhat unbelievable figure of Scarborough, seemingly a sort of cross between Bryan and Grover Cleveland but actually supposed to be based on the character of Senator Beveridge, shines as a creature of sure integrity amid the fetid business of buying votes and manipulating the machinery of government for "the interests." But *The Cost* is mainly a story of business double-dealing. *The Plum Tree* is almost wholly given to politics, and it illustrates, as nothing else could, the vagueness of Phillips's theories of government. As Mr. Hicks has pointed out, the attitude of Senator Saylor—who tells the story—shifts with bewildering speed. Now he looks upon the delivery of a Mid-Western State into the hands of Big Business with contempt for his own part in the deal; and now he regards his career as a sort of Nietzschean justification of himself. But Saylor is chronicling his ascendancy to power in his middle age, at a time when his point of view would long since have hardened. Saylor's father has been an Old Republican, a man of ideals, and the son goes into politics for revenge, since the way to honest preferment as a public servant has been blocked for him by a corrupt politician. He wants power so that he may revenge himself by preening his feathers on the topmost bough of the plum tree, in full sight of the vultures whom he has tumbled off. And to win through he learns all the effective off-color practices in the book of the things-as-they-are, although he loses his one true love in the process.

But Saylor is only a means to an end. He is not shaped by the logic of biological development, and the mitigation of circumstances; he is, rather, taken as an arbitrary expostulating figure. The causes of his "selling out" early in life to corruption, which should have been the story, are not exhibited in word and action, in the manner of the good dramatist. Phillips, through Saylor, simply tells us a fact or two about the Senator-Boss's youth. Saylor has been selected, one feels, in order that the novelist may have a good vantage point to view the springs of political corruption, from the ward to the White House. Mr. Hicks says *The Plum Tree* omits "none of the steps in the creation of political power." In a broad sense, this is true. But what is lacking is the stray, revelatory detail that illuminates more than itself. We miss the juicy contretemps, the humor of the "wood-chuck" session in the New Hampshire State Legislature that redeems *Coniston* from the junk pile. *The Plum Tree* is, despite its accurate documentation, obviously the work of a reporter who "gets up" his facts from the outside.

And the philosophy behind *The Plum Tree* is "gotten up" for the occasion. All Phillips seems to have to offer as cure is an "honest" politician, the Senator Scarborough of *The Cost*. But how this politician is to keep his party honest, how he is to maintain his ranks without the usual tricks of dispensing patronage, how he is to finance his campaigns without giving at least a few implied promises in return for the sinews of war—how, in brief, he is to hold back the pressure of the interests whom Saylor has come to represent, is not disclosed to us, either implicitly or explicitly, by Mr. Phillips, the Progressive crusader and friend of Beveridge. Nor has Mr. Phillips done the only honest thing in default of an answer—he has not become a Manichean, nor yet a cynic. He simply goes on hoping, along with his whole generation.

THE most hopeful of men in those most sanguine of days was the incorrigible middle-class dreamer, Booth Tarkington, whose habit of optimism, chained to an ingrained belief that it was good to get on and therefore good to make money, has probably robbed him of a permanent place in American literary history. Of the generation of Churchill and Phillips, he has paralleled their writing careers almost exactly. Commencing with his own analogy to *Richard Carvel—Monsieur Beaucaire,* which *McClure's* published—he soon found himself working side by side with Phillips and Churchill in the orbit of political fiction. This was some years after his graduation from Princeton, whither he had gone from Phillips Exeter and Purdue, and after a happy childhood in the midlands, where his father was a prosperous lawyer. Tarkington even anticipated Phillips and Churchill in throwing his novelist's hat into the political ring. For his *The Gentleman from Indiana,* written about a college boy who goes back, somewhat as Tarkington himself went back, to work with the home folks and edit the local paper, was issued in 1899. A flabby philosophy, or at least a philosophy which has become flabby in terms of the American situation, animates this novel, but the Hoosiers of that distant day, who looked upon General Lew Wallace of *Ben Hur* as the type artist, were not a very ironic or contemplative lot. They still thought of life in terms of the old swimming hole, of Riley neighborliness, even as industrialism grew and Indiana politics paralleled Ohio's in general corruption. The theme of

The Gentleman from Indiana is incredible, what with the editor's miraculous escape from death after smashing the vice ring and defying the political boss, and what with his subsequent nomination for Congress. *In the Arena,* a collection of short stories which was published in 1905, is something better—although Tarkington betrays his "goo-goo" complex at the very opening, when he quotes with approval an "old-timer": "What we most need 'in politics' is more good men.... There are many thousands of young men belonging to what is for some reason called 'the best class,' who would like to be 'in politics' if they could begin high enough up—as ambassadors, for instance. That is, they would like the country to do something for them, though they wouldn't put it that way. A young man of this sort doesn't know how much he'd miss if his wishes were gratified. For my part, I'd hate not to have begun at the beginning of the game."

The "old-timer," if such a babe-in-the-wood can be properly called an "old-timer," would have been shocked if Lincoln Steffens had appeared on the scene to tell him that what we really most need is good men in back of politics; that the cure for political democracy is industrial democracy. But the "old-timer," being Tarkington himself, would never have been sufficiently shocked to put the horse in front of the cart. The use of the word "game" is significant in that it betrays the common American insistence that nothing is to be plumbed to the bottom, nothing to be taken seriously if seriousness is to lead to pessimistic conclusions. In the stories that follow the "old-timer's" introduction, Tarkington, who "served" in the Indiana State Legislature for a period, demonstrates, in spite of himself, that politics is no "game" for the poor devil whose life depends on the decisions of the representatives. *Boss Gorgett* is somewhat specious, but *The Aliens,* for all its underscored humor, mainly at the expense of the immigrant, is, in reality, grimly ironic. A first-class artist would have made it either five times as savage at the expense of those who exploit the alien vote even to the point of virtual murder, or five times as objective, and furthermore he would have substituted irony and pity for easy humor. *The Need of Money,* with its corruption of a slow-witted country bumpkin in the Legislature, has the faults and virtues of *The Aliens. Hector,* a tale of the egotist in politics, good as it is, should have fallen into the hands of Ring Lardner—for Tarkington's Hector is Lardner's busher so far as his unquenchable egotism goes, and he demands the impassive Lardner stare and the scientist's cold handling. However, for all its shortcomings, *In the Arena* contains some of the best character work, done from the outside, that Tarkington has given us. And in this connection it is interesting to record the novelist's conversation with Theodore Roosevelt, a conversation that followed the publication in the magazines of the stories of *In the Arena.* The experience in the Legislature, Tarkington has written, "was lively, enlightening, and in one or two particulars infuriating—for there were operations that could not be viewed with humor—and when it was over I published as short stories some studies founded upon observation. Straightway I was in trouble... this time with a powerful and authoritative critic. He was at that time President of the United States, and he sent for me to come to Washington.

"'Do you understand what you're doing to politics?' he inquired.

"'Why—why, no, sir. I haven't noticed anything. I've only been in the State Legislature and nobody seemed to—'

"'I'm not referring to your membership in that assembly,' he interrupted with some sharpness. 'I'm speaking of the stories you're writing about politics and politicians. Do you understand their effect?'

"'Well, I—I hadn't heard of any. One of my aunts told me she'd been reading them, but that's all I—'

"'Never mind,' he said. 'Everything published in that magazine has some effect, and what you're publishing in it now is the darker side of politics. Do you deny it?'

"'No, I—'

" 'Certainly you don't. What's your object?'

" 'Well, I thought that perhaps if people could be made to realize some of the worst things that do go on they'd want to remedy them. I thought they'd—'

" 'You're absolutely wrong!' he said with his well-known decisiveness. 'It's precisely what they don't do. They say to themselves, "Ah, I thought so! Politics is too dirty a business for any decent person to mix with; I'll keep out of it." You're helping to crystallize the feeling that politics is "no business for a gentleman." ' "

Well, it was no business for a gentleman in the day of the dinosaurs; the gentlemen of that day played politics through their lieutenants, one of whom was Theodore Roosevelt, as I hope to demonstrate in a later chapter. But from a man who posed as a "scientist," Roosevelt's denunciation of Tarkington seems more than a trifle quaint. The effect of T. R. on the course of American literature is a subject for pondering, and an essay. Did he pull the teeth of writers? One recalls his effect on Owen Wister, who toned down his Western sketches to please his great friend. It is true that Tarkington went on from political fiction to a general realism, as both Churchill and Phillips tried to do, and in one novel, at least, *Alice Adams,* he succeeded in letting character create its own story. But the softness that was in him when he recorded, with some pride, the conversation with Roosevelt has come to the top in every novel since *Alice Adams,* and "the tragedy of Tarkington" has become a commonplace in American critical discussion.

IT IS a pity that the most persistent digger for political phenomena of the decade, Lincoln Steffens, wasn't a born novelist. He did try his hand at political fiction when his muck-rake days were over, but for the most part his stories—which he wrote for *McClure's* in 1914, 1915 and 1916—were simple Socratic dialogues between Mr. Steffens himself and persons connected in one way or another with politics. In his story of "The Dying Boss"—Iz Durham of Philadelphia—the action narrows down to a death-bed conversation about the morality in general of the political machine. Steffens informs Iz, who is a first-class sentimentalist, that his crime has been disloyalty to the common people from whose ranks he sprang. "You, all of you—not you alone, boss, but all of you: ward leaders, State leaders, all the national political bosses—you all betray them." The boss, who has always plumed himself on his character as a straight-shooter, is nonplussed for the moment, but Steffens makes it all right by proving to him that "we can't any of us quit doing the particular wrongs that are required of us in our business." "You can't play a crooked game straight."

The story of "The Dying Boss" is staged, as are Steffens's other fictions: "The Reluctant Briber" and "The Boss Who Was Bossed." "The Reluctant Briber" is obviously built on the career of Mellen, who was forced to go into politics or relinquish his job as head of the New Haven road. The figure who stands for Mellen comes to Steffens to get his advice on how to go straight in his business, but learns that it is impossible. So he tries to be an "honest" crook, one who realizes what he is doing. In the end, however, he "sneaks"; he couldn't stand the gaff. And Steffens answers: "If enough want to do this, won't the 'system' be retired?" But Fred Howe knew the answer to that: there are always people who will take a chance.

THE Steffens stories, however, are pitched at the right angle: they attempt to deal with human beings in the act of making moral decisions that affect their conduct with other people. Steffens, of course, being limited to conversation, could not carry out his plots in terms of subsequent activity, but he was working in the right direction. If he had had the novelist's equipment he might have transcended the work of Churchill, Phillips and Tarkington. For he knew that a dramatic novel—which is to say, a good novel—must swing around an absolute. This absolute forms the axis; it gives cohesion and proportion to a work of art. It may, of course, be a negation, in which case the resulting novel will be, as Thomas Mann's *The Magic Mountain* or Proust's *A La Recherche du Temps Perdu,* ironic, making mock of the attempts of people to attain standards. But the political novelists of the decade of muck couldn't grasp the fundamentals of dramatic fiction. Winston Churchill had a perfectly good set of Christian values to work with, but he was unable to find suitable symbols in life to illustrate his meaning, and he lacked the fiber necessary to take the ironic point of view. Thus, as we have seen, his Christian character, Austen Vane, was compelled to walk upon the fringes of politics, making speeches, but unable to come to grips with the situation. Austen could have come to grips in two ways: by compromising, which would have been the cue for irony, or by pushing his philosophy through in terms of action, in which case the logic of the situation would have made him into a revolutionist and a Christian socialist. Similarly, Jethro Bass, if he had come to grips with a situation in terms of his conversion, would have been compelled to choose between back-sliding and revolution.

The only ironist of the decade who wrote political novels was Brand Whitlock, whose *The Thirteenth District* was a fumbling, ineffectual attempt to satirize a weak politician who double-crosses the keeper of his destiny. The trouble with Whitlock, as I have indicated elsewhere, was that he was a poor power philosopher; he didn't have a firm grasp on his absolutes. Whitlock pities his Garwood because he cannot remain honorable in his dealings with the man who makes him a figure of promise. But if Garwood had been loyal to his friend, he would still have been disloyal to Whitlock's own Single Tax philosophy and Tolstoian anarchism. Edge and point are lacking in *The Thirteenth District* because Whitlock himself has wavered at the point of declaring his values to himself.

But the political novel as a *genre* is somewhat suspect. It is dramatically off-center. All its problems are decided, spiritually, before the political sphere is reached, since politics is *negotiation.* One can easily make drama out of a decision leading to a negotiation, or out of a decision resulting in a refusal to negotiate, but hardly out of the act itself. In the case of Norris's *The Octopus* Magnus Derrick's high moment comes before he goes into politics—the rest is a study of degeneration, and a matter for irony. The most representative novelists of political problems in the muck-rake era—Churchill, Phillips and Tarkington—lacked facility for irony. It remained for Elliot Paul to write a really good ironic political novel in his *The Governor of Massachusetts,* but that came two decades after the sputter and fume of the Rooseveltian years.

CHAPTER SIX

The Economic Man

☆

THERE are corresponding patterns in the decade of muck. The "good-bad" man theory of American delinquency in the art of being ruled did not satisfy the philosophical Steffens for long, as we have seen. It did not satisfy Brand Whitlock. It had sufficed Churchill, Phillips and Tarkington in their stories of the political arena, but it could not, in the face of its obvious superficiality, satisfy the American novelist for long, even during the years of some of the worst problem fiction ever committed to paper. Just as the muck-rakers of the political structure learned that in back of political corruption was economic pressure—that, in short, political corruption was merely a function of renewal in State organization by those in a position to make effective demands—so the novelists made a similar discovery. From 1903 to 1908 was the heyday of the political novel—and it was a novel exactly as profound as the mind of Theodore Roosevelt, no more, no less. But parallel with the development of the political novel went the development of the economic novel—the discovery of the economic man. Behind politics stood economic power, economic desires, of which the fights for franchises, for voiding of old legislation, for privileges in new fields, were merely reflexes on the plane of threat and negotiation and chicane. Dreiser, during these years of discovery, was reaching the sound conclusion that the stuff of the novel resided in Charles T. Yerkes's appetites, not in the duplicity, the moves on the chess board, of Yerkes's lieutenants at the Philadelphia City Hall or at Springfield, Illinois. One of the few real chances for good political fiction might have been found in the story of Altgeld of Illinois, who, in breaking his own political career, provided the mythic material for an American tragedy. But Whitlock, who had known Altgeld, was satisfied to concentrate on lesser fry—on the negotiators; and the North German who was so congenitally "sot" in his ways as to refuse Yerkes and rise against Grover Cleveland has only an incidental place in *The Titan*.

Similarly, the political novel has only an incidental position in American fiction. The mood of the decade of muck, as it deepened, was for facts, facts, facts—economic facts, as it happened, since the middle-class world was out of joint, and people had little time for the data of esthetics or of the soul. And inasmuch as politics was a matter of the incidence of economic facts in the sphere of negotiation, the novelists who grew up with and succeeded Churchill, Phillips and Tarkington—even including the later incarnations of these writers themselves—wisely decided to let politics become subject for pamphleteering and the election booth.

Documented fiction became the fashion. Characterization was forgotten when it became known that coal barons cheated the lesser economic man—the laborer—at the tipple. Jack London turned from his studies in primitive psychology *(The Call of the Wild, The Sea Wolf)* to a lecture on the Marxist conception of surplus value in *The Iron Heel*. Hutchins Hapgood utilized the novel to make plain the distinction between the hobo and the yegg. David Graham Phillips and Upton Sinclair became fascinated by the details of money-changing in Wall Street. Robert Herrick looked wistfully from the campus at Chicago University into the offices of his own lesser Titans and Financiers to see what made the wheels of the System revolve. And, ultimately, Ernest Poole plunged into the maelstrom of a dock strike to chart the lines of cleavage of the class struggle. And single men and women in conflict, the basic data of all good fiction, were, while not completely forgotten, at least subordinated to the paraphernalia of the new, the changing, the astoundingly difficult American nation.

What was the reason for the sudden insistence on the inventory? Why did American writers fail to turn a period of *sturm und drang* into fiction with a preservative quality? Granville Hicks, in seeking specifically the key to the failure of Robert Herrick, finds the diminished worth of *The Memoirs of an American Citizen* correlative with an auctorial dislike of the industrial process and its ultimate possibilities for an augmented human life. This dislike, which was undoubtedly a part of Herrick's make-up, may be the reason for a lack of gusto in one of America's pioneer naturalists. But more germane to the inventory bias of the American fiction of those years is the lack of immersion in the given subject material. Dislike of the actualities and the Utopian possibilities of one's theme, if it is strong enough, may provide the very emotion needed to galvanize fiction to greatness. Eliot's *The Wasteland* is great; Robert Herrick's fiction is not. The notion that one ought to pass by what one cannot love is an unctuous aberration of Ludwig Lewisohn; it certainly does not explain Proust, Mann—or Edward Dahlberg, to name an American Proust of the "scum proletariat." No, dislike of the given American theme of the early twentieth century will not explain the lapses of Herrick, of Phillips, of Sinclair. What does explain them, so far as I can see, is the lack of immersion. The slow gathering of impressions, the exposure of the human sand to the ripples of the tide—these could not be indulged in by the writers of the decade of muck. Problems were there to be solved, immediately; the American middle class, threatened by the Marxian centralization of control of capital that would be exposed by the Pujo investigation in 1913, could not wait; nor could the novel wait. So, while Dreiser brooded, soaking in the impressions and sorting them out, the Herricks, the Sinclairs and the Londons rushed their elongated pamphlets into print. The novel had gone back to its journalistic origins; it had become a muscle to punch men to action, not a thing to be savored by those seeking a basis for reflection upon human destiny.

In the light of the tradition into which they had all been born, how could the American novelists of industrialism do good work in their chosen field? Robert Herrick came from a cultured university background of Cambridge, Mass.; Hutchins Hapgood had the same misfortune. William Allen White, a belated Tennysonian Victorian of Kansas, as H. L. Mencken will have it, was so bound up with country life that the possibilities of the Progressive years appealed to him mainly because they were the possibilities of preserving the farms from the encroachments of the machine. Jack London's élan was a frontier élan; he who had marched with Kelly's Army into Iowa was no son of the pavements. Phillips and Tarkington, both of them, came out of the Indiana that had nurtured Meredith Nicholson and James Whitcomb Riley. Upton Sinclair's background was that of a poor relation in a series of Southern communities—a *milieu,* by the way, that has had little representation in his fiction. Dreiser alone, among the historically important fiction writers of the pre-War years, had fallen, in his youth, in the path of the machine. He knew Pittsburgh as an experience; Sinclair, London, Herrick and the others knew industrialism solely in the guise of takers of inventory. So, while Dreiser succeeded in writing fiction, his contemporaries cast up balance sheets. They had facts, facts, facts—and they draped them around the appropriate symbols. They were pamphleteers of the Progressive movement.

THE most effective pamphleteer of the Progressive movement was the socialist, Upton Sinclair, whose novel of the meat-packing industry, *The Jungle,* actually reached up to Theodore Roosevelt and Albert J. Beveridge to punch the government into pure-food legislation. When muck-raking was adolescent, Sinclair was busy with autobiographical fiction, with day-dreams of a career as a Shelleyan seer, with his first and ill-fated experiment with marriage. Up to 1904 his radicalism was a matter of personal ferment, of the psychology, as he later told Floyd Dell, his biographer, of a "poor relation." He had no theory of the State; he was merely against any and all oppression. Yet he had his own private feelings about life in the United States, and when he met Leonard D. Abbott and George D. Herron, the latter a socialist who became Woodrow Wilson's war-time agent in Switzerland, he was enraptured by the discovery that other human beings thought as he did, and actually had a rationale for the thought. Herron staked him, in a dark hour, to enough money for financing the writing of *Manassas,* a novel of the Civil War which has some claim to permanence. And while he was finishing up *Manassas* in 1904 in a makeshift shelter in the woods near Princeton, N. J., Sinclair read *The Appeal to Reason.* He had spent the year with the consequences of the institution of chattel slavery, reading some five hundred books centering on the Civil War, and consulting as many as five hundred more. Meanwhile he and his wife, with one child on their hands and no knowledge of birth control, were practicing a puritanical chastity. Sinclair had watched the agony of his wife in childbirth, an account of which forms the backbone of the first volume of the autobiographical novel, *Love's Pilgrimage,* and he had spent a winter with a gloomy, changeful young woman whom Platonism in marriage would eventually cause to rebel. The echo of the "embalmed beef" scandal of the Spanish-American War reached Sinclair's ears in 1904, and the explosion that was to result in *The Jungle* came. He put everything that was troubling him into *The Jungle*—the agonies of a young husband and a young wife with no money, the questionings of a tender conscience which had realized, at last, that chattel slavery had merely given way to wage slavery, and the carrying power of a psychic energy that was dammed up by insufficient knowledge of the world in a land of Comstocks. The result is a book of power; *The Jungle,* it can be said categorically, stands with *The Call of the Wild* and *The House of Mirth* as one of the three really respectable American novels not written by Henry James between 1901 and the publication date of *Jennie Gerhardt* in 1911. And James, at this period, was hardly an American novelist.

The goodness of *The Jungle,* as literature, is a matter of inexplicable luck; it is the only good novel that Sinclair was to do in his muck-raking phase within the period of the quest for social justice. *King Coal,* which came in 1917, and which Parrington has incongruously singled out for commendation, is, by contrast, a mere illustrated lesson in the art of robbing the miner of his surplus value. *The Money-Changers* and *The Metropolis,* the first a novel based on the Wall Street "bankers' panic" of 1907, and the second a story of the licentious antics of the gilded rich of New York, are, too, merely illustrated lessons in the social effects of plutocracy. They are, doubtless, good pamphleteering; they have their value. But *The Money-Changers* has not outlasted the lifetime of the elder Morgan, and *The Metropolis* has died with the demolition of the châteaux of the titans on Fifth Avenue. These books belong with the fiction of David Graham Phillips, whom, by the way, Upton Sinclair praised to the point of extravagance in 1927. "It is nothing less than a conspiracy of our kept critics," he wrote then, "which deprives this magnificent talent of its influence." And there, in that praise, we have Sinclair, the man to whom anything is good, provided it be an attack on the System. I wonder what Mr. Sinclair will make of the curious fact that Isaac Marcosson, sedulous ape to all capitalist successes, has written the book to vindicate Phillips?

Upton Sinclair might be used as a metaphor or a simile in a physics textbook to make palpable the law that for every action there is an equal and opposite reaction. For the author of *The Jungle, The Goose-Step* and *The Brass Check* is the reactive type par excellence. This jumping to the equal and opposite extreme, which has its unquestionable value as social dynamics, as the career of Rousseau has shown, began, with Sinclair, at an age when most boys have nothing more serious on their minds than the perplexing question whether cigarettes can best be made of cornsilk or dead leaves. The young Sinclair was brought up in the post-bellum South, amid the still regnant code of Southern chivalry. It was a decadent society he knew for the first ten years of his life, and he made, from his experiences with it, a few generalizations that would seem to contradict the notion that a socialist state will automatically solve many of the ills of an industrialism run for private profit. It is in these generalizations, notably the generalization about liquor, that Mr. Sinclair's weakness as a socialist lies.

In the days before the Civil War, and after it, all Southern gentlemen, as Mr. Sinclair says, drank whisky in its multiple forms—juleps, toddies, hot-scotches, eggnogs, punch. These drinks were the "most conspicuous fact" in Upton Sinclair's boyhood, for his father, the youngest offspring of a long line of naval officers, was successively a whisky salesman and a drummer for straw hats and men's clothes; and the entertainment of buyers involved a good deal of crooking the elbow. A periodic drunkard, the little drummer wavered between taking the pledge to abstain forever from the demon rum and falling off the wagon with éclat. In *Love's Pilgrimage* Upton Sinclair introduces us to his hero, Thyrsis, as he is hunting his father through Bowery saloons and gutters. The opening scene of this novel sounds like a tract for the W. C. T. U., but we have it on Mr. Sinclair's word that the novel was based on literal truth. And given such a father, and such a rum-flavored childhood, it was but natural for the reactive Sinclair to become a teetotaler and a prohibitionist.

And here is the curious thing about it: we have, in Upton Sinclair, a socialist who doesn't blame an uncongenial environment, but rum itself, for the ruin wrought upon a man. He does indicate, in *King Coal,* that bad working conditions can drive a man to the dram shop for forgetfulness, but he is not willing to rest his case there. He must do away with rum itself. If he had not rushed off to the equal and opposite extreme from that of his father, and had thought about the matter a bit, he might have reached the conclusion that perhaps the life of a drummer, no less than the life of a coal miner, was not very exhilarating, that perhaps his father drank because he was unhappy—that, in short, drink doesn't "get" people until something else has. If Mr. Sinclair had mulled this over a little, with due regard for what might be called social chiaroscuro and less regard for the strict black-and-white of the matter, he might have realized that prohibition will never cure the unhappiness and the sense of atrophied personality that lead to drink, and that, failing this cure, unhappy man will find compensation in the bottle as long as green things grow.

The attitude of Upton Sinclair towards liquor sets the pattern and the rhythm for his whole career. As the "Don Quixote" of the American Revolutionary movement, he has not been concerned so much with a rigorous economic analysis of society as he has with a series of moral reactions to extreme forms of exploitation within this society. It is one thing to say that finance capitalism contains within it the seeds of recurrent unbalance, and eventual dissolution—that it is built on certain contradictions that must inevitably pull it down. Once one has got that point settled one way or another, one can go on with one's work with a certain amount of intellectual firmness. But with Upton Sinclair, the intellectual conviction did not come first; what was primary, as we have said, was the psychology of the "poor relation" whose fate, from childhood, was to live in the presence of wealth that belonged to others. The rest followed when Shelley, Goethe and other romantic rebels came within his ken. Mr. Sinclair's conversion to socialism, it will be seen, was the opposite of Mr. Edmund Wilson's, which came only after an investigation of American conditions that had started under "progressive," or "pragmatic," auspices. One feels a little less certain of the intellectual value of Mr. Sinclair's forty books when one reflects that a Kansas childhood, in a fanatical "dry" community, would probably have made this Don Quixote into an ardent supporter of Al Smith, and that residence in Russia of to-day would inevitably throw him into the clutches of the Ogpu because of a free-speech demonstration in the Red Square.

However, when all the objections have been made (and they are objections that have kept a goodly audience from taking Mr. Sinclair with the seriousness he deserves), one must admit that emotion plays its part, and a very superior part, in stirring men to action. The emotionally-conceived "noble savage" is, anthropologically, non-existent; yet upon his shoulders rested the revolution of the eighteenth century. If Upton Sinclair hadn't seen the blinding light on the road to Damascus, he would never have hurried forth, bubbling with energy, to Chicago, staked by the editor of *The Appeal to Reason,* to write a novel about the stockyards. The journey to Chicago came in October of 1904.

The genesis of this novel shows how the muck-raker worked. At the end of a month, Sinclair tells us, he had his data, he knew the story he meant to tell, but he *had no characters!* In other words, he had taken his inventory of an industry, and must fit the people to it. The result was saved for literature because Upton Sinclair could project his own story into the form. Jurgis fell victim to the stretch-out and speed-up of J. Ogden Armour in Packingtown—just as Sinclair had fallen victim to the stretch-out and speed-up of working for sixteen hours a day for Street and Smith over a period of several years turning out woodpulp stuff. The terrible ordeal of Ona, Jurgis's child wife, finds an emotional parallel in the story of the vicissitudes of the young wife in *Love's Pilgrimage,* the novel which Mitchell Kennerly was to publish in 1911, and which was to have its effect on Floyd Dell and hence upon a good deal of the autobiographical fiction that grew up in the path of *This Side of Paradise.* Even the sudden conversion of Jurgis to socialism at the close of *The Jungle* is true, in spite of the objections of some critics that it is the equivalent of a "terse admonition," and thus artistically false. For Jurgis's conversion is like Upton Sinclair's own conversion;

it represents the sudden "falling down of prison walls" about a mind. It is exactly the sort of conversion that a poor harried individual, caught in the sweep of forces that make no moral sense, would undergo. The objection has been made that it "solves" nothing; but *The Jungle,* with its full recital of the stenches, the bickerings, and the production of human slag, that was the stockyards, is not designed as a solution. It is a call to action. Jurgis's hypothetical career as a socialist, with possible backsliding, very properly belongs to an unwritten book, a book that Sinclair, whose mind is not a meditative one, is not fitted to undertake.

By the chance cross-fertilization of autobiographical knowledge with an inventory of the social incidence of the packing industry we have a powerful novel. And the powerful novel, when it was put forth in February of 1906, had its repercussions in high places. Macmillan's, which had contracted for the book, had turned it down, but an independent investigation, undertaken by a lawyer for Doubleday, Page and Company, Sinclair's new publishers, upheld the factual content, so the bombshell was hefted into the world. The explosion, as Sinclair said ruefully, reached the stomach, not the heart, of the country. The packers replied in a series of articles by J. Ogden Armour in the *Saturday Evening Post,* a magazine that wavered between muck-raking and apologia for the muck-raked, but the counteractive influence was not sufficient. The Armours didn't dare bring suit against Sinclair. Shortly the novel was being read by Roosevelt, and by Beveridge, and a pure-food law which was languishing in a House committee prior to the usual burial after an insincere passage by the Senate was suddenly, at the President's behest, galvanized to life, and provided with a meat-inspection rider. The government also commenced its own investigations of the packing industry, and the Armours became frantic. *The Jungle* had done its work; it was one pamphlet of the decade of muck which led to a direct, tangible, immediate reform, and, as such, may properly be called the crown and culmination of the whole literature of exposure.

Sinclair, of course, had been more interested in obtaining redress in the shape of improved working conditions for the employees of the Packingtown he had so gruesomely described. But the novel failed of its major extrinsic intention; it failed to have any directly ascertainable effect on working conditions. However, with Sinclair's subsequent fiction, and with the work of Hutchins Hapgood in *The Spirit of Labor,* for example, *The Jungle* probably did much harrowing of the ground for the tentative and feeble growth of a more humane spirit in industry. Sinclair's pamphleteering at least put the implications of the capitalism of the titans in imaginative form for the common man to read as he ran.

It is easy to patronize Upton Sinclair. He has not worked in the spirit of scientific inquiry, and is thereby open to an attack from the logician. Yet he is, fundamentally, an impressive personality, likable, even breezy. He has not "sold out"; even his support of the War, which certainly was not undertaken in the spirit of an intelligent socialism, was derived from the set of courageous moral values that had moved him from the start, even before he had become a socialist. His radicalism is, as a matter of fact, older than Marx's; it is the radicalism of the eighteenth century, which derives from a belief that man is perfectible. A potentially "good" world, converted by Woodrow Wilson, might, Sinclair considered, make a just peace, and turn to socialism as the next step.

With Sinclair in the ranks of the socialist pamphleteer novelists went Jack London—the "yakclunnen" who is a staple in the literary diet of Scandinavia and Soviet Russia, and whose stories so pleased Lenin. In every way London inspires considerably less respect than Sinclair. He was theatric where

Sinclair was sincere. Both writers made great sums at different times. But where London, who flaunted his flannel shirt, and who signed his letters grandiloquently with "Yours for the Revolution," spent the profits from his enormous magazine output on his ranch at Glen Ellen, which he planted with some 30,000 eucalyptus trees, Sinclair threw all of his away on idealistic projects. The $30,000 derived from the success of *The Jungle* was sunk in the phalanstery experiment at Helicon Hall, where the young Sinclair Lewis acted as janitor. Hearstian journalism, sordid, eyeless, pounced upon the experiment, magnifying it into a super-Oneida community, with free love setting the pace. And poor Sinclair found himself the center of an insane persecution, which only let up after Helicon Hall had burned, and after the scandal heaped upon his first wife had died down. But Sinclair was incorrigible; when he made more money, later, he embarked upon a scheme to back the Soviet moving-picture producer, Serge Eisenstein, in the making of a great film of Indian life in Mexico. Sinclair's radicalism sprang from a good heart; London's, on the other hand, was suspiciously febrile, and seemingly bound up with his admiration for the "abysmal brute" and "dominant primordial beast" in man. He protested, once that "rampant individualism" had been effectively hammered out of him, and socialism hammered in. But he always knew where his bread was buttered; he was not honest with respect to his own fundamental cynicism, which expressed itself in his overweening care for his own acres. To the last, he remained—not only Ernest Everhard of *The Iron Heel,* but the Burning Daylight who was the financial buccaneer and the romantic who sought peace on a farm of his own. "The revolution is here now," London told his listeners in the years when Debs was gathering a large following. But he never acted, purely, on the assumption. He actually resented a mayor advocating municipal ownership—it made socialism too "respectable." London, it is to be feared, was a socialist because it gave him the ego-soothing feeling of high danger; not because he advocated it as a way of life, or regarded it intellectually as inevitable.

Nevertheless, the man had a fine glow about him—and the hidden motives of a pamphleteer often make no connection with his actual effect. The vigor which marked every undertaking of London, canalized to radical ends, has had its impact on thousands, although London himself once remarked that his work had brought the revolution ten minutes closer. *The People of the Abyss, The War of the Classes, Revolution, The Iron Heel*—all of them are vibrant documents, hard-hitting pamphlets from an age of hard-hitting pamphleteering. With Sinclair's work, with some of Whitman's poetry, they are America's revolutionary tradition in imaginative literature.

The élan of the frontier, which expressed itself in the back-trailing "demand" movements of General Kelly and "Jumbo" Cantwell's groups of "Coxeyites" in 1894, and, later, in the up-surge of the I. W. W., was London's natural heritage. The father of the novelist had been a trapper in Canada, and had come to San Francisco in 1873, where he was, for a time, a member of the police force. Jack London was born in 1876. He spent his earliest youth on a truck farm at Alameda, and on a wild ranch in San Mateo County. At the age of ten he was selling papers on the Oakland waterfront, and picking up a penny as a pin boy in bowling alleys and by sweeping out saloons. Later on he became an oyster pirate, an occupation which gave him material for his *Tales of the Fish Patrol.* By the time he was seventeen he was a confirmed alcoholic and waterfront bruiser, and perhaps only a trip into the North Pacific on a sealing schooner saved him from the sudden death which took his boon companions in the pirating business. London was shocked to learn of this death when he returned to San Francisco, in 1893, from the sealing expedition. So he decided to become respectable. For a time he worked in a jute mill and as a coal heaver; then, wearying of "honest labor," he set out to catch up with the Coxeyites of General Charles T. Kelly. His diary of the Kelly march, kept from the time of his departure from San Francisco until he deserted the "commonwealers" at Hannibal, Missouri, forms the basis for some of his book on tramp life called *The Road,* and is indispensable to an understanding of the popular ferment of the early nineties.

London's tramp experiences convinced him that brains, not brawn, ruled the roost. He decided forthwith to get out of the ranks of the underdog who worked with his hands to the end of scrabbling a bare living. Back in California, he accomplished the incredible feat of preparing two years' work for admittance to college in three months' time—a fearful ordeal which he later put into the autobiographical *Martin Eden.* But the college education which he fought so hard to attain displeased him; he remained at the University of California for approximately a mere semester, deserting, as had Frank Norris, because of the uninspiring instruction. He tried to write, but had the usual beginner's bad luck. Then, suddenly, information reached San Francisco of the Klondike Gold Rush, and London, the son of the trapper of the Canadian wilds, was off to the North. He came back with scurvy (which he cured by a diet of raw potatoes), and without any gold. But he struck pay dirt in his stories of the frozen North. Picking up where the Frank Norris of *Moran of the Lady Letty* had left off, London commenced turning out red-blooded fiction of men, women and dogs under primordial stress. His top work, *The Call of the Wild,* which was published in 1903, was the result of his flyer into the Klondike.

The socialist London was born of myriad experience—plus a reading of the literature of early American socialism. The evolutionary process of Herbert Spencer, the "blonde beast" morality of Nietzsche, and the worship of science—all of these were articulated, in London's mind, with the economics of Karl Marx and with the zeal of the working-class solidarity movement which is the subject of glowing pæan in London's essay on "Revolution." In 1902 the new convert to socialism went abroad, to dip into the City of London's East

End. His experiences among the human wreckage of an empire were related, in 1903, in *The People of the Abyss,* his first pamphleteering work.

The crown of London's socialist pamphleteering is *The Iron Heel,* which was published in 1908. Much of this book is a cogent, simplified, and very effective, exposition of the theory of surplus production and surplus value. On its informative level it runs parallel to even so recent a book as William Z. Foster's *Toward Soviet America.* All of the Marxian rationale is in it. The contradictions of capitalism, so Ernest Everhard tells unconvinced college professors and ministers of the gospel, make periodic depression inevitable, and final collapse only a question of time. When a crisis approaches, the owners, bent on preserving their own superior position, shift the burdens to the workers and to the farmers. The middle sort of man—the shopkeeper, the small dairyman, the small rancher—is squeezed out by monopolistic capitalism, which undersells until its small-time rivals go to the wall and join the proletariat. And the only thing that will "cure" capitalism, and free the world, is the socialist revolution, which, of course, will be violent, for no owning class ever gives up without a struggle.

Everhard, who is a Martin Eden with a message, a "Wolf" Larson of the intellect, pours his brute energy into the struggle. But the Oligarchy wins out—for centuries. Here London shows the undeniable literary effect of W. J. Ghent's *Our Benevolent Feudalism,* with the exception that in London's Wellsian phatasmagoria of an abortive revolution staged for 1932, the oligarchy—or the "Iron Heel"—proves anything but benevolent. It breaks the socialist thrust mercilessly, and drives it underground for an intolerable period.

The Iron Heel illustrates, perhaps more obviously than any other socialist document, the weakness of Marx in prognosis. London bit off the official theory of revolution, that it must, of necessity, be violent, and that it is inevitable. He failed to realize that, in a nation that is ostensibly democratic in structure, there are safety valves, such as the income tax.

Free capitalism results, inevitably, in a larger and larger class of unemployed, yes, but the dole, forced at the polls, and cannily administered, can put off the evil day of necessary uprising. Then, too, London underestimated, as do modern strict Marxians, the power of the dying lower middle class to kick back in the form of Fascist movements—movements that buy a certain tolerance and artificial continuance from the State as the antidote to Communist success. The fact that revolution is a long, devious, often undramatic process in most cases, with ultimate success depending on a varied attack, both on the positive and negative sides, escaped London, the doctrinaire, just as it escapes orthodox Marxists to-day. There is no need to minimize the nature of the class struggle in saying this; the class struggle is basic. But positive recourse to physical attack is not the whole of force. Revolutionary France was, in good measure, already a bourgeois nation before 1789—the comedies of Molière prove as much. Physical violence has been likened to the high fever that accompanies the final stages of the disease attacking an outmoded order. An oligarchy as strongly entrenched as the one London visualized in *The Iron Heel* would never have permitted the show of force that is in the novel; his oligarchy was not at the high fever stage. London made no study of the devious, only sporadically violent, stages of the bourgeois revolution in nations other than France. Such a study would not have served his clean-cut myth-making purposes. And so *The Iron Heel* does not convince as a prophecy; it remains an interesting pamphlet of an interesting time.

London and Sinclair were, both of them, potential romantics who were inverted by the pressure of their times. The idea of social justice, troubling all of America to a greater or lesser degree in those days, had its almost universal effect on the sensitive equipment of the creative writers—only an occasional Edith Wharton could escape troubling herself with the economically unbalanced implications of the rising industrialism.

And even Edith Wharton's work is, as *The House of Mirth* demonstrates, fundamentally bound up with the change that was coming over America—the fate of Lily Bart is a function of the passage of power from the hands of those fitted to practice primitive capitalism—such as trade and the collection of rents—into the hands of the investment bankers.

In the nineties a promising naturalist group had gotten its start, only to see its exemplars—Frank Norris, Hamlin Garland—carried away by crusading zeal. And in the 1900's more naturalists were drawn into the movement agitating for social justice. Robert Herrick was one potential naturalist who was diverted to fiction with a "moral," "problem" content; Ernest Poole was another. And besides the naturalists, romantics other than Sinclair and London were captured for the movement. William Allen White of Emporia, Kansas, wrote "problem" fiction. So did Winston Churchill and Booth Tarkington, as we have seen. None of the problem novelists—neither Herrick, nor any of the potential romantics—had the proper immersion in the *milieu* which had forced a preoccupation with the idea of social justice upon them—the *milieu* of the growing industrialism that was transforming the nation.

ROBERT HERRICK, a young man with a Puritan background, tried to saturate himself with a *milieu* from the outside, and succeeded as well as could be expected in *The Memoirs of an American Citizen,* published in 1905. The novels of Herrick are not negligible; they are honest attempts to explore the problems of a nation which had shifted from old moorings. But they are not great, by any means; they could not be great, for Herrick had no sustaining tradition for the industrial novel upon which to rest. The novel of industrialism had had its early practitioners, the best known of whom is the John Hay who wrote *The Breadwinners* and published it anonymously in the eighties. But *The Breadwinners* is not even a respectable beginning. An ingenuous defense of property rights, by a man who proclaimed himself a real democrat, it lacks the charm which is an indubitable part of Hay's letters. The strikes of Gilded Age America affronted Hay, the child of America's expansion; he lost his balance when he came to do the economic counterpart of Henry Adams's *Democracy*. He, too, lacked immersion in the new *milieu*. He made, merely, a panicky reaction.

In 1913, Edwin Bjorkman, looking about him for a "national" novelist, fixed upon Robert Herrick. Herrick, he wrote, was as "'national' as strikes, panics, country-wide unrests, 'booms' reaching from ocean to ocean, political and ethical fluctuations." But Bjorkman had not known Dreiser, who had come up through the world which Herrick had tried to discover from the outside. There is something of the kid-gloved investigator about Herrick. A Harvard graduate, with an education in Europe tacked on, Herrick had made the teaching of English his profession. At the age of twenty-six he had been called from the M.I.T. faculty to the new University of Chicago, where he was to organize the English department along Harvard lines. Chicago fascinated the young Easterner, as it had fascinated another exquisite, Henry B. Fuller. But it was the fascination that the bird feels in presence of the snake that has transfixed it with beady eye. Herrick was particularly struck by the "immorality" of business in the Chicago of the Wheat Pit, of the city of the earliest use of the gangster to settle problems of industrial markets, and of Charles T. Yerkes. He tried his own "Titan" in *The Memoirs of an American Citizen,* the story of Van Harrington, the sausage-maker, who attempted to create his own ethical justification for monopolistic exploitation. The philosophical weakness of this novel, one of the weaknesses which puts it definitely below *The Titan* and *The Financier,* lies somewhat in Herrick's felt necessity to provide Van Harrington with a new, a Darwinian ethics. It is questionable that the titans needed a "new" ethics—the data of Calvinism were there to sustain the tender-minded among them, for Calvinism insists upon the parable of the talents, and the "elect" need not question the whys and wherefores of worldly success. As a matter of fact, Van Harrington's ethics are a rationalization—and the man himself realizes it. It is Herrick rather than Van Harrington who is sincerely wrought up by the moral questions raised by monopoly.

But the main weakness of *The Memoirs of an American Citizen* lies in its "slenderness at the pith"; it simply lacks the marrow of *The Titan* and *The Financier.* It is a wholly "gotten up" book. It is true that Dreiser had to undertake considerable documentation for his "trilogy of desire," but it was not the documentation of the takers of inventory. He needed merely a skeleton of an actual career; the "feel" of the America he was depicting was in him, soaked up during his peregrinations about Chicago, St. Louis, Pittsburgh and New York. Facts, a hundred critics to the contrary, were accessories to Dreiser; he had the real thing in his bones.

A good deal of Herrick's work is, like David Graham Phillips's, an exploration of the problems of marital relationships in a society which had exalted its womenfolk to the position of petted spenders. But in *A Life for a Life* Herrick attempted to work out, on the plane of a misty symbolism, a projected "cure" for the evils, the "immoralities," of the new industrialism. This novel abandons the attempt at naturalism completely; its figures are those of the morality play. The banker, Alexander Arnold, is Satan; David Grant, a foundling who is in a fair way to make a success in the game as it is played, suddenly sees the light, and literally abandons his worldly goods to follow Christ among the poor. The novel plays upon two themes—the theme of cure by revolution, which is abandoned as the false cure, productive of only more violence and tragedy, and the theme of cure by the application of Christian principles, symbolized by the act of the banker's daughter, Alexandra Arnold, who turns over her estate to provide a home for foundlings. Here the naturalist of *The Web of Life* (1900)

—a novel in which Herrick made the amoral observation that "in striving restlessly to get plunder and power and joy, men weave the mysterious web of life for ends no human mind can know"—quit the attitude that existence is fundamentally incomprehensible; one must break through the web, and choose the human values of a David Grant or a reformed Alexandra Arnold. But the founding of a foundlings' home leaves the central problem—the problem of the approach to power—untouched. Here, Herrick had nothing to say. Herrick's implied advocacy of Christian "works" simply does not operate on a large enough scale to have any fundamental effect; *A Life for a Life* is, thus, as much a "Goo-goo" book as any of Winston Churchill's.

Herrick's fear of the results of industrialism found an analogue in Kansas, where William Allen White, in intervals of leisure seized from a daily struggle to get out a newspaper, turned occasionally to fiction. White's many books are very important to an understanding of the temper of the average human addition to the Progressive movement, whether the book in question be a biographical work such as *Masks in a Pageant* or *Woodrow Wilson,* or one of two novels, *A Certain Rich Man* (1909), and *In the Heart of a Fool* (1918). White's sole concern with the Progressive movement—the reason why he fought so assiduously for Theodore Roosevelt and, later, for a Woodrow Wilson whom he personally had a hard time liking—lies in the Progressive promise to right the balance between industry and agriculture. White's fear of the sleazy side of industrialism went into *A Certain Rich Man,* the story of John Barclay's capitulation to the forces that were pumping American business full of profitable water in the years following Appomattox. A good deal of this novel is credible; what is not is John Barclay's sudden conversion at the close to the forces of righteousness, when he gets rid of every "dirty dollar" he had amassed in a lifetime of manipulation. *In the Heart of a Fool* followed the same pattern of values as *A Certain*

Rich Man, with the countryside painted as the source of all human virtue. Industrialism, William Allen White implies, kills neighborliness; ergo, it is wicked. Finance is the modern devil, separating man from man.

THE novelists who set out to explore a changing America in the period from 1901 to 1915 generally made the mistake of trying to get inside of something which was fundamentally alien to their own dying world. Ernest Poole, whose novel, *The Harbor,* was published in 1915, saved himself from this mistake. Like Herrick and Sinclair, the young Poole wished to understand the conflict of interests which was killing the small business man and bringing in the world of corporate control. As the brother-in-law of Walter Weyl, radical economist, Poole wished, too, to arrive at an understanding of the growing labor problem. Syndicalism was in the air in 1915; the I. W. W. had succeeded in organizing strikes at Lawrence, Mass., and at Paterson, N. J. Bill Haywood had escaped capital punishment at the trial for murder of Governor Steunenberg held at Boise, Idaho, where Clarence Darrow, Heywood's attorney, had bested the young William E. Borah, prosecutor, in a duel of wits. The American world was trembling with portent, as skittery with fear as it ever has been.

To understand this world, Poole chose as his fictional vehicle, not a Van Harrington, not a labor leader, but a young and bewildered writer who had grown up in Brooklyn, close by the harbor of New York. This young writer passes through three natural phases—the phase of worship of art, typified by a Latin Quarter interlude, the phase of worship of efficiency, symbolized by his engineer father-in-law, who is attempting to apply the planner's creed of Stuart Chase to a chaotic New York harbor, and the phase of recognition of his friend Kramer's contention that justice comes only to those who will fight for it. Bill, Mr. Poole's writer, is finally involved in doing publicity for the forces of organized labor in a great dock strike—a natural point of contact with the class war for a writer. *The Harbor* is a stirring book, shot through with a wild rhythm, a sort of Research Magnificent in the world of industry. All of the problems raised by the growth of a great port, all of the contradictions, which Veblen was to explore, of the engineer in a profit economy, all of the quakings which a recognition of the fact of the class war would induce in a young man with a sensitive conscience and a wife and child to support—these are the vibrant material out of which *The Harbor* is made. It is a fitting book to serve as the culmination of a period.

The Harbor, by its definite stressing of the issue of political control, throws all of the preceding industrial fiction of the decade of muck into perspective. What did the movement toward bringing the economic man into the novel succeed in doing? It was, at best, auxiliary to the muck-raking campaign. It made little effort at the patient understanding of the greatest novelists. It suggested many problems, but shied away generally from a rigorous portrayal of the conditions necessarily attendant upon solution. Perhaps the human material was not there for a portrayal of conditions attendant upon solution. Hutchins Hapgood, in *The Spirit of Labor,* attempted a fictional biography of Anton Johanssen, a Chicago labor leader, but only to arrive at the conclusion that Samuel Gompers had to sidestep and compromise with capitalism to get along and retain a hold over his forces. "Yes," says Anton, "Gompers is a sidestepper, I must admit. But it is better than having always a panacea that doesn't work." And if labor itself, in the large, chose to go along with Gompers, what could the poor novelists do about abolishing the contradictions of capitalism? The best they could do, since they were unable to see any sure way out in terms of American potentialities, was to go consciously along or be dragged unwittingly along with the Progressive movement—a movement that called attention, and then called attention again, to the need for social justice, without quite knowing what could be done to handle a dynamic system that made for monopoly and attendant exploitation in spite of all the anti-trust laws in the world.

CHAPTER SEVEN

Philosophical Progressivism

☆

EVERY movement of any vitality reaches a point where it brings forth, as if by law, its philosophers, those who systematize its thought; and the years of the quest for social justice were no exception. The *sturm und drang* of that gusty pre-War period had its inevitable impact in the study on a widely diversified group of scholars who were, nevertheless, united in their common feeling for the pathology of the American spirit. One by one, as the voters were clamoring for Theodore Roosevelt or following the exposures of frenzied finance in the pages of *Everybody's* or moving on to Armageddon with a group of inspired men at Chicago, the volumes came forth from the study. J. Allen Smith published his *The Spirit of American Government* in 1907—and the "economic interpretation of the Constitution" was henceforth to be reckoned with. Herbert Croly dropped his *The Promise of American Life* into the controversy about a nation's future in 1909—and both Roosevelt's "New Nationalism" and the *New Republic* were born, as strange a pair of brothers as ever came in the same litter. John Dewey's *School and Society,* a product of 1899, was followed with an increasing number of papers dealing with democratic education, education for active service as against the education for "conspicuous leisure" which Thorstein Veblen had so elaborately spoofed in his chapter on "The Higher Learning" in *The Theory of the Leisure Class* (1899). After investigating the *History of Tammany Hall* in 1901, only to see most of the copies of the resulting book mysteriously bought up after publication, Gustavus Myers, working with benefit of Marx, brought out his three volumes on the *History of the Great American Fortunes* in 1909 and 1910—and no one could complain thereafter that the genesis of American capitalistic increment had not been thoroughly explored and reduced to formula. In *The Wine of the Puritans* (1908) a young man named Van Wyck Brooks, just out of Harvard, sought to determine the effects of the Puritan metaphysical passion on the quality of both American life and American literature—and his stray paragraphs have flowered in a magazine literature of self-critical articles whose proportions, if estimated, would be staggering, and whose producers include every one from Stuart Chase to James Truslow Adams. The years of the Wilsonian ascendancy—1912 and 1913—witnessed the publication of Walter Weyl's *The New Democracy,* Walter Lippmann's *A Preface to Politics* and Charles A. Beard's *An Economic Interpretation of the Constitution of the United States.* With the appointment and confirmation of Justice Brandeis to the Supreme Court in 1916, the neo-democratic forces at last got a man on the tribunal which Gustavus Myers, in 1912, had demonstrated in his *History of the Supreme Court of the United States* to be, if not property-conscious, at least subconsciously disposed to interpret in the interests of the propertied. Brandeis belongs to the list of the progressive philosophers not only for his judicial opinions, but for his *Other People's Money* of 1913 and 1914—an accurate and lucid, and systematic, diagnosis of the centralization and perversion of credit, the life-blood of the system which Myers, Smith, Croly, Veblen, Dewey, Lippmann and Weyl were either attacking or seeking to channel for social uses.

The men I have enumerated cannot, of course, be herded into a single corral and labeled "strictly belonging to the Progressive era." They touch hands with the past at innumerable points. A Henry George, a Henry Demarest Lloyd, a Bellamy, had provided earlier intellectual pabulum, which had been seized upon, in the opening years of the 1900's, by figures as diverse as Tom L. Johnson of Cleveland, Robert La Follette of Wisconsin, and Charles Edward Russell of Vermont and New York. These men, in turn, did their part in helping to create a situation, in terms of word and deed, calling for new systematic thinkers, new pathologists of the democratic spirit. A broad social movement always has a deep continuity, which, though it may often go underground for a time, must inevitably be present for the tapping if the imaginations of men are to be touched. And the men who provided the philosophical systematization of the 1912 progressivism, whether Rooseveltian or Wilsonian, were, each in his own way, integers in a broad movement that had reached America in the seventeenth and eighteenth centuries and had come to an early efflorescence in Jefferson, Patrick Henry and Tom Paine. With the growth of the plutocracy after the Civil War this movement had been channeled off to the farm border, where it was manifest in a series of periodic revolts which culminated, as we have seen, in the Populism of the nineties, and which had seeped through to the twentieth century by way of certain key figures who kept alive the spirit of Jefferson, the Grange and Henry George during the Spanish-American War and its aftermath of what Veblen called "conspicuous waste." Rolling up from West to East, and joining forces with city reformers like Tom Johnson and "Golden Rule" Jones, the spirit of Populism met the spirit of socialism in the larger urban centers. The rise of the Left in America, which had been made possible by a half century of immigration from the congested centers of Europe where Marx's predictions of the class war seemed all too sane, inevitably conditioned, to a small extent at least, even those Progressives who presumed to speak for the Jeffersonian state. Weyl and Lippmann had to reckon with industrial unionism and the ineluctable encroachments on that shibboleth of an earlier liberalism, "freedom of contract." From 1900 to 1912 the vote polled by Eugene Debs steadily grew; the I. W. W., America's version of the Anarcho-Syndicalist movement, became strong enough to organize and run the Lawrence and Paterson strikes in the East; and these two facts alone account for certain passages in Lippmann's buoyantly youthful *A Preface to Politics. The Appeal to Reason,* a socialist weekly published by Julius A. Wayland in Girard, Kansas, reached 500,000 readers in the rural and the smaller city districts, and its articles must at least have prepared a few thousand readers for the spread of neo-democratic, if not for socialist, doctrine. Nor can the effect of Graham Wallas and the Fabians be dismissed as totally negligible; they were read and discussed in the colleges, affecting such figures as Lippmann, although it is perfectly true that the experiment in social democracy would have gone along without them.

In back of all the social thinking that went to make up the body of doctrine which I have called "philosophical progressivism" were great seminal minds. Charles A. Beard, who imbibed much materialistic wisdom from *The Federalist,* might have been a good Jeffersonian gentleman and an able scholar if he had never encountered European thought, but it is highly doubtful if his work on the economic origins of Jeffersonian democracy and the American Constitution would have been as searching, as articulated, if he had not run across both Marx and Hegel in his salad days. The spirit of Hegel—with his thesis, his antithesis, his synthesis—runs through the canon of Beard, holding it always close to the earth and to the psychology of men living under the shadow of shifting institutions. And it was Hegel who brought Dewey to instrumentalism. Without benefit of Marx, it is difficult to see how Gustavus Myers could have read meaning into his studies of the origins of the great American fortunes. Brandeis, a believer in smallness and in competition, and in the preservation of these by State interference if necessary, touched hands not only with the Populism of the West of his youth, but with the Rousseauistic spirit of '48. Veblen, the greatest pathologist of the entire group, has admitted his debt to Marx. Herbert Croly, a "sport" among the philosophers of social justice in that he considered Alexander Hamilton a greater man than Jefferson, was undoubtedly influenced by Hobbes, but his plea for the Leviathan State, the strong Hamiltonian government with centralized control, was given a humanitarian color by his Comtean background; he grew up in the "religion of humanity"; and the strange cross-breeding of Hamilton with Comte resulted in the "New Nationalism." Brooks, the first social critic of the movement to work from purely literary documents, took Taine and Marx for his intellectual masters—and both were as much "genetic" thinkers as the Hegel of Dewey's early loyalty or of Charles Beard's treatment of historical sequence.

It is evident from the foregoing that many strands may be woven into a going social movement. But in spite of the presence of Marx in the thinking of many of the philosophers of social justice, in spite of the spread of socialism and the recognition, by Brandeis, Weyl and others, that the doctrine of freedom of contract could no longer be held sacred, the prescriptions of virtually every philosophical progressive took the line of what George Soule has called American "economic fundamentalism." They practically all believed in curbing the plutocracy by instituting controls and checks in the interests of the "little fellow." The stress of all of them, save Myers and the later Veblen, is upon the pathology of modern industrial society, not upon any necessity of changing the fundamentals. Even as the earlier Populists, they were, in the words of Charles Edward Merriam, "on the side of individualism as against socialism, and democracy as against plutocracy; and on the side of collectivism where necessary to curb monopoly or unfair competition as they conceived it; but not for the type of collectivism implied in the labor theory and the ideal of industry administered by the standardized union association of men, in which all stood upon the same level of production and compensation regardless of individual differences in capacity. They were for a progressive income tax, but not for a single tax on land; for an inheritance tax to prevent swollen fortunes, but not for common ownership of capital."

But no matter where they stood, since property—not necessarily in its real, but also in its personalty forms—was at the basis of the society which the philosophers of progressivism were, in one manner or another, attacking, it is mandatory to begin a discussion of the whole movement with the historian of the genesis of American ownership. That historian was Gustavus Myers, once an orthodox campaigning socialist, now, in a somewhat meditative sixth decade, withdrawn from the front-line trenches.

When Gustavus Myers reached his majority in March of 1893, the historic panic of the nineties was only a few weeks in the offing. Myers, who was born in Trenton, New Jersey, an ugly industrial town, had grown up in the harsh atmosphere of exploitation, political corruption and overcapitalization, and by the time of the anthracite coal strike—when President Baer of the Philadelphia and Reading Railroad was exclaiming: "The rights of the laboring man will be protected and cared for, not by labor and agitation but by the Christian men to whom God in his infinite wisdom has given control of the property interests of this country"—he had become a convinced socialist. Tammany Hall and the history of the public franchises of New York were the first subjects to gain his attention, which was that of the "indefatigable mole" burrowing deep among lost, strayed, buried and faded records. The *History of Tammany Hall,* published in 1901 and reissued in 1917, was a brave book, and an invaluable book, and every critic, every historian, of the New York Democracy since 1917 has had frequent recourse to it, whether they have given credit and thanks to Myers or not. A pride of research and a considerable pugnacity required to get his facts listened to were two of the young Myers's dominant characteristics; and since pride and pugnacity invariably breed opposition, they have left the older Myers a bit battle-worn. The young man, as indeed the older, had also a blunt predilection for stating the ungarnished truth—a predilection which often led him into a heavy-handed, socialist-pietistic irony, ineffective now, but readily explicable in terms of its pre-1912 social context.

The *History of the Great American Fortunes,* in three volumes, sounds like a long, "Oh, yeah?" to Baer's citation of the gifts of "God in his infinite wisdom." If God indeed has placed the control of the property interests of the country in the hands of certain Christian men, Myers's testimony would seem to indicate that He had selected the devil as His agent of transfer. For Myers discovered the history of large accretions of property in America, as elsewhere, to be largely a matter of plunder and preëmption, whether legal or otherwise. Cleverness, cupidity, strength and the ability to organize a State in the interests of preserving plunder and preëmption—these, rather than the more social virtues, were at the back of the development of the American continent. The State, Myers saw clearly enough, was not an abstract entity which, somehow, cared for all its citizens; it was merely a fulcrum which the strong employed for their own uses in lifting the public domain, the public utility franchises, the mineral deposits, the rights of way, into their own capacious pockets. And, good socialist that he was, Myers considered one predatory pry worth another—the weak, by combining to become strong, might seize and hold the fulcrum for their own more merciful uses. It is the socialist hope which gives the *History of the Great American Fortunes* its snarling overtones—and the snarl is fully as justified as the Baer hypocrisy.

A child of the Gilded Age, Myers was primarily interested in the power politics growing out of the decision of the Civil War—the politics of the Vanderbilts, the Goulds, the Russell Sages, the Morgans, the Elkinses and the James J. Hills, in short, the men who made America what it is to-day. But as a conscientious student Myers began at the very beginning, with the growth of the first fortunes in land and in rents, with the growth of the Astor family as the landlords of New York. To a large extent, he blocked in a factual justification for *Progress and Poverty*—for all his greatest fortunes, one discovers, were matters of getting a stranglehold on a monopoly, whether that monopoly be of land, of a right of way, of credit in a tight situation, or of a supply of defective rifles in time of war.

The early industrial developments, "as exemplified by mills, factories and shops," which followed the seizure of land in the East and which preceded the construction of the great American railroads, led to no swollen fortunes—a fact which Henry George might have made much of if he had been disposed to implement his defense of non-monopolistic capitalism. With factory warring against factory, and with supply and demand delimiting the opportunities for sudden factory growth, "fortunate was the factory owner regarded who could claim $250,000 clear." But land had been a different matter, as John Jacob Astor had demonstrated, and land for railroads, to be stolen or cajoled from the government along with subsidies for building, offered a juicy opportunity for those who had observed the methods of attaining to inordinate wealth. It was simply a matter of persuading or packing a legislature, by bribery, "community of interest" or the offer of stock, as the builders of the canals and the capitalists of the great Western land companies in the Mississippi and the Ohio territories had shown. And under cover of the "idealism" of the Civil War, when truly patriotic men were plugging at their erstwhile countrymen across the fields of Bull Run or Antietam, the corruption of state and national governments in the interests of the railroad systems gathered irresistible momentum.

Myers traced the ramifications of the art of capitalizing public utilities and other natural monopolies through the careers of Cornelius Vanderbilt, of Jay Gould, of the Morgan who was railroad consolidator and security underwriter as well as banker, of the Stephen B. Elkins who sat at the center of a web of many transactions, whether in coal, coke, oil, lumber or railroads. He investigated the "big four" of the Pacific coast —Collis P. Huntington, Leland Stanford, Charles Crocker and Mark Hopkins. The details of the Myers books need not concern us here; it is sufficient to note that his facts came, like Ida Tarbell's, from the records of legislative investigations, of legal controversies, of Supreme Court decisions. He had the facts—and if he dealt with them in a certain spirit of gloom, if he had the habit of calling attention to what now seems obvious by moralistic intrusions upon the record, he may plead considerable provocation. Myers's attitude towards his facts, towards the society of the dinosaurs, if it has robbed the anatomist of the great American fortunes of a certain quality of preservative serenity in his writing, should not, in any case, be used to excuse the objects of his attack. It is a favorite trick of apologists for the *status quo* to make game of the zeal, the febrile manner, of the Gustavus Myerses and the Upton Sinclairs of this world, thus diverting attention from the methods of an Armour or a Jay Gould; and to this trick the *History of the Great American Fortunes* is wide open. But the *History* is, nevertheless, a great work and an honest work—and the pity of it is that it has not brought leisure to its author. At the very least it has played an important part in killing respect for the "divine right" theory of the Baers.

THE *History of the Great American Fortunes* came as a factual climax to a decade of investigating and agitating the connection between plunder economics and politics. The new century had opened, as we have seen, with the detailed impertinences of the muck-rakers, but as late as 1908, in his *Mr. Crewe's Career,* Winston Churchill could still write as if the economic basis of politics had not existed in the early days of the Republic. With the coming of the Jacksonian overturn—so Churchill said—the "unintelligent" and the venal took charge of our politics, and with the development of the railroads corruption became general and magnified. Corruption means, of course, the attempt to divide service between two masters, the general weal and the individual desire for profit; and the founding fathers, in Churchill's eyes, were wholly innocent of divided loyalties. They had been solely devoted to the concept of the nation as a whole.

In general the historians, with the exception of McMaster, accepted the Churchill version of the national story. Federalists themselves, they had little difficulty in identifying virtue with the Constitutional Convention. But the disclosures of a Steffens, a David Graham Phillips, a Tarbell, set the newer historians to thinking. If economic need, and economic desire to expand, so these historians must have argued to themselves, is behind the manipulation of municipal, state and national government to-day, then is it not reasonable to suppose that human nature functioned in the same way yesterday, and the day before yesterday? Lincoln Steffens has told us, in his autobiography, that he made the discovery, when a student at the University of California, that the founding fathers not only did not, but did not desire to give us democratic government. But he kept the notion to himself. It was not until 1907 that a fine Jeffersonian gentleman, Professor J. Allen Smith of the University of Washington, made an extension of the muck-rakers' discovery backward into our history, and laid profane hands upon the most reverend Constitution of the United States. In his *The Spirit of American Government,* which, so Parrington has told us, meant a great deal to the Progressives of 1907, Smith called the Constitution a "reactionary" document, and the "economic interpretation of the Constitution" was formally born. Charles A. Beard, working at Columbia University, made a subsequent study of the economic origins of the Constitution that was detailed and precise where Smith's work was sketchy, but the seed was sown by Smith—as, indeed, it had been sown in the nineties by the implications, if not the direct statement, of the Turner thesis.

"Constitutional government," Smith said, "is not necessarily democratic." The Declaration of Independence, of course, was —but with the return of peace, the classes which so largely represented the wealth and culture of the colonies regained the influence they had lost when to be conservative was to be Tory. Moreover, many who had been ardent democrats during the rebellion became reactionary in the hard times that followed. And when the framers of the Constitution met at Philadelphia, democracy—the excesses of which had been blamed for the chaotic money situation and demonstrations such as Shays's Rebellion in Western Massachusetts—was "the very thing which they wished to avoid."

That Professor Smith was hinting directly at an economic interpretation, rather than the common "democratic versus aristocratic" dualism of John Fiske and McMaster, is proved by his quotation of Adam Smith's statement, that "civil government, so far as it is instituted for the security of property, is in reality instituted for the defense of the rich against the poor, or of those who have some property against those who have none at all." And as if profiting by this gleam from the *Wealth of Nations*, Charles Beard, in his *Economic Interpretation of the Constitution of the United States,* carried out an elaborate study of the economic interests in the states in 1787—or at least as elaborate as was possible, given the fragmentary and dispersed character of the records. Beard proceeded from the obvious to the so-called "inadmissible." To begin with, as everybody knew, there was a large disfranchised class in the United States of the post-revolutionary Populism—the slaves, the indented servants, a fair-sized group of men who were disqualified by property tests, and women. Among the property owners, who were entitled to the vote, were those whose interests were in realty, a group consisting of the small farmers, the manorial lords and the slaveholding planters. The two latter classes, in spite of individual differences of opinion, naturally combined against the small farmers of the back-country, who formed a homogeneous group from New Hampshire to Georgia. And allied with the manorial lords and the masters of black chattels were the men who were interested in personalty, whether in money, in public securities, in manufactures and shipping, or in capital invested in the will-o'-the-wisp of Western lands.

Both Beard and Smith discovered, or re-discovered, that the Constitutional Convention had been mainly organized by the great landholders, and by those interested in preserving and increasing their equity in personalty. "Most of the members," said Beard, "came from towns, on or near the coast, that is, from regions in which personalty was largely concentrated," and, furthermore, "not one member represented in his immediate personal economic interests the small farming or mechanical classes." Moreover, "of the fifty-five members who attended, no less than forty appear on the Records of the Treasury Department for sums varying from a few dollars up to more than one hundred thousand dollars." "It cannot be said, therefore, that the members of the convention were 'disinterested.' On the contrary, we are forced to accept the profoundly significant conclusion that they knew through their personal experiences in economic affairs the precise results which the new government that they were setting up was designed to attain." And the State ratifying conventions, Beard disclosed, were generally diminished replicas of the Philadelphia gathering, where the "rich, the well-born and the able" had their will behind a smoke-screen of the preamble, "We, the people...."

The Beard book, with its convincing array of facts from the olden documents, should have been sufficient to silence the critics of the less concrete J. Allen Smith—although the President of Beard's university, Nicholas Murray Butler, apparently never forgave the most intelligent member of his political science department for producing the facts. When Butler was asked on an occasion, "Have you read Beard's last book?" he gave answer, "I hope so." At least that is the story current among the present faculty at Columbia. And when the War came, and Professor Henry Wadsworth Longfellow Dana was in trouble for his pacifist views after America's entrance, Beard, although heartily believing our participation on the side of the Allies both justified and inevitable, took up the cudgels for academic freedom, and his resignation was accepted with some alacrity. But his "economic interpretation" led to no open break—it was too formidably documented for that.

Professor Smith, in his book, had cut through the maze of facts to underlying principles and motives, and had not taken the trouble to trail his research behind him on the page. He said, patly, that the aim of the Convention was to limit the direct influence of people on legislation, and that the members represented wealth and the conservative forces. The popular notion that the Convention, in framing the Constitution, was actuated solely by the desire to impart more vigor and efficiency to the general government was, he insisted, only part of the truth. To complement "vigor" and "efficiency," the framers wanted to establish a government of great stability and freedom from change—and the result, what with the system of "checks and balances" that is our heritage from the Philadelphia of 1787, is a modern government that is about five times as inflexible, and much less democratic, than the government of Great Britain. Of course, as Smith said, the framers didn't want to carry the system of checks upon the majority "too far"; hence the new government had the "form" of a democracy. But, with the process of amendment made extremely difficult, and the Senate put at one remove from the people (where it remained until 1913), and the Supreme Court standing as the final check, the government bequeathed to America at Philadelphia was certainly a long way from an open democracy. And as events have since proved, the "form" fell an easy prey to the plutocratic elements within American society. The "wisdom" of the fathers, Smith summed up, has largely defeated (1), the popular choice of candidates; (2), a clear expression of majority opinion; and (3), responsibility of government to a popular majority. "We thus see that true party government is impossible under a constitutional system which has as its chief end the limitation of the power of the majority." And in this connection, it is perhaps well to raise a query: If America ever has another revolution, will it not be because the cumbersome system of "checks and balances" has "checked" once too often, and "balanced" us on the edge of an abyss?

To prove his point of "non-representation," Smith recalled to mind that eleven general elections had resulted in a House of Representatives that had no political support in any other branch of the government—a situation that is impossible under the modern British system, where a party stands or falls upon its ideas. And an American party, Smith further reminds us, may have a nominal majority in all branches of the government, and yet lack the power to enforce its will, since an amendment, to become law, must run the gauntlet of more than a majority of the States. In carrying his explorations beyond the boundaries of national government, Smith discovered that both state and city were also organized on a plan of "distributed powers and diffused responsibility"—again the checks and balances that enabled a predatory few (as Lincoln Steffens also learned) to stave off popular retribution and control.

The basic trouble with our government in the twentieth century, in Professor Smith's eyes, was that it had grown out of the exigencies of eighteenth-century conditions. In the Age of the Enlightenment, to devise checks was simply to limit the over-riding power of a tyrannical aristocracy. When the founders of the United States' system moved on to an approximation of democracy, they carried with them a pernicious habit of thinking—vestiges of cerebration induced by the aristocratic order. Under the régime of democracy, the devising of checks works to preserve an aristocratic leaven within the common lump. But this leaven does not work to the amelioration of the lot of the whole. It does not lead to "liberty" in any sense other than that of "liberty" to do with property and property rights what one will. And in a corporate age, an age of trusts, this is no "liberty" for the common man at all.

At the close of his "long and arid" (but, in reality, extremely interesting) book, Beard quotes some general conclusions that should be displayed here:

"The movement for the Constitution... was originated and carried through principally by four groups of personalty interests which had been adversely affected under the Articles of Confederation: money, securities, manufactures, and trade and shipping."

"No popular vote was taken directly or indirectly on the proposition to call the Convention which drafted the Constitution."

"The propertyless masses under the prevailing suffrage qualifications were excluded at the outset from participation (through representatives) in the work of framing the Constitution."

"The Constitution was essentially an economic document based upon the concept that the fundamental private rights of property are anterior to government and morally beyond the reach of popular majorities."

"The Constitution was ratified by a vote of probably not more than one-sixth of the adult males."

"In the ratification, it became manifest that the line of cleavage for and against the Constitution was between substantial personalty interests on the one hand and the small farming and debtor interests on the other."

"The Constitution was not created by 'the whole people' as the jurists have said; neither was it created by 'the States' as Southern nullifiers long contended; but it was the work of a consolidated group whose interests knew no state boundaries and were truly national in their scope."

IN THE light of Charles A. Beard and J. Allen Smith, it becomes doubly evident that the Progessivism of 1902-12 was mainly an attempt to over-ride the spirit of the Constitution, and return to the Declaration of Independence; and to recreate the Constitution in the interests of the people—or, rather, the twentieth-century equivalent of "the small farming and debtor interests." The attempt was rendered the more difficult because of the Supreme Court, which, in Professor Smith's words, had virtual power to "enact"—a power which Oliver Wendell Holmes, Junior, writing in the eighties, said should not belong to it. But "shoulds" and "oughts" meant little to Justice Shiras in the nineties, when he reversed his decision on the income tax, thus enabling the Supreme Court to declare it unconstitutional. Nor did the palpable import of the Sherman Anti-Trust Act mean anything to the Supreme Court when the phrase, "combination in restraint of trade," was applied to labor unions. In fact, the actions of the bench so went against the grain of the developing Progressive philosophy that Smith's statement, that "under the guise of an independent judiciary we have in reality an independent legislature, or rather an independent legislature and judicial body combined," soon became a commonplace. The commonplace was at the base of Roosevelt's furious championship, expressed in heated terms to William Roscoe Thayer, of the recall of judicial decisions in 1912. Did the founders intend that the Supreme Court should have the power to "enact"? Beard found it difficult to believe otherwise. "The keystone of the whole [governmental] structure," he wrote, "is . . . the system provided for judicial control—the most unique contribution to the science of government which has been made by American political genius. It is claimed by some recent writers that it was not the intention of the framers of the Constitution to confer upon the Supreme Court the power of passing upon the constitutionality of statutes enacted by Congress; but in view of the evidence on the other side, it is incumbent upon those who make this assertion to bring forward positive evidence to the effect that judicial control was not a part of the Philadelphia program. Certainly, the authors of the *Federalist* entertained no doubts on the point, and they conceived it to be such an excellent principle that they were careful to explain it to the electors to whom they addressed their arguments."

The economic function of the Supreme Court was learnedly and exhaustively discussed by Gustavus Myers in his *History of the Supreme Court,* which reached the public in 1912. In decision after decision Myers uncovered the class bias of the judges—lending great point to the dissenting opinion of Justice Holmes, an independent on the bench, who, in a bakeshop case, had handed down a minority report to the effect that "this case is decided upon an economic theory which a large part of the country does not entertain.... The Fourteenth Amendment does not enact Mr. Herbert Spencer's *Social Statics."* But whatever Mr. Justice Holmes might think, or Gustavus Myers might call "class bias," the Supreme Court stood, through Taft's Administration and the time of the "rule of reason" as it was applied to "good" and "bad" trusts, firmly upon the eighteenth-century shibboleths of the "freedom of contract." Roscoe Pound might object to "mechanical jurisprudence," Justice Holmes might urge that "the life of the law has not been logic; it has been experience," but "class bias" remained "class bias." However, with both Wilson and Roosevelt running for the Presidency in the Autumn of 1912, it looked, for the moment, as if America might—possibly—at last get a new deal.

IF TWO pathologists of the American spirit—Thorstein Veblen and the young Harvard graduate, Van Wyck Brooks—were right in their diagnosis of that spirit, it was high time for a new deal. Brooks, writing some years after 1912 in his *America's Coming-of-Age,* spoke of the wistful hunger of those days just prior to the War—when "new" was tacked on to every social philosophy then in the making: the "New Freedom," the "New Nationalism," the "New Woman," et cetera. (That was long before the battle over the "New Humanism.") Veblen, commencing a brilliant series of operations on national complacency in his *The Theory of the Leisure Class* (1899), bothered himself very little with the wistfulness of aspiration, preferring rather to stick to mordant analysis of conventions and of "middle-class" morality.

The figure of Veblen, remote, complex and aloof, is one of the most curious that ever walked through the American university world. A child of Scandinavian parents, he had grown up in a pioneer Minnesota community of the sixties and seventies, and perhaps he sucked in from the atmosphere the dislike of General James B. Weaver and Ignatius Donnelly for the over-riding processes of industrial development which, in the hands of business men, were squeezing the farmers of the Middle Border with the device of an appreciating currency. After a hard youth he studied and was graduated from Carleton College, where, ironically enough, he was taught by Professor John Bates Clark, one of the foremost apologists for *laissez faire* in America. Ultimately Veblen was to become the most formidable opponent of Clark among American economists. From Carleton, which was a small denominational college, the future adversary of Gilded-Age capitalism went on to Johns Hopkins, and thence to Yale, where in 1884 he took his doctor's degree for a dissertation on Kant. But Veblen did not stop with orthodox philosophy, for he also won a prize at Yale with a study of the panic of 1837.

Nor did he stop with economics. When J. Laurence Laughlin picked him up and procured him a job at Cornell in 1891, Veblen was an adept in Norse literature, in Icelandic mythology and in Cretan history, and in much curious lore going back to neolithic times. The sweep of his mind awed his graduate students, according to the testimony of those who studied under him, and the vast reaches of his learning enabled him, as Lewis Mumford has said, to break down "the conventional division between economics, ethnology, anthropology, psychology and the physical sciences." But the erudition of the man hurt him as a teacher; he knew too much to suffer fools gladly, and the conventions of the college town irked him.

Ithaca was no place for a Veblen. But when Laughlin took his protégé with him to the University of Chicago, where, in spite of the Rockefeller endowment, a considerable atmosphere of intellectual freedom reigned, the morose young sociologist expanded in the company of John Dewey and Jacques Loeb. He remained at Chicago from 1892 to 1906, going on to Leland Stanford in that year, stopping later at the University of Missouri, and winding up as a lecturer after the War at the New School for Social Research in New York, along with Charles A. Beard.

The university career of Veblen is, on the whole, meaningless; he has no history, as Paul T. Homan has said, "but the history of his thought." Essentially a satirist, he had the Clarence Darrow technique of expressing the obvious in such a lugubrious, straight-faced manner that what common folk are apt to act upon as horse sense seems, in the Veblen idiom, to be ridiculous nonsense—as indeed it is ridiculous nonsense. Mumford has spoken of his "desperately accurate circumlocutions," his willfully "elephantine" manner, his "American mechanism of the impassive face and the solemn exaggeration." This exaggeration once took Mencken in completely. His satire "never had the need to depart from description," but under the cold exterior of the man who took refuge in an elaborate ritual there was the Don Quixote, hating sham and cant and exploitation and tilting at them in his own way.

Divorced from the manner, which was habitual and unbreakable, the contents of the Veblen books could very well be boiled down into a sizeable essay. The flavor of the man would be lost; but his influence might grow with a simplification of his thought. He may have been a fine critic of art and culture, as Mumford has claimed, and his definition—that "the canon of beauty requires expression of the generic. The 'novelty' due to the demands of conspicuous waste traverses the canon of beauty"—may be profoundly true. Yet how much more barbed for the memory is Louis Sullivan's expression of the same truth: "Form follows function; function creates form." It is as a phrase-maker calling attention to distinctly economic data that Veblen's genius is at its highest—as a phrase-maker and as an economic distinction-maker. His descriptions, colored indefinably with the quality of the epithet, —"conspicuous leisure," "conspicuous waste," "conspicuous consumption," "pecuniary canons of taste," "pecuniary aptitudes," and so on, thrown out into the society of 1899 when the "captain of industry" was glittering in all his magnificence, sent deep beams of light into the recesses of American psychology at the century's end.

The most vital of Veblen's distinctions is that between "industry" and "business," which was implicit in his *Theory of the Leisure Class,* and which took on sharpness and clarity in his *Theory of Business Enterprise,* a book that explored the mystical bases of modern capitalism. In splitting "business" and "industry" apart, Veblen showed, once and for all, that the former was a matter of the price and profit system, by which certain favored individuals attempted to acquire as large a money income as possible, while "industry" was a matter of organizing, by means of the "instinct of workmanship," the technological resources of mankind in order to produce the most goods with the least effort for the satisfaction of material wants. The functions of the engineer and the business man, Veblen argued in a series of books commencing with the *Theory of Business Enterprise* (1904) and continuing through *The Vested Interests and the Common Man* (1919), and *The Engineers and the Price System* (1921), were radically opposed. Business, so he demonstrated, was carried out according to the rules of onslaught, capture and plunder learned during mankind's most warlike stage—the savage tribal hunting stage —while "industry," or the natural desire of men to carry through a necessary job as effectively as possible, was a survival from an even earlier culture, that of the peaceful neolithic man.

The development of the great technology, culminating in the late nineteenth and early twentieth centuries with the inventions making for mass production, had moved the engineer, the technician, to the fore. And in the machine age the business man, whose sole urge is to take advantage of the price system and to buy cheap and sell dear, runs squarely counter to the "instinct of workmanship" which is the pride of the technological mind. In 1919, when Veblen was at work on his analysis of the *Vested Interests* (he defined a "vested interest" as a right to get something for nothing), the I. W. W. were inspiring a fear of "criminal syndicalism" in the hearts of those who cried "sabotage" at the Wobblies. But Veblen, with his habit of discrediting the postulates upon which all classical, *i.e.*, "conventional," economics rests, undertook to show that business men habitually engaged in "sabotage" of the industrial system—in fact, made their living by an orderly campaign of sabotage. Collusion to insure profits, Veblen said, must inevitably work toward the "conscious withdrawal of efficiency" whenever the market appeared to be glutted, and the price trend down. Pecuniary gain, in short, had nothing in common with maintaining maximum industrial efficiency in the interests of getting the largest amount of goods into the most hands at the cheapest price.

In his earliest books Veblen took no "moral" stand; he was simply the observer, cutting across all taboos. He criticized the "deductive" elements in the thought of Marx as quickly as he criticized them in Adam Smith. But in *The Vested Interests and the Common Man,* which came to publication after the Bolshevik triumph in Russia, the Don Quixote in Veblen triumphed over the Jove—and the Syndicalist sympathizer was openly revealed. *The Vested Interests* praised the I. W. W. as the "exuberant" and "untidy" vanguard of dissent that would, ultimately, make the world over in the interests of the technologist, he whom George Soule, translating Veblenese for the readers of the *New Republic,* has called the "organizing man." And the Non-Partisan League, "large, loose, animated and untidy"—"agricultural syndicalists"—Veblen named as the natural agrarian complement of the I. W. W.

"To these untidy creatures of the New Order," he said, "common honesty appears to mean vaguely something else, perhaps something more exacting, than what was 'nominated in the bond' at the time when the free bargain and self-help were written into the moral constitution of Christendom by the handicraft industry and the petty trade." And the book ends with Veblen, the moral exhorter, remarking, "And why should it not?" But alas, as Veblen himself had said, "It is not that [the I. W. W. and the Non-Partisan League] are ready with a 'satisfactory constructive program,' such as *the people of the uplift* require to be shown before they will believe that things are due to change." The italics are mine, and they prove that Veblen, although he has been temporarily displaced since 1921 by the statistical method in economics, and although his theories may have failed to account for the prosperity of 1925 and after, had always a keen insight into the hearts and minds of the people. He knew the power of those who constituted the "vested interests" and their camp followers, the agriculturalists who were hopeful of an advance in the price of real estate, and the reactionaries of the American Federation of Labor, dependent on the crumbs from the table of Dives and unwilling to try to seize a place in the kitchen and the garden for their own uses.

WHERE Veblen is weak, and where he has led a generation of economists—the generation of Stuart Chase—astray, is in his lack of a power politics, the same lack that has sent Henry George into limbo as a complete systematic thinker. All that Veblen had to propose for the supervision of an economic system reared on modern technology was a plan for a hierarchy of technical experts. His "social control," as Paul Homan has acutely observed, is not postulated; he offers no prospective means by which the technical experts may be expected to oust the high priests of the price and profit system. The "vested interests" still stand in the way of *carte blanche* for the technological hierarchy. Yet in *The Vested Interests and the Common Man,* Veblen does indeed more than hint at his plan—and his plan is that of men as diverse in temperament as Edward Bellamy and Daniel De Leon, industrial representation and control. For what have the portents of the I. W. W. and the "agricultural syndicalists," the Non-Partisan League, meant, if not just this? And even though he may be chary of "control," we owe Veblen a debt for his work toward emancipating social philosophers from the bondage of orthodox categories. "Progress" he spoke of as "cumulative change"; economics, he said, was not a "system of deductive logic." He died in 1929, at the crest of a period of "progress," and at a time when men were "deducing," from the spectacle of a "New Era" and the antics of the stock market, an eternal plateau of prosperity. Few there were to do him reverence at his death. But now he shines like a star of the first magnitude.

LIKE Veblen's, the first work of Van Wyck Brooks—who was ultimately to create for the generation of 1912-1922 a consciousness of the needs and possibilities of American literature in his best books, *America's Coming-of-Age* and *Letters and Leadership*—was an inquiry into the psychology of the exploiting man. Called *The Wine of the Puritans,* it was published in 1908, a year after the author's graduation from Harvard, the socialist Harvard that preceded the era of the "esthetes." Brooks was twenty-three years old when he wrote that book, but it is a mature man's book, for all that. In its pages one may discover the whole Puritan-pioneer rationale that was strong meat for a decade—the rationale that dissected the American as exploiter and victim of exploitation. It is surely no accident that when Brooks was working on his thesis, Theodore Dreiser was mulling over the story of Yerkes for *The Financier* and *The Titan.* Brooks, however, did not rail against the "interests." As Waldo Frank has said, he "has essentially a non-political mind." But his criticisms of "prosperity" in *The Wine of the Puritans* had their political implications—McKinley and the "Full Dinner Pail" were still, in 1908, the secret desire of many in the Republican Party and in America.

The most uncanny thing about *The Wine of the Puritans* is its prophecy. "I am perfectly sure," Brooks remarked in 1908, "that we are on the edge of an age of satire." At that time Thomas Beer was writing execrable poems about ancient Babylon for the Yale *Literary Magazine;* Sinclair Lewis was celebrating the glories of the ivy-bedecked Yale campus for the same publication; Henry Mencken was scarcely a portent; and there were still some years to go before the advertisements for Ring Lardner's "You Know Me, Al," were to appear in the pages of the *Baseball Magazine.*

The crown of Brooks's work was to come in *America's Coming-of-Age* and *Letters and Leadership,* books in which he raked the entire field of "direct expression" in America. He spoke, in 1918, of Dreiser's characters as "insulated against human values"; and Robert Shafer got around to the same criticism, possibly thinking it original, ten years later. In *Letters and Leadership* Brooks complained of Whitman that he had "a large share of the naïve pioneer nature, which made it impossible for him to take experience very seriously or develop beyond a certain point," and this criticism was made germane to the whole American habit of crude booster optimism. And of Henry Ford, Brooks asked in 1918: "Has it never occurred to us to compare Mr. Ford's face with Mr. Ford's recent career [on the Peace Ship]?" The dualism of Mr. Ford was the dualism of America—and of the "Progressive" forces: he wished to "do good," yet he wished to preserve the *status quo*—exactly the dualism of the trust-busting Roosevelt, as we shall see.

To "DO GOOD" and to preserve the *status quo;* to make the lion and the lamb, the Garys and the Gomperses, as Gilson

Gardner puts it, lie down together—such, in brief, was the hope of more than one Progressive as 1912 drew nigh. And if it was not precisely the program of the formulators of the "New Nationalism" and the "New Democracy" and the writers of prefaces to politics, it at least has a germ of truth when applied to them. Herbert Croly, in his *The Promise of American Life,* did not exactly hope to leave the *status quo* untouched, but he wanted the "vested interests" to give up their evil practices as if by acclamation. Walter Lippmann, although he toyed with the enchanting idea of Guild Socialism (which is a form of democratic syndicalism), was similarly sanguine of a peaceful renunciation on the part of the powerful. Walter Weyl, a brother-in-arms of both Croly and Lippmann on the *New Republic* after 1914, was more inclined than either of his colleagues to go to the point; his *The New Democracy,* published in 1912, insists that "control of political parties is the very beginning of political democracy." Weyl had a sobering realization, which both Croly and Lippmann were apt to forget, that "money buys publicity, orators, advocates"; hence "we must control the party through its purse." And to control a party through its purse evidently entailed, in Weyl's very intelligent estimation, preliminary work in equalizing income and opportunity, which, in turn, demanded a strong labor movement. Otherwise, with the plutocratic elements of society in control of the necessary sinews of war, all talk about "democracy" shot away into the upper air.

There is a great deal of this rumination in the upper air in Croly, and in Lippmann's otherwise brilliant *A Preface to Politics,* which was written under the twin influence of Graham Wallas and Lincoln Steffens. Croly did believe, it is true, that industrial democracy implies the necessity of a strong union movement, fully recognized, and an elimination of the open shop and the concomitant threat of the "scab." And in *The Promise of American Life*—a book whose influence spread in a wide circular ripple to touch men as diverse as Theodore Roosevelt and Robert Morss Lovett—Croly advocated a recognition of the crucial position of labor in any real program for democratization of the industrial machine. But by far the greater part of *The Promise of American Life* indulges in vague hopes rather than in concrete proposals.

A streak of religiosity in Croly led him to make a mystical fetish of "nationalism." It is true that he spoke of a strong centralized government as a technical means of problem-solving on the scale made mandatory by machine technology, but he was forever skipping away from the realities of politics to refuge in phrases like "national interest," "the nationalization of reform," and so on. These phrases, which every one can parrot and Presidents frequently do, are as empty of content as "the good, the true and the beautiful." The "national interest" under capitalism must inevitably mean the full satisfaction of the bargaining power of the group interests within the national orbit—which, of course, can add up to jingoism, extreme Jeffersonian decentralization, Know-Nothing-ism, plutocracy, or the application of the Single Tax. In other words, talk of "national interest" means nothing until you have talked out every possible antecedent question—a process which didn't particularly attract the mystic in Croly, who was Hamiltonian "with a difference," the difference being his mystical streak.

Croly was born in 1869, and went to Harvard when that university was turning out idealistic young men—Norman Hapgood, Robert Morss Lovett, William Vaughn Moody. He died in 1930 at Santa Barbara, California—some eleven years after the failure of Woodrow Wilson at the Peace Conference had caused him to lose hope, in good measure, for political reform. A child of the Comtean "religion of humanity" (Edmund Wilson says he was the first person in America to be baptized in the credo of this most desiccated of religions), he believed in the efficacy of "taking thought" and urging your fellow-men to righteousness. And *The Promise of American Life* is a Comtean book. It has all of Comte's own latter-day predilection for distinction-making in terms of "ought," and it likewise has Comte's lack of a program situated in human power-groups. Comte himself, it will be remembered, had to fall back upon a hope that the "best minds" (in mid-century France, virtually the minds identified by the Positivists with Catholicism and Royalism) would, in a sudden though unlikely zeal for human perfectibility, administer the central government in the interests of the formulæ of the "religion of humanity." And Croly, similarly, trusted to the "best minds" of America.

As analysis, *The Promise of American Life* meant a great deal to the Progressivism of 1912, inasmuch as it shaped the speeches of Theodore Roosevelt, who was enamored of the phrase, "the New Nationalism." In this book Croly gave the ancient discussion of Jefferson versus Hamilton a unique twist —and a twist that is not wholly justified. He agreed with Roosevelt that Hamilton "was much the finer man and much the sounder thinker and statesman," and he objected strenuously to Jefferson's "intellectual superficiality and insincerity." All Jefferson had, so he argued, was an "indiscriminate faith"; the Jeffersonian mind couldn't see any antagonism between "liberty and equality"; while Hamilton realized that "genuine liberty" would result in "fruitful social and economic inequalities." But Hamilton, Croly continued, perverted the American national idea as much as Jefferson did the democratic idea. What the twentieth century needed, in Croly's opinion, is a strong Hamiltonian state administered to Jeffersonian ends.

Historically, the fallacy of Croly's objections to Jefferson lies in an unwillingness to keep American conditions steadily in mind. If Croly had pondered the lesson of Turner, he would have realized that the Jeffersonian appeal, and whether Jefferson did or did not take over the Federalist machinery without admitting his *volte face,* had less to do with either the "profundity" or the "superficiality" of American democracy than had the presence of an open vent to the west. It was Tennessee, not Jefferson, that made Andrew Jackson. And the régime of political "lethargy" which Croly complained of, the state of "superficiality and insincerity which ever since [Jefferson's terms as President] has been characteristic of official American political thought," was inevitable simply because a majority of Americans seemingly had little need of the state save as a good uncle to grant them subsidies in the shape of tariffs, or land in the shape of rights of way or of quarter-sections. It is only when economic opportunity is closed (as it was, eventually, for the Middle Border farmer after the Civil War) that "sincerity" comes back into political thought. It certainly came back with the appearance of Robert La Follette in Wisconsin. There is never a lack of "sincerity" when sincerity is the natural reflex of desperate conditions; conversely, there is a general wallowing in hokum whenever political leaders seem supererogatory, as they did during the late period of Coolidge prosperity.

The idea of a "mystic" national America kept Croly from a sympathy with any international labor movement, according to Edmund Wilson, who has been Croly's one keen critic. And the failure of Croly to pierce through to the economic basis of war and peace caused the *New Republic,* which had been started in the wake of the Bull Moose movement with the help of Mr. and Mrs. Willard Straight, to support American participation in the World War in defense of "the Atlantic world." Just as Woodrow Wilson could not make a triple distinction between democracy, plutocracy and kaiserism, so Croly failed to see the War as the inevitable result of an overripe capitalistic system in which all participants were equally implicated. He let the side with the "best manners" persuade him. And it is here, most glaringly, that his lack of a power-politics shows; he failed to situate his "national" idea in any group whose interest it was to create a world in which the economic rivalries that lead to war should be outlawed. He hoped to work with one plexus of rivalries, and trust somehow to gain a world in which rivalries would be impossible. It was the old Winston Churchill trick of trusting power to vote itself out of control.

Like most Americans of his generation, and ours, for that matter, Croly distrusted organization along class lines, which alone can give "sincerity" to politics. He could not see that talk on the part of labor leaders of a "national interest," when bread and butter were what they were worrying about, or prattle by shopkeepers about the "good of the whole" when room to grow was their heart's desire, was in itself the worst type of insincerity. He could not see that any "new nationalism" must be a compromise among group interests according to strength—and that for "sincerity" one must keep the group interests firmly to the fore, whether it be a frightening process to the timid or not. And because he failed to think in realistic terms, the "New Nationalism" fell prey to Theodore Roosevelt, an "agnostic" in economics who yet had no qualms about prescribing for every one.

Walter Weyl is in a somewhat different category. *The New Democracy* is *The Promise of American Life* minus mystical trust in the "religion of human brotherhood." Otherwise, although Weyl is obviously a Jeffersonian sympathizer, *The New Democracy* differs about as much from the democraticized central state of Croly's dream as "The New Freedom" of Woodrow Wilson differed to all practical purposes from "The New Nationalism" of Theodore Roosevelt—which, in the words of William Allen White, was the difference between Tweedledum and Tweedledee. But Weyl's exposition had a clarity and a hard sense of reality, and a running between-the-line flavor of Mephistophelian appreciation of the irony of life, that Croly lacked. Weyl put his industrial and social program for a democracy on a firm basis of self-interest—enlightened self-interest. He attempted to demonstrate, on a broad scale, that whosoever is denied long enough will end up by spreading rot through a whole society, or by a gory attempt to take what he considers his just deserts. "Like the trade union," he said, "the democracy must always be open at the bottom." It must "cure the slum to prevent its own destruction by the slum." "Its instinct to live as well as its justice and clemency impel the democracy to this course." "The instinct to live"—in that phrase Weyl shows his grasp of the fundamentals of political action. An ameliorative radical, he recognized firmly that the "right to tax" meant the "right to destroy." With Croly, he believed the fate of democracy probably rested "with a government ownership of some industries, with a government regulation of others, with publicity for all (to the extent that publicity is socially desirable), with an enlarged power of the community in industry, and with an increased appropriation by the community of the increasing social surplus and of the growing unearned increment [by which] the progressive socialization of industry will take place." But after the War, after the rape of liberal ideals at Paris, Weyl, in a book that was to propose the "concert of the classes," admitted that there was "little hope" of the laborer being satisfied with "reforms and concessions dealt out to him by other social classes in a spirit of wisdom, caution or humanity" (Croly's hope), for "it is out of the very progress of labor that the problem of labor arises." In other words, the more that labor gets, the more power it has, the more it will feel it can demand. Weyl did not live to finish his book—but it would have been truly interesting to see the working out of his "concert of the classes." Weyl, like Stuart Chase and George Soule, was looking for a "third alternative," but, unlike either Chase or Soule, we may be sure he would not have been afraid to investigate the political implications of his alternative. Whether it would have involved an alliance between the spirit of the I. W. W. and the spirit of the Non-Partisan League, or whether it would have taken the tack of the Guild Socialists, or whether it would have led to Norman Thomas, we do not know.

Walter Lippmann, perhaps the most brilliant simplifier of his generation, proceeded to supplement, as it were, the books of Weyl and Croly with his *A Preface to Politics* in 1913. *A Preface to Politics* is an endearing book and a young book, part magnificent and part mistaken. Its incidentals are extremely intelligent; its criticism of the Chicago Vice Report, that curious survey which advocated self-control (on three to twelve dollars a week) as the cure for prostitution, is a classic of pragmatic argument. In this criticism Lippmann cut through to the economic origins of prostitution in any large city, and incidentally exposed the shallow pretentions to any specifically "moral" reform. But in defining politics, government and the State, Lippmann was only partly realistic; he made the mistake of Croly, and spoke in glittering phrases, such as the necessity of harnessing "political power to the nation's need." He observed, quite accurately, the feebleness and the harm of the unenforced Sherman Anti-Trust Act; here, like Croly, he was on solid ground. But in chastising the individualist business men and politicians of the eighties and the nineties, he could be guilty of a thundering fallacy: "Such a [constructive] statesmanship would in the eighties have *prepared for the trust movement.*" Here, again, in the italicized phrase, is the "liberal" confusion of representation (which is the politician's honest business) with disinterestedness. There could have been no such "constructive" statesmanship as Lippmann desired in the eighties for the very obvious reason that group power was so allotted in Congress as to prevent it.

Lippmann spoke, cogently, of the necessity for keeping close to human psychology when talking of politics. In pointing out the reasons for Tammany's superiority to "government by an up-town club," to a goo-goo administration that would be splendidly indifferent to the humble needs of the slum dweller, he proved that Lincoln Steffens had taught him well. But when he got around to writing sentences like this—"Instead of telling business men not to be greedy, we should tell them to be industrial statesmen, applied scientists, and members of a craft"—he ignored his own advice completely; he looked at carnivorous teeth and called them herbivorous. A man who could write that admonitory sentence had lost, temporarily, all insight into the human heart, which in the aggregate, is a greedy heart; he had lost his grasp on the power basis of politics; he had ceased to keep human psychology in mind. It is a pity that Thorstein Veblen's distinction between business and industry did not catch Lippmann at the impressionable age when he was listening to Wallas and Croly. It might have saved him from a criticism, expressed recently by a member of his own newspaper guild: "Walter Lippmann never seems to realize there are *people* in this world."

WHILE Croly and Lippmann, Weyl and the rest of the Progressive Americans were looking for political reform to carry America out of the woods of plutocracy, John Dewey was looking to the school. This Hegelian who became an instrumentalist, this author of *School and Society* (1899) and *Democracy and Education* (1916), came to be America's foremost advocate of a system of education which would train children consciously for the "levels of democratic striving," and for leadership in a democracy. But Dewey, like Croly and Lippmann, has been a bad power philosopher. He has remained blind to the impasse into which he has run. Hoping for the salvation of democracy through primary and secondary education, he fails to see that this education can be no more than a reflex of the very political situation—government by Koenig men or Tammany men, Vare men or Grundy men—that he sincerely deplores in his statements as a leader of the League for Independent Political Action. As an instrumentalist, Dr. Dewey ought to be the first to know that the stream of mass education can rise no higher than its source in political representation; the school board is inevitably of a piece with plutocratic control in city hall and legislature. Certain endowed schools, no doubt, might be able to put the Dewey theories into very fruitful practice; but regeneration of the body politic as a whole must come from some source outside the public school. The Rousseaus of this world owe nothing to education which is a reflex of the *status quo;* they become great diagnosticians and prognosticators because of their independence of the *status quo.* This fact may mark them down as pathological cases—but psychopaths, in time of imminent change, are often the very quintessence of "instrumentalism."

FINALLY we come to Louis D. Brandeis of Boston, who represents the intellectual attainments of the generation striving for "the New Freedom"—or "the New Democracy"—at their highest voltage. More than Justice Holmes, who merely believes intellectually in the right of a people to experiment, even to the denial of the pursuit of happiness, Brandeis was the flaming humanitarian answer of the Progressive movement to those who considered the phrases of constitutional guarantee —"freedom of contract," "due process of law"—as forever preventing a democratic majority from instituting the eight-hour day, the minimum wage. Brandeis was the first member of the Supreme Court thoroughly to immerse himself in an elaborate study of the human incidence of all phases of an economic question before rendering a decision on that question.

When Woodrow Wilson appointed Brandeis to the Supreme Court, the Boston "people's attorney," who had led the fight against the New England transportation monopoly which the New Haven road tried to effect with such dubious results, was pretty generally regarded as a dangerous radical. The late Clarence W. Barron, founder of the *Wall Street Journal,* reports a conversation with a Boston lawyer who accused Brandeis of having "poisoned" the mind of Woodrow Wilson. But the appointment of Brandeis was the most logical move the author of *The New Freedom* made in two terms as President. For Brandeis brought to the attack on the growth of a plutocracy what reformers usually lack: a passion for concrete detail and a gift for elementary arithmetic. Where Bryan had inveighed vaguely against the "money trust," shouting that we "cannot afford to put ourselves in the hands of the Rothschilds," Brandeis, using the material spread upon the books by the Pujo investigation, wrote an accurate diagnosis of the abuse of savings by investment bankers in his *Other People's Money,* published in book form in 1914.

The Pujo committee, sitting in 1913 as the Congressional climax to a decade of muck-raking, proved beyond the shadow of a doubt that a vast concentration of money and credit had been effected through the activities of J. P. Morgan and Company, the National City and the First National Banks of New York, and the bond houses of Kuhn, Loeb and Company, Lee, Higginson and Company, and Kidder, Peabody and Company. The concentration had been made possible through interlocking directorates, stockholdings and other forms of domination over banks, trust companies, railroads and industrial corporations, and Brandeis considered the fact of a money monopoly a danger to democracy. In his *Other People's Money,* relying in good part for buttressing material on the history of the New Haven road which was Morgan-controlled and Morgan-junked, Brandeis attempted to show that no one man could serve two masters with probity or acute judgment. If bankers sit on the Board of Directors of a railroad, Brandeis argued, their judgment of the need for a new security issue is inevitably clouded by their divided loyalties. On the one hand they are asked to give untrammeled advice as to the necessity and the best means of disposing of the security issue; on the other, as investment bankers in the security underwriting business, they are necessarily interested in creating as high a percentage for the marketing of the securities as can be gained. The result is a special cut taken out of the public by the investment banking community. Concomitantly, overbearing percentages taken on security marketing means an agglomeration of the resources under control of the "money trust"—and this means increased speculation, the racketing up and down of the business cycle, and general public discomfort and spoliation.

Brandeis was no complete champion of small business. But, in the words of Max Lerner, "wherever monopoly has taken the place of former competitive units he wishes to restore and maintain competition; where, in a competitive situation, unfair practices threaten the competitive equilibrium he wishes to curb them and so maintain the plane of competition; where competition is impossible or undesirable due to the nature of the industry he wishes to pattern the system of control as closely as possible upon . . . putative competition." This is the philosophy of the Progressives of 1912, virtually as stated by Charles Merriam. That it is due to crumble under the irresistible force of "bigness," leaving the problem one of control of the bigness, seems obvious to-day—as obvious as the impossibility of reviving the Progressive movement. The figures cited by Professor A. A. Berle, Jr., and Gardiner C. Means in their recent *The Modern Corporation and Private Property* must indicate that Brandeis has been working against the grain of inevitable historical development. Yet, in his insistence that such matters as hours of work, insurance of employees' health, and allied desiderata, are not beyond State regulation if the fulcrum of government can be seized long enough to pry them out of the opposition in control, Brandeis has done invaluable work in creating a mental climate favorable to the program of labor. He has never been guilty of the national mysticism of a Croly, nor has he been sanguine, Lippmann-fashion, of the capacities of highly interested men to act with a god-like disinterestedness. Like his colleague, Justice Holmes, he knows that justice for men and classes ultimately rests on force; that justice is taken, not granted. He has ever been the wise psychologist—with La Follette, the most intelligent of the Progressives who took over the ideas of the Populists in an attempt to make them nationally effective.

CHAPTER EIGHT

The Progressive Mind in Action—La Follette and Roosevelt

☆

LA FOLLETTE becomes the hero of the piece; Roosevelt, the showy—although not consciously diabolical—villain.

We have seen the part played by men like Tom Johnson of Cleveland, U'Ren of Oregon, Altgeld of Illinois, in the working of the Progressive leaven, but none of these men became a national figure. The Progressive movement, in the years before 1912, came to be symbolized in a national way by three leaders: Bryan, Roosevelt and La Follette. Bryan, however, showed repeatedly that he couldn't win through to office; he could only run, stir up a fuss and fall back. His value was that of ambassador of the rural crowd. Roosevelt and La Follette, on the other hand, had genius for politics as well as agitation; they were elected to office on the basis of their expressed ideas.

Each man had his own type of courage; each had a magnificent will. Their backgrounds, however, were as different as homespun is from silk. La Follette was a born democrat; Roosevelt came closer to the English ideal of the disinterested gentleman in politics—which implies disinterestedness within a class orbit, of course. It was no aberration that dictated Roosevelt's genuine detestation of Thomas Jefferson. And if Roosevelt never referred to the people as a "great beast" in public, he was not one to suffer fools in denim shirts gladly. La Follette, in contrast, had a mystical faith in "the people";

he believed that, provided there was plenty of light, the common man would find his own way. The superior population of Wisconsin was excuse enough for his credo.

Roosevelt, born in New York in 1858 of the still dominant Knickerbocker caste, was always able to live on inherited wealth; money was of no more importance to him than it was to his Manichean college mate, Boies Penrose. Freedom from economic worry caused him to take the kid-gloved reformer attitude in exaggerating the importance of abstract morality as divorced from fundamental necessities; never having been tempted, he couldn't understand temptation. This mistake of assuming the relevance of the Ten Commandments to be constant, even in a jungle society, was never made by La Follette, who, nevertheless, was as exacting in his standards of morality in public office as Roosevelt. La Follette, in fact, demanded much more than Roosevelt of public servants. But he did not expect the "Big Bill" Haywoods and the 'Gene Debses to maintain the amenities of Knickerbocker society in the midst of imperative economic warfare.

Roosevelt's inheritance bred in him a certain philosophical irresponsibility. He was not interested in ideas—which is to say that he was a careerist, a showman of his own personality. He might have gone the way of so many of his fellows; he might have dabbled in the law, done a little hunting, followed the migrations of the social seasons. His showmanship might have been limited to chasing the fox with superior skill; it might have been circumscribed by yachting at Newport or on Long Island Sound. But a weak body, shaken in youth by recurrent spasms of asthma, and weak eyes that rendered him unfit for baseball or football, caused him to rebel against his physical heritage in such a way that he exalted a certain synthetic primitivism; he must climb mountains, jostle with cowboys on the round-up, meet the "bad men" on their own ground and on their own terms. He must turn his back on the playing fields of the polite world; and with the need of this primitivism went a corresponding rejection of polite values. "I'll make my body," he told his father. And when somebody objected that politics was too vulgar a business for the Knickerbocker patrician, he answered that "if this were so it merely meant that the people I knew did not belong to the governing class, and the other people did—and that I intended to be one of the governing class."

By stepping out of his social context, Roosevelt was forced to make a game of life. His background of inherited wealth, with its assumed concomitant of *noblesse oblige,* engendered in him, it is true, a certain feeling of responsibility; but it was never whole-souled. Since he was making a gift of his life to the commonweal, since he was playing a game, there were privileges he might assume, laurels he might demand for the victory. He was making a career; the career should make him.

And so, at crucial moments, consistency, proclaimed philosophical principle, the assumptions he made at beginning points and in his books on ideals, went casually by the board. "Get action," he said, "do things; be sane, don't fritter away your time; create, act, take a place wherever you are and be somebody; get action." But (so a philosophically responsible person might ask) action for what?...Do what things?...Be sane in what way, and for what reason?...Employ your time how, and to what end?...Create what?...Take a place for what program?...Be somebody to what good?...Isn't all this admonition to place and action simply another and more febrile way of keeping up with the Joneses?

Indeed, if one makes a thorough scansion of Roosevelt's career, the exhortation to strenuous living, the eternal harping upon activity, the crashing words and writhing visage, all seem a little pathological. Action becomes a drug; Roosevelt just an American version of the Rimbaud myth. "The great game [of life] in which we are all engaged" comes down to a childish pirouetting over a void—and Roosevelt was always afraid to look into the void. This is the very negation of spiritual courage.

How different it is with La Follette! It was never "get

action" with him, never "take a place and be somebody." It was "put through a specific railroad or income-tax law, and you will find action enough on your hands." "Create a railway rate and valuation board, and you won't have any time to fritter away." "Don't mind whether they call you insane or not if you are certain you are not compromising your principles." "Refuse to take a place unless it is for some specific end." "Create a progressive movement within the Republican Party and you will find you are somebody."

La Follette was words and deeds in close tandem; Roosevelt was words—and an occasional deed for the sake of the record, or to save face. La Follette was a man who sought to make strict economic analysis the basis of his laws; he never talked without facts, the best available facts, and the University of Wisconsin faculty came, characteristically enough, to replace the lobby in his home State. But Roosevelt was, confessedly, "rather an agnostic in matters of economics"; the tariff bored him. With all his interest in cultural and scientific matters, he never understood the spirit of the laboratory—which was the one hope of the Progressive, or Liberal, movement.

Certainly Roosevelt had no realistic definition of government, no philosophical grasp of the nature of politics. Politics, by definition, is primarily the organization by legislation and control of the means of life; it is based pretty largely on economic desires and it reacts upon economics in turn. An "economic agnostic" has no more business running for legislative or executive office than an ibis has at the North Pole. But Roosevelt, the "agnostic" ("I do not know"), never had any hesitation about injecting himself into the forefront of the political fight. Like so many Americans who were still confusing the imperatives of the stomach with the voice of God, he conceived of politics as a sphere for the dramatics of Protestant morality. The result was a vast confusion about standing at Armageddon (with Boss Bill Flinn of Pittsburgh) and battling for the Lord (who was on the side of the biggest slush fund). And the worst of it is, Roosevelt was perfectly sincere about his Armageddon stuff at the moment of utterance. He may, as Medill McCormick said, have understood the "psychology of the mutt," but it was a subconscious understanding, soaked in at the pores. If Roosevelt had only understood the springs of his activity one would be justified in calling him a demagogue, but one would never be justified in calling him unintelligent.

Opinions differ on Roosevelt. But even his firmest friends admit a certain weakness in fundamentals; they see his primary value as the sort of person who "sits on the bulge," curbing excesses on the part of labor, on the one hand, and capital, on the other. Roosevelt dramatized the antithesis of "predatory wealth" and "predatory poverty"; he couldn't see, this man who administered "antiscorbutics to socialism," that predaciousness cannot be eliminated until the simpler antithesis of wealth and poverty has been reduced to a synthesis. Gilson Gardner, one of the wisest of tired radicals, sums up the Roosevelt tightrope act in a pithy paragraph. "More honesty," he offers as the Roosevelt credo; "By George, they mustn't do it. The rich must be fair and the poor must be contented—or, if not contented, at least they must be orderly. I will tell them both. No restraining of trade by the great corporations and no rioting by the toiler. Give me the power and I will make them behave." The ideal may be laudable. But just what class of people is there left *to delegate the power?* A middle class? Yes, for a while, but a middle class cannot exist permanently in a dynamic society that is creating "great corporations" that need restraining. The "great corporations" must be blotted out or made one corporation beyond the pale of manipulation for private profit. This, Roosevelt never could bring himself to realize. He had too many nice friends who were part of the corporation system.

Opinions differ, too, on La Follette. He was a man who was strong on analysis, and weak, as it turned out, on prognosis. But scratch a man who slights his caliber of character, such a man as Mark Sullivan or Roosevelt himself, and you will find a born compromiser. Roosevelt couldn't understand La Follette because he couldn't understand patience and devotion to an idea. In his book on *Pre-War America* Sullivan speaks slightingly of La Follette's "anti-railroad bias," his "almost perverse bent toward visualizing himself in the rôle of martyr." But just a few pages away from the criticism of La Follette, Sullivan himself admits everything that La Follette ever said against the railroad practices of the eighties, nineties and early nineteen-hundreds. And any one who has read the La Follette autobiography will know that the anti-railroad "bias" was only part of a cogent, dynamic economic philosophy, and that it can no more be called bias—in the sense that bias implies an element of unreason—than a mathematician can be called pig-headed for insisting that two and two are irrevocably four in every world but Lewis Carroll's. Certain conclusions flow from certain premises; La Follette's premises may have been proved without twentieth-century social grounding, but his railroad conclusions flow inevitably from his primitive capitalistic postulates. Sullivan, in his skimming way, lets the case against the postulates go; the word "bias" saves him from thinking through to his own position.

La Follette was always a man to try to square practice and theory. And consistency in word and deed must necessarily seem a little grim to a man like Mark Sullivan, who says that La Follette was "all grimness." But it is highly questionable that La Follette had any fundamental streak in him that "made the wearing of a hair shirt a pleasure." He may, of course, have made a virtue of the necessity; it is the way of the human organism to try to like what it has to like. Undoubtedly he became morose. But men like Donald Richberg, who knew La Follette as well as did Sullivan, and who, like Sullivan, have real fondness for the memory of Theodore Roosevelt, tell us that "Battle Bob" was a man of deep and tender affection, not only for his intimates but for all mankind. Richberg came to this conclusion after being mightily angered, as were so many of the Roosevelt Progressives, when La Follette refused to leave the Republican Party in 1912.

Certainly the La Follette autobiography doesn't radiate any more grimness than is necessary to a fighter who has gone his way alone for many years. Mark Sullivan objects that this "grim" man probably never in his adult life threw back his head for a hearty laugh. Fola La Follette, with a daughter's partisanship, contradicts this impression of eternal seriousness. In any case, the belly-laugh is the prerogative of the simple-minded; a sense of irony, which La Follette had in private, must inevitably restrict its operation. And the "grim" man was far from being acidulous; he is more than kind in his autobiography to faded statesmen like John Sherman, William McKinley and William Jennings Bryan. No historian with a sense of values will give these men so much consideration in the history books of the future. Richberg makes a fruitful comparison of the La Follette mind with that of Bryan. Bryan would not yield on points on which he was sure. "He believed in his Bible—'from cover to cover.' Alcohol was evil. He would not yield to Satan or the Demon Rum. On economic issues he was not sure. He advocated compromise."

Another man who had no business in politics; another churchman strayed from his pulpit! Roosevelt, too, was pretty certain on moral issues; he was dogmatic about "race suicide," the devil's business of divorce. ("Smash divorce-ridden Newport," he would exclaim.) La Follette, on the other hand, was not so sure concerning religious and social issues. "He recognized mental life as an experiment. But material existence was more nearly fixed. Economic inequalities and hardships were real—subject, he felt, to relief by law. He had definite rules for economic justice and for political action to enforce the rules. Here he was uncompromising."

And rightly so. For no one has proved more conclusively than both Bryan and Roosevelt that "half a loaf" in legislation is apt to dull the appetite for the whole loaf. La Follette was always willing to be beaten; he knew he could bound back with renewed vigor, and with more strength added to his followers. But Roosevelt, who was always willing to take half a loaf, finished his days in the White House with a pitiful amount of achievement to show for them, as we shall see. It was the La Follette grimness, the Wisconsin tenacity, which persisted in carrying the Progressive fight through the Taft Administration. There is no perversion of the truth when La Follette says the cause of the Progressives fared better and made more converts when the confusing, contradictory figure of Roosevelt was daring lions to do their duty in the center of Africa. It was the La Follette following, nothing less, which forced the country to the point of accepting the Woodrow Wilson of *The New Freedom.*

The business of dismissing La Follette as a demagogue has persisted, even as the habit of regarding Roosevelt as an effective President still persists. But soon the biographies will begin to appear, and La Follette will take his rightful place at the head of the pre-War Progressive movement. A demagogue is, by definition, a person who consciously misleads the mob to promote his own advantage. Demagogue is, also, a word that is cast up by people on the defense as ink from a retreating squid. This ink all but engulfed the portent from Wisconsin in the early days of his fight. Lincoln Steffens went to Milwaukee expecting to find a demagogue in La Follette; he had no doubt that the man was a charlatan and a crook. Hadn't it been dinned into his ears often enough by those who urged him to be fair to both sides? A banker told him that the "little giant" of Art Young's famous cartoon was nothing more than "a crooked hypocrite who stirred up the people with socialist-anarchist ideas and hurt business." "Good," said Steffens, "let's begin with the evidence of his crookedness." But the banker had more feeling than facts, and a corporation attorney, brought in to convince Steffens, contradicted the banker by saying that La Follette wasn't dishonest; he was only a fanatic. The banker broke in to say that La Follette would "spread socialism all over the world," but the attorney said he was more of a Populist. Hadn't he taken votes away from the socialists of Milwaukee? This contretemps converted Steffens; he came to believe, on further reconnaissance, that La Follette, if something of an actor, was yet a "sincere, ardent man." It was characteristic of him, Steffens said, that he remained as Governor in Wisconsin for months after his election to the United States Senate, simply to follow through State legislation that was dear to his heart and convictions. "A fighter for peace," was the Steffens verdict. "A dictator dictating democracy."

And Frederic C. Howe, who will probably be La Follette's first biographer, came back from the 1924 campaign through the West with the belief that La Follette was "probably the best-loved man in America."

The "best-loved man in America"? A crooked hypocrite? A Populist fanatic? Or was he, simply, the last bona fide democrat? "It is hard," said Senator Borah in 1925, after being told of La Follette's death, "to say the right thing about Bob La Follette. You know, he lived one hundred and fifty years." But clearly, we have here a man of uncommon abilities, since people without force or character do not inspire these contradictory utterances. Clearly, we have here a man who could touch millions on the quick.

Physically, La Follette was a little man. But he was impressive enough to be called "the little giant." His personality was not one of easy winsomeness; he didn't appeal to voters in any baby-kissing, glad-hand way. After the World War, with most of the Progressive program lying about in shattered débris, he showed his disappointment; he was at times bitter. But bitterness is sometimes an index of the original faith of a man. This was certainly true in the case of La Follette; he had given a great deal, and had seen it all swept away. It is silly to call the man egotistical in a tone of reproof; what person who believes in himself, and is willing to fight for the prevalence of his beliefs, is not self-centered? We need "egotistical" men of the type of La Follette.

We also need men with a passion for distinction, provided the distinction be not shoddy. La Follette's hunger was not for shoddy, but he was sometimes vain. The passion for distinction caused him to dress the part of Senator once Beveridge had remarked on his country clothes. Donald Richberg objected to his spats. His hair, worn pompadour fashion, made him seem taller than he was. This flaring mop inspired a sonneteer to write:

When Bob La Follette with defiant glare
Leaps forth to smite the foemen of his land,
Five feet he soars into the zenith and
Six inches farther soars his fretful hair....

The same sonneteer, George Fitch, called him the "capsule statesman with a whirlwind's way," a description that was made palpable to members of the Senate almost upon the advent of La Follette in Washington in 1906 during the frenzied jockeying that attended the passage of the Hepburn Act. This bill perhaps meant something in the way of establishing a precedent; it embodied the admission, on the part of the Aldrich-ridden Senate and the Administration generally, that railroads could be controlled by law. It also gave objective significance to the general feeling that the Supreme Court's decisions which had pulled the teeth of the Interstate Commerce Commission must not be allowed to stand forever. But as a measure to "get the railroads out of politics," as a work of economic statesmanship, it didn't mean very much. And it was not at all to the liking of La Follette; it provided, as he so earnestly pointed out to Roosevelt, absolutely no touchstone by which railway rates could be fixed in the just interests of all. The most that could be obtained under the Hepburn Act was rule-of-thumb justice on the part of the Interstate Commerce Commission after complaints had been made by shippers or passengers. And the "broad court" review provision meant that judge-made law could over-ride the Hepburn Act just as it had over-ridden the Interstate Commerce Commission Act of 1887. The Hepburn Act was only a wedge.

La Follette, fresh from his victory in Wisconsin, saw all this plainly. In 1903 the Wisconsin Legislature, under his direction, had created a railroad law which replaced a percentage tax on gross earnings (which the railroads falsified) by a tax on the physical valuation of the property, as is the case with other property. And in 1905, before leaving for Washington, La Follette had witnessed the passage of a railway rate-making law based on a fair return on this physical valuation. He was already an old hand at scientific legislation—or legislation that at least attempted to be scientific. There is a catch in the physical-valuation method of rate-making, as will be made apparent, but at least it meant the end of watered railroad stocks and balloon bonds. The Hepburn Act did not even guarantee this much, and La Follette was quite right in spraying it with ridicule.

Now, the "unwritten law" of the Senate stipulates that new members shall be seen and not heard; but to La Follette this smacked of the gag. His speech on the rate bill consumed the major part of three sessions. The Aldrich clique, thinking to haze the young recalcitrant, was conspicuous by its absence from the chamber, leaving Kean of New Jersey behind as a lone watcher to sound the alarm in case of emergency. But La Follette turned the enemy's flank by a shrewd and dramatic gesture. "I cannot be wholly indifferent," he announced to gallery listeners, "to the fact that Senators by their absence at this time indicate their want of interest in what I may have to say upon this subject. The public is interested. Unless this important question is rightly settled, seats now temporarily vacant may be permanently vacated...." The junior Senator from Wisconsin proved a good prophet, for six years later twenty-four of the standpatters who had refused to listen to him had passed from the upper house.

La Follette's behavior during the attempts to pass the Hepburn Act is indicative of his general and very effective method. Roosevelt, yearning for the approval of the historians, simply wanted legislative action; he demanded paper results to show for his term in office. He was not at all unwilling, as events proved, to take any compromise he could get. Hence the approval of a slightly amended "broad court" review provision. Hence his blindness to the need for scientific rate-making. La Follette, however, preferred to be huddled off in a corner by himself rather than acquiesce in a bad measure. He took his medicine—and proceeded to introduce a railway valuation bill at every succeeding Congressional session. President Taft gave his approval in his annual message of 1910, and La Follette's bill became a law on March 1, 1913.

The fate of the La Follette bill is instructive. For reasons not apparent in 1913, the physical valuation idea hasn't worked out very well as the basis for rate-making. There are a number of tragic misconceptions at the heart of it. The Interstate Commerce Commission, under the La Follette scheme, doesn't fix rates in reference to the costs of providing adequate service on the one hand, and the need of shippers and passengers for low-cost transportation on the other. The owners of railroad securities, clamoring for dividends, preclude this. And La Follette, being a good primitive capitalist in 1913, was careful to take the security holders into account. But he failed to see that no absolute connection exists between the physical cost of a railroad and its earning capacity. A railroad in a desert region might cost millions and earn nothing on the investment. How could "fair" rates be fixed to insure it an adequate return? Again, it proved difficult to determine "original costs." The value of a railroad, so it turned out, could be construed in only two ways: it might mean the cost of reproduction of the property, or it might mean the amount of money it would sell for. Obviously, these are fluctuating matters. Further to complicate the picture, the sales price of a railroad is determined by the rates charged, by the profit the road is able to make.

A "fair return" on the value of the property, once fixed by law, may, in turn, alter the value; rates cannot be set without affecting the sales price of a road, either by pegging it, raising it or depressing it.

All of this proves that dividends and scientific rate-making are not compatible unless the I. C. C. is to have "confiscatory" powers. In his 1924 campaign for the Presidency, La Follette advocated public ownership of the roads—a Bryan proposal of two decades previous. Had he come to see a fallacy in fixed dividends? We cannot be sure. But as we have suggested, the La Follette provisions for railroad valuation at least made an end to the racket of stock-watering which was worked so assiduously on the Morgan-controlled New York, New Haven and Hartford before the War. It meant that directors could no longer sell their own trolley lines to their railroads at a tremendous profit—the profit to be taken out of the passenger and shipper. It meant that the crude anarchy of cut throat competition between roads was at an end. Ineffective as it is, no one, not even the railroads themselves, would abolish the I. C. C.

The fate of the La Follette hopes for scientific regulation of investment-built industry means the defeat of the Progressive dream of a social democracy. It means that we shall have either State capitalism (Fascism), a form of Communism, or the old-familiar business cycle repeated *ad nauseam*. And the defeat of the Progressive dream marks the downfall of La Follette as the builder of the new America which he envisaged. But as a man, he remains admirable. Statesmen of the future will emulate his spirit, his scientific attitude, his willingness to be beaten rather than compromise a fundamental principle.

La Follette, indeed, did live one hundred and fifty years. He was a man out of an old United States. Born in June of 1855, of Huguenot parentage, in a two-room log cabin at Primrose, Dane County, in Southern Wisconsin, his roots went back into that agricultural America which was dear to the heart of Jefferson. His father was a Kentuckian from a Hardin

County farm that was half a mile distant from the birthplace of Abraham Lincoln. A man of the soil, the young Robert Marion knew the dirt farmer, the common man. "The people," he said, "have never failed in any great crisis in our history"—and by "the people" he meant the farmer and shopkeeper folk of his youthful environment. All of the young La Follette's circumstances were of the pre-technological age. The wonder of it is that he came so well to understand the needs of the urban factory laborer! His first friends, as he said, were "hard-headed old pioneers from New England and from Northern Europe who thought as they plowed," and, moreover, thought to their own conclusions. These "old pioneers"—New Englanders, Norwegians, Germans of the '48 migration—were all swept up into the Granger movement that was agitating the Middle Border States when La Follette was a youth. His earliest memories were of anathema called down upon the railroads. It was plain to the hard-headed farmers that the railroad was just another form of highway; if it could invoke the right of eminent domain, calling upon individuals to give up their property or their country's property in the interests of the general welfare, then didn't this same general welfare, from any logical standpoint, imply the right to public control of the roads? A reading of a dog-eared copy of Henry George's *Progress and Poverty,* which he borrowed from a blacksmith, convinced La Follette that the reasoning of these old farmers was sound—although he never went to the length of some Single Taxers who believed that any one had the right to run a train over tracks, irrespective of the need for maintaining a uniform service.

The seething agrarianism of the seventies, when the Patrons of Husbandry gathered in country schoolhouses and at the corner stores, left its permanent mark on La Follette; it made him a firm democrat. Hadn't he seen the blessed "people" taking their affairs into their own hands and dealing with them with some show of effectiveness and logic? Even as late as 1923, when on a visit, with his son, Robert, Jr., to Soviet

Russia, the old warrior was not convinced that democracy could not be made to function with the tools of primitive capitalism—with equal small units of production and exchange all working for themselves, and by this contributing to the general good. He looked the Soviet union over . . . and invited its leaders to visit a real commonwealth, the State of Wisconsin! It is easy to say that he had become blind to the complex realities of a technological age, but good collectivists were not made on the American Middle Border of the seventies and eighties. We have no socialist here! Another agrarian, Joseph Bailey of Texas, was quick to denounce Bryan for advocating government ownership of the railroads and telegraph lines; yet Bailey was with the wing of the Democratic Party which demanded government regulation of the roads, and no one fought harder than Bailey for the income tax. La Follette, though in a purer form than Bailey, was of the same independent agrarian breed; even in 1924, when he ran for President on his third-party ticket, he obviously cared more "to break the combined power of the private monopoly system over the political and economic life of the American people" than he did for the planks calling for public ownership of the railroads and water power. The same old shibboleths, the same old phrases, that were magic to the common man of the Rooseveltian decade were furbished up for this last third-party effort to win. They are, for that matter, still doing duty for political leaders in 1932. . . .

All of his life La Follette thought in terms of the individual competing with other individuals to wrest a living from soil and environment. But the individual must be free to compete on equal terms. In this advocate of primitive capitalism there burned a mighty zeal for justice. It cropped out in his college days, when he was filled with an "overmastering sense of anger and wrong and injustice" at the fraternities for dictating nominations caucus-fashion for student office. The granger movement of La Follette's youth had dramatized the devil in terms of the oppressing railroads; when he came to political maturity the wrongs of Wisconsin, and of the United States as a whole, were still the result of unfair practices on the part of the common carriers. Hence this instinctive "dramatic tragedian," this youth who had won a prize with an oration on the character of Iago in a State collegiate oratorical contest, this man whose greatest admiration was Bob Ingersoll, concentrated his emotional fire upon the old devil of his youth. In 1874 Wisconsin had elected a Democratic Governor; a comprehensive law for regulating the roads had been passed, and a railroad commission instituted. Other States had experimented with anti-railroad legislation; Texas, for instance, under Governor Hogg, succeeded in creating a railroad commission in 1891 after years of agitation. John H. Reagan, United States Senator from Texas, and a pioneer in the fight for Federal railway regulation, resigned to head this commission. But in Wisconsin the "old gang" weathered the early storm; flagrant violations of the law followed, and the carriers embarked on a program of systematic corruption of the State. What happened in Wisconsin was a commonplace of American political life in the eighties and nineties. The one Governor whom the agricultural and dairy interests had been able to elect in Wisconsin between 1874 and 1900 could do nothing; the railroad lobby had tied his hands. And so, when La Follette finally came to power in the State in 1900, at a time when the rest of the country was enjoying its post-Spanish-War breathing spell, the time was overdue for effective action.

LONG before this, La Follette had had his first intoxicating taste of political battle. He knew how to wait; he knew when to strike. Bred in poverty, working his way through the University of Wisconsin by running a college newspaper, he had long since acquired the will to endure. At the very first stage in his career he had found bosses of the orthodox type intolerable. In contrast to Theodore Roosevelt, his entry into politics owed nothing to the men in control of the primaries. He had ridden into office, in fact, by making a point of dispensing with the boss.

This first brush with the machine came immediately after he had left college. The office of District Attorney of Dane County looked a likely plum to a poor young man, and he resolved, with characteristic directness, to have it. Boss Keyes told him he was wasting his time; but La Follette thought he knew the farmers of Dane County. One of them objected, "Ain't you over-young?" but on the whole they must have liked his spirit, for in January of 1881, La Follette was sworn in as District Attorney, having defeated his opponent by ninety-three votes. He had his start; and he was thus early making a beginning at building up his own powerful and flexible political machine. His opponents have never tired of pointing out the "boss" in La Follette; they have also never succeeded in remembering that a boss is to be judged by the fruits of his leadership. La Follette was a boss, but he did not betray his constituents into the hands of special privilege; the cardinal sin of betrayal of one's class—which, as we have seen in Lincoln Steffens's story, was the main sin of the boss as a type—could not be imputed to La Follette.

As District Attorney, La Follette worked so hard that he had a breakdown at the end of each term of court. His energy, which was colossal, had always to contend with nervous and digestive disorders; throughout his life he was recurrently threatened with complete collapse of health. But sickness did not interrupt his work. He must have satisfied the Dane County farmers, for he held the job until he won the Republican nomination and election to Congress in 1884. When he came to write his autobiography, in 1912, he had changed his mind about crime; he had come to see, he said, that wrong-doing often grew directly out of the sins and injustices of society; but when he was upholding justice in Dane County he glimpsed only two things: the law and the individual. His zealousness won more and more voters, and his influence came to extend beyond the bounds of his home county. A first term in Congress was followed by reëlection in 1886, and again in 1888, but, as a Republican, he lost his seat in the great Democratic landslide of 1890. Although he was neither very important nor very effective in Congress, these early terms were integral parts of a Progressive education. He witnessed, in Washington, the mechanics of legislation for special privilege; he learned about the ways of the lobby; he discovered, by practical observation, what he had learned in a passive, theoretical way from Henry George: that the way to make money quickly is to get a strangle hold on a natural monopoly. The creation of the Interstate Commerce Commission in 1887 interested him more than any other legislation during his three terms in the House, but the meaning of the Sherman Anti-Trust Act was not lost upon him. And simply that John Sherman's name was attached to this act was sufficient to make La Follette reverence the Ohio politician for life.

When he first entered Congress, La Follette was assigned to a place on the Committee on Indian Affairs. It was the customary minor disposal of the Congressional neophyte, but La Follette, with the pertinacity and scholarliness which he, more than any other Progressive, was to display throughout a lifetime of economic statesmanship, attacked the problem as if the future of the Republic depended upon it. A land bill with a provision calling for the ratification of an agreement made by two Northwestern railroads with the Indians for rights-of-way through the Sioux reservation looked suspicious to the new member. Not only did the bill provide for the opening of 11,000,000 acres of the reservation to settlement; it also guaranteed to the railroads certain exclusive rights that smacked of an inside deal. Provisions for "terminal facilities" and "station privileges" running into hundreds of acres made it look as if the railroads were taking for themselves all the best town sites. La Follette said as much. "Bob," argued a member of the Committee, "you don't want to interfere with that provision. Those are your home corporations." But home corporations were the very corporations which

La Follette hated most. The pressure brought upon La Follette by Philetus Sawyer, blunt lumber man who represented Wisconsin in the Senate, availing nothing, the Wisconsin Republicans called in Henry Payne, the secretary of the Republican State Central Committee and one of the most skillful of the tribe of lobbyists. But Payne failed too. "La Follette is a crank," he said; "if he thinks he can buck a railroad with 5,000 miles of line, he'll find out his mistake. We'll take care of him when the time comes." But La Follette got his amendment through; the town-site job was not a part of the final Indian bill.

What is most apparent to a later generation is the naïveté of the young La Follette in the presence of pressure and graft. But the eighties lacked the disillusioning benefit of the whole coming literature of social protest; they had been fed "kings of fortune" pap; the voter didn't "know too much" in that age of innocence. Far from bringing him to a cynical view of the function of legislation, the encounter with Sawyer and Payne only served as prelude to the fight on the old gang in Wisconsin which was to have its birth in the nineties after La Follette had left the House. It so happened that Sawyer was the blundering instrument which provoked La Follette to his battle. Before the nineties, in Wisconsin as elsewhere, the interest on State funds was considered a perquisite of the State Treasurer. But the forces of the Populist revolt were raising an objection to this cavalier appropriation of the people's money, and the commonwealth of Wisconsin was making an attempt to recover the lost interest from the bondsmen of ex-treasurers. La Follette's brother-in-law was a judge in the case; Philetus Sawyer, a bondsman. The stage was set.

The whole truth of the contretemps is lost in controversy. But the La Follette version, which is circumstantially backed, tells of the offer of a bribe. La Follette flared up; Sawyer, frightened, gave the show away by issuing a proclamation of innocence before any public accusation had been made. "It was the turning point, in a way, of my career," La Follette said later.

Whatever the relative merits of the case may be, the facts of the aftermath are important in Progressive history. The Sawyer machine, of course, banished La Follette to an uneasy Coventry. The ostracism hurt La Follette, but it made him. Without newspaper support, with virtually no financial backing, he commenced to build up his anti-Sawyer bloc within the Republican ranks. A new boss fought an old one... and the old one was not equal to the terrific pressure which the young boss could put on. The La Follette forces were beaten in 1894, in 1896 and in 1898. But with each Republican State convention it was evident that La Follette's strength was growing. In 1898 he dictated the Republican platform. It so happened that Governor Scofield had taken advantage of his railroad pass to ship a cow free in a crate, and La Follette was not slow to see the political capital in a picture of Scofield's cow gazing ruminatively from the front pages of the papers. That would bring the railway abuses home to the farmers! Ridicule thus came to his side in the fight on the railway pass evil, but it couldn't force the Republican Legislature to redeem the campaign pledges of 1898. However, 1900 was another story: La Follette became Governor in that year, elected by the largest majority in Wisconsin history. The prairie fire built up against the railroads by the Populists was sweeping one State, at least. And the fire grew hotter as La Follette was returned to the Governor's office in 1902 and again in 1904.

Conditions were just exactly right for the crusader and the reformer in 1900 and immediately thereafter. Large masses of Americans were still thinking in terms of "right" and "wrong" when they meant "individual representation" and "bloc representation." And La Follette's political principles were just the sort to appeal to the child of the Protestant reformation. Anything that was dishonest and unfair in dealings between individuals, he argued, was dishonest and unfair in dealings between corporations and individuals. It was just as reprehensible for a railroad to dodge taxation as for an individual to steal from his neighbor. If it was wrong for an individual to bring pressure to bear on a friend at the polls, it was equally wrong for big business to exercise pressure in gaining control of the machinery of government. If murder was outlawed, then it was just as wrong for companies to fail to use all available means to protect their employees from injury and death.

In the face of caucus politics, where bribery was a commonplace, La Follette proposed a philosophy of the delegation of power that was as direct as the man himself. He revealed it, characteristically enough, at the college which oil built when he spoke before the students at William Rainey Harper's new University of Chicago on February 22, 1897. In a speech called "The Menace of the Political Machine" he outlined a system of direct nominations for all county, State and legislative offices, the nominations to be made by both parties on the same day, and by means of the Australian ballot system. "Abolish the caucus and the convention," he said; "go back to the first principles of democracy; go back to the people." But the Republican Party, to La Follette, was sacrosanct—at least until 1924. Parties, he urged in 1912, were born, not made. His answer to the Roosevelt bolters, who had effectively scotched the La Follette chances *within the Republican ranks* for 1912 or 1916, was that a march to Armageddon meant the cancellation of all the Progressive gains within an existing powerful party. Better capture machinery that had already been created, he said with an excellent show of logic, than try to build anew. Events in 1912, 1916 and 1924 have proved him temporarily right.

La Follette's specific achievements were many, although not all of them have withstood the attrition of the years. In 1902 an amendment to the Wisconsin constitution did away with the corrupting railway pass evil. In 1903 came the first State-wide direct-primary law to be passed in the country. The railroad-tax law followed, and in 1907, after La Follette had gone to the Senate, the State railroad commission was given jurisdiction over all public utilities. A railway rate-making law, a progressive tax on inheritances, and an act introducing the merit system in the State civil service came in 1905. The extension service of the State university was a La Follette idea, and laws in the interests of workmen's compensation, pure food and public health were written upon the Wisconsin books by the Progressive forces. Nearly all of the La Follette provisions were challenged, but none was ever pronounced unconstitutional. And all of them influenced the course of legislation in other States. Oregon followed two years after Wisconsin in the adoption of the direct primary. By 1913 the popular election of Senators was a national reality, and by 1915 the direct primary was the norm in three-quarters of the Union. Books were written about the "Wisconsin Idea"; one of them, by that title, was issued in 1912 with a curious preface by Theodore Roosevelt, who took occasion to remark that "unfortunately too many of the men in public life who have seemed to attempt [reform] have contented themselves with enacting legislation which, just because it made believe to do so much, in reality accomplished very little." These words apply so well to Roosevelt's own reforms; it almost sounds as if he were commenting upon the Hepburn Act of 1906! But Roosevelt was, at that time, laying his eggs, cuckoo-fashion, in the Republican nest built by La Follette in a decade of work.

Nationally speaking, the La Follette reforms are not as tangible. He was in opposition during most of his time in the Senate. First, there was the Aldrich combine to buck; then followed the Taft régime; then eight years under a willful Democratic President who came to consider La Follette one of "a little group of willful men expressing no opinion but their own." And then, crowning irony, the Harding normalcy put a term to the work of two decades of storm and stress. But the years were rich in activity. La Follette played a leading part in the formation of railroad, banking and labor laws. The creation of the Department of Labor, the Federal Trade Commission and the Federal farm loan system bear the marks of his handiwork. He was primarily responsible for the hours of service act of 1907, which limited the number of consecutive hours a railroad employee could be kept at work continuously. The employer's liability act of 1908, which modified the common-law rules to favor railroad employees involved in personal injury actions, was inspired by La Follette. We have mentioned the railroad valuation act of 1913. Other tangible legislation includes the section of the postal appropriation act of 1912, requiring the management of newspapers to file with the Postmaster General semi-annual sworn statements showing the personnel and ownership of the business. The seaman's act of 1915 brought relief to a class of workers whose conditions were particularly rancid. And, near the close of his career, it was La Follette who introduced the resolution under which the investigation of the naval oil leases proceeded. As a member of the opposition, he fought the Payne-Aldrich and the Fordney-McCumber tariffs and the Taft project for reciprocity with Canada—a false "reciprocity" which favored the American manufacturer as against the American farmer. He objected strenuously to the Armed Ship bill of 1917 that made war with Germany a certainty; he held out against war with the Central powers; and he condemned the Versailles treaty.

In all of La Follette's speaking and writing the work of a keen analytical mind is obvious. As Ray Stannard Baker pointed out in *McClure's* for December of 1905, he had "one quality sometimes lacking in reformers, thoroughness." Mark Sullivan, with customary slipperiness, says that La Follette was for "heavier" taxation of the railroads in Wisconsin. This is nominally true, but it implies a distinction that cannot honestly be made. For the railroads weren't "soaked" by La Follette; they were merely made to pay their share. La Follette was for "equal" taxation—which Sullivan doesn't mention. As the basis for this taxation, La Follette's commission, so Baker said in 1905, made "the most thorough investigation perhaps ever made by a State into railroad affairs. . . . For about two years, four or five skilled accountants have been at work in the main offices at Chicago and other cities, of all the railroads that traverse Wisconsin." La Follette came to the Senate with this work behind him. Sullivan, in analyzing La Follette's attitude toward the Hepburn Act, insists that he was more "radical" in the Senate than at home in Wisconsin—and the implication is that the growth in radical sentiment was due to a jealous animosity toward Theodore Roosevelt. This is the purest distortion; La Follette advocated precisely the same things in both places.

La Follette's god as an orator may have been Bob Ingersoll; he may have been charmed by the rhetoric of Shakespeare in his college days; but clarity, simplicity, fairness and force are the qualities of the La Follette writing and speaking style. His understanding of the historic process was as keen as that of the Marxians or the Marxian revisionists, but he came to non-Marxian conclusions. With the fate of the railway valuation act and the anti-trust legislation in mind, we must accept the La Follette conclusions as non-viable. La Follette's greatest weakness was that he hoped to turn back the clock, as it must seem to us now; he put his trust in a farmer-shopkeeper class as a generating force, whereas we, who are born into an industrialized world, must put our trust in the implied threat of labor. But short of the conclusions, La Follette's analysis of the growth of industrialism must be accepted. It was not a jaundiced analysis; La Follette was not blind, although many have said he was, to the argument which justified the historic development of private interests in America. While the country was expanding, he argued, when capital was scarce and competition strong, the encouragement of the growth of private interests often seemed the best, and possibly the only, way to secure the highest public interest. Our forests seemed unlimited, our plains as empty as the sea. But private interests, fed upon easy public favors, became abnormally strong—and never more openly strong than between 1885 and 1891, during La Follette's terms in the House.

La Follette's analysis of the growth of American industry, which he embodied in his famous speech at the annual banquet of the Periodical Publishers' Association in Philadelphia on February 2, 1912, may have seemed like a travesty of the facts to Owen Wister, but to us it must seem true to the point of platitude. In this speech La Follette divided the industrial history of the country into four periods. The first—the day of the individual and the partnership in manufacturing—continued for about a century after Jefferson had declared for a government of "equal rights for all, and special privileges for none." This period, of course, had La Follette's full approval; to him, it seemed like the veritable Golden Age. It was the day when most business was conducted under the natural laws of trade—demand, supply, competition. "Like all natural laws, they were fair and impartial; they favored neither the producer nor the consumer." But as the country developed there was a demand for a new business device to unlock the treasures of field and forest, the mountains of coal and iron. The modern corporation came into being to meet the demand, and we embarked on the second period of our business life. Men associated their capital, and, employing the representative principle upon which the country was based politically, voted for and elected presidents, managers, boards of directors, and clothed them with powers sufficient to the business at hand. But the natural laws of trade—supply, demand, competition—still ruled the market.

And then, as La Follette, good believer in economic democracy as the foundation for political democracy, said, the evil hour was upon us; the third period dawned. It was the period of the combination of corporations, the new day heralded by the incorporation of the notorious South Improvement Company of the Rockefellers. It was time for a Morgan, a George Baer, a Havemeyer, to nullify the laws of trade, to combine to set prices and limit production. The business of the country, to use La Follette's phrase, was "Mexicanized." And this period merged rapidly into the fourth and final period, the period of the combination of combinations. All this is so obvious to-day that few people object to the proposal to abrogate the anti-trust laws, which are observed in name only, anyway. The combination of combinations is here to stay; the question is, who will run these combinations, and for whose benefit? But the end result of the historic process was not apparent to the young La Follette from the Middle Border of the seventies and eighties. As with the muck-rakers, his emotions lagged behind his ability to make a picture in analytical terms.

La Follette's tariff views were a trifle inconsistent with his praise of the "natural laws of trade." He was not an absolute Free Trader, since this doctrine, if applied thoroughly, would enable exploiters of labor in foreign countries to take advantage of an America that, presumably, would not always exploit its working men. La Follette, always strong for the expert (he had never seen the uses to which a Wickersham Commission might be put), believed in a body of skilled economists sitting to investigate and discover actual differences in labor costs between American and foreign products. "We do not wish to have the tariff below that difference," he announced in 1912, "but we realize that we cannot accept the statements of interested manufacturers." The protective principle, however, should not be used to protect inefficient management, nor should it be allowed to lead to the exhaustion of our natural resources. The laborer and the farmer alone should benefit from the tariff. As a "reciprocity" man, but not in the Democratic sense, La Follette advocated a high tariff on tropical and semi-tropical products in order to build up "trading capital."

La Follette, in short, was a "little American" in the matter of the tariff, just as he was on all subjects. He was ranged with no dominant tariff group. Taft "reciprocity" with Canada seemed to him a flagrant abuse of the farmer, whose products were to be favorably admitted to the United States in exchange for the favorable admission to Canada of our manufactured goods. The Democrats who believed in a tariff for revenue only were patently soft-headed. And the Aldriches and the Dingleys were obvious representatives of the industrial interests alone.

To those who think of the world as the economic unit, and any tariff at all a barrier to cheap consumption, the La Follette tariff views are anathema. But La Follette, who had what Professor Frederick A. Ogg calls a "lack of world-mindedness," always considered "America First." When the War came, his hatred of it was apparently overweening, but it was entirely logical. Indeed, if Wilson had had La Follette's inability to think in world-terms, we might have been spared a wholly useless crusade. La Follette realized what the War would do to the Progressive movement; with Jane Addams, he foresaw that the conflict would "set progress back a generation." As he moved about the Senate, working after April of 1917 in the shadow of ouster proceedings, he had an instinctive vision of the débâcle of "normalcy." But with high courage he filibustered against the Armed Ship bill that made the War a certainty for us. He became one of "a little group of willful men expressing no opinion but their own."

Wilson, who poured out his wrath upon La Follette (who had done so much for the reforms of the first Wilson Administration), gave the *coup de grâce* to the Progressive movement when he and Tom Johnson's old-time lieutenant, Secretary of War Newton D. Baker, issued the call for conscription. To the eyes of 1932, La Follette's course seems a little pathetic ... and Wilson's a calculated bit of horror. To fight and die —for loans! Those who bracket our participation in the War and the Morgan loans, *New Masses* fashion, are not far from wrong, even though, as C. Hartley Grattan has pointed out, the banking community was pro-ally before the loans were made. La Follette realized the nexus. "We have grounds for complaint against Germany," he admitted, but we had grounds for complaint against the Allies, too. (Newspapers distorted his first statement to read, "We have *no* grounds for complaint against Germany.") The United States, he continued in a notable speech, had not pursued an impartial policy in dealing with England and Germany. England had begun the violation of American rights by unlawful seizures and searches; England had closed the North Sea by sowing it with mines, and had thus provoked the submarine *revanche*. Was not a mine as much a menace to American shipping and American lives as the torpedo? And if Prussian autocracy was distasteful, what about oppression in Ireland, Egypt, India? If Germany had its Kaiser, who was a symbolic threat to democracy, what about Russia and its Czar? And of the espionage bills, and the forced conscription of the A. E. F., La Follette said he feared they were a sure sign that the War did not have the popular backing of the whole people.

La Follette's last phase was rather pitiful. With common sense on his side he had arraigned Roosevelt for splitting the Republican Party in 1912. Yet in 1924, La Follette was getting old; his time was growing short. He had seen the dying Penrose, a flabby thing of skin and bones, come back to power with the accession of Harding. Perhaps the time had arrived—at last!—for a third-party movement. Corruption in Washington, the high tariff which had supplanted the Underwood rates, the post-war agrarian discontent, the Red hunts and the repressive tactics which had brought a virtual end to the I. W. W. and the labor movement as a whole—all these seemed to offer soil for the growth of a new party. So La Follette swallowed the bait of the Conference for Progressive Political Action, and headed a third-party ticket. With Burton Wheeler of Montana for Vice-President, the party polled close upon 5,000,000 votes. Trade unionists, socialists, farmers, Progressives, the A. F. of L., the Scripps-Howard newspaper chain and the liberal weeklies, all flocked to the La Follette standard. And the old phrases of the Rooseveltian insurgency were once more pressed into service—perhaps unavoidably.

The old cries of the opposition to Bryan were pressed into service, too. The Republicans said La Follette was endangering property relations (the third-party platform called for government ownership of railroads and water power). La

Follette was called a Bolshevik—blessed new word for the outworn cry of "anarchist." And, as Frederic C. Howe has pointed out, the people did not all vote as they had shouted during the La Follette tour of the West. Wage earners were intimidated as they had been in 1896; Coolidge and Prosperity triumphed. But for all that, La Follette captured Wisconsin, and ran second in California, Idaho, Minnesota, Nevada, Montana, North Dakota, Oregon, South Dakota, Washington and Wyoming. He swept the Jewish districts in the cities which had been the strongholds of the Socialist Party. The approximation of five million votes was a real tribute to "Fighting Bob" La Follette—the more so because they were polled in a year which saw the farmer's purchasing power increased over what it had been in some time. But it was only a personal tribute; the failure of the La Follette party to hold its lines doubly proved his contention, made in 1912, that parties are born, not made. There was no hope for Progressive Political Action in Coolidge America.

ON JANUARY 6, 1919, Roosevelt died—and is it too much to say that the "moral" age in American politics died with him? Bryan, it is true, would live to face the cameras at Dayton, Tennessee, but he had gone into political eclipse at Baltimore in 1912. La Follette would linger on to lead his forlorn hope in 1924, but that would be the final gasp of an agrarian idealism in the days of the New Era. And Wilson, though still nominally a liberal, would or could do nothing in his last days in the White House to stop the Red witch-hunting of his Attorney General, A. Mitchell Palmer.

The Roosevelt myth grew apace after his death. For ten years the memory of the looming teeth, the impetuous "By George," the emphatic "I've done nothing that wasn't absolutely right and proper," would continue to bemuse the commentator. Joseph Bucklin Bishop, Charles Willis Thompson, Owen Wister, all of whom wrote from close acquaintance, were blinded by the remembered brilliance of the sun itself.

Hermann Hagedorn suffered, and still does, from the delayed adolescence acquired from the Roosevelt of Spanish-War days. Lord Charnwood's biography, representing the English point of view, sounded as if it had been written by the British Press Bureau—as, indeed, in a way, it was. But at the end of a decade a change for the more wholesomely astringent was felt. Thomas Beer, in his *Hanna,* sniffed about teeth and spectacles like a cat inspecting a new house—and objectivity was thereby born. In his autobiography Lincoln Steffens waved away the myth that had grown up around T. R. as a police commissioner. With the best will in the world, Steffens still could not avoid giving the impression that Roosevelt's accomplishment in Mulberry Street was mainly pictorial—a faint prefiguration of Smedley Butler's adventures among Philadelphia's vice rings. And Walter Millis, in *The Martial Spirit,* uttered some second thoughts about Las Guasimas which should have occurred to others long before.

All this was preliminary. But in 1931 came two biographies of the man that attempted to give him in sum. The first, by Walter McCaleb, was excellent for two reasons: it attempted to tell the truth about the Panama Canal steal, and it set forth the facts about the panic of 1907, in which Roosevelt was played for a sucker by Gary and Frick, whose representations resulted in the swallowing by United States Steel of its biggest rival, the Tennessee Coal and Iron Company. The second, by Henry Pringle, is a more complete job. But both biographies suffer from an unwillingness on the authors' parts to think things through. When Dr. McCaleb comes to the war years he is himself blinded by the sun, and his book dissolves into dubious rhetoric. Mr. Pringle, too, has a hard time making up his mind about the War. Neither one tackles the tremendous three-cornered fight that went on, under the phrases and flag-waving, between the factions of Woodrow Wilson (which looked to the community of nations within an international league), of La Follette (which believed in putting home houses in order before attempting a world synthesis), and of Roosevelt, who believed in *la gloire,* and the "big stick," and anti-war pacts only when all the nations should become as civilized as the United States of America.

The curious thing about Dr. McCaleb and Mr. Pringle is their return to the opinions of Roosevelt held by his saner contemporaries. The little vanities of T. R., the bullyragging and bulldozing, the mercurial uncertainty of the man, were quite apparent to Harry Thurston Peck early in the muck-rake decade. "His courage," Peck wrote, "was of the French, rather than of the Anglo-Saxon type. It was allied with a certain nervousness which could perform the most daring deeds if they were deeds of action, but which became restive and almost uncontrollable when patience and grim endurance were demanded." Here we have the complete antithesis to La Follette painted before the Wisconsin Senator had become a national figure. Peck, echoing his contemporaries, was particularly struck by Roosevelt's use of the personal pronoun. He tells an amusing, though probably apocryphal story: "In writing one of his earlier books he used . . . 'I' so frequently that his publishers were compelled to order from a type-foundry a fresh supply of that particular letter." Peck quoted, too, a story about Theodore Roosevelt and John Hay. The charming Hay, diplomat to his finger-tips, remonstrated gently with Theodore for using the word "big" too frequently in one of his early messages. "Big," said Theodore, with visible annoyance, "is a good strong Anglo-Saxon word! I like to use such words as that." Yet Roosevelt, the lusty, was unable to appreciate Lincoln's harmless fondness for smutty jokes in which good strong Anglo-Saxon words predominated. The masculinity of Roosevelt, in truth, was always a little febrile; the courage likely to waver. Even the Booker T. Washington luncheon incident at the White House, for which Roosevelt has been praised or damned many times with no half tones, seemed, to Peck, an example of Dutch courage. Roosevelt, Peck surmised, was "afraid of being thought afraid" to ask the Negro to lunch. And blocs could make T. R. back down. When H. C. Evans, a Pensions Commissioner, angered the G. A. R. by exposing frauds in the pension legislation, Roosevelt, fearing the loss of the soldier vote, removed him from office by "promoting" him. McKinley, a weaker man than Roosevelt in many ways, had not done this; in fact, he had staunchly refused to touch Evans's job. The facts that Evans was "promoted," and that an equally honest man was put in his place, do not compensate for the lack of courage shown by McKinley's successor. But, on the credit side of the ledger, Peck was careful to note that Roosevelt "...brought in, as it were, a stream of fresh, pure, bracing air from the mountains to clear the fetid atmosphere of the national capital."

This admiration for the "pure, bracing air," coupled with a sane analysis of Roosevelt's essential character, is part of the attitude towards the apostle of the strenuous life which both Pringle and McCaleb rehabilitate. No one in his right mind would condemn T. R. in toto. One cannot, upon a full review of a remarkable life, remain either a Roosevelt idolator, or—if one warms to wistfulness—a Roosevelt hater. Roosevelt had his physical courage, no one doubts that. His romanticizing of the wilderness will always have its appeal. His admiration for soldiers (Cromwell, Moltke), his love of war for its own sake, his family affections, his childlikeness, his flashing humor, his social charm, his bullying, his willingness in an explosive moment to call a man guilty before he had been proved guilty, his wistful hedging-away from the problems of an afterlife, and, finally, his lack of inwardness, will always combine to make a fascinating study in personality. But more than any of these characteristics, the one that most stands out is the Rooseveltian inability to think things through. Roosevelt scored heavily against Woodrow Wilson when he struck off the phrase, "weasel words." But no one knew the uses of weasel words better than T. R. himself, as La Follette has conclusively shown in his autobiography in the section that reviews Roosevelt's public statements as a Progressive.

Roosevelt was always quicksilver to the touch—and one

can only sympathize with La Follette's unwillingness to commit the Progressive cause in 1912 to such an unpredictable man. There is good evidence that Roosevelt had promised his support to La Follette in 1912, or at least had made a "tacit" agreement not to interfere with the La Follette boom. Gilson Gardner, when he gets ready to release his story of the 1912 campaign, should be able to clear up this point once and for all. In any case, Gardner carried the "tacit" agreement to La Follette in such a way that an assumption of a promise is the only workable hypothesis. But Roosevelt, when the country seemed on the verge of a rebellion against conservative politics, broke the implied promise; La Follette was shelved by the Pinchots, by Gardner and the Scripps papers, and by Cummins of Iowa; and the master of Oyster Bay marched out of the Chicago convention to form the Progressive Party. Here, in this gesture, we have the complete rationalizer contradicting his anti-third-term utterance of several years back.

Roosevelt was always willing, at any time, to contradict himself, by word or deed, if by contradiction he could further his career. His friends will be quick to say, "No, no." But there are so many major issues on which he shifted ground at the precise moment when his career was involved that charity balks at the attempt to find excuses. He became a Progressive when the Republican Party threatened to become Progressive—but it should not be forgotten that he fought La Follette in Wisconsin in 1904, and he was willing to enter a "gentleman's agreement" with Nelson Aldrich not to disturb the McKinley home policies if he could have a free hand in the conduct of foreign affairs. He reversed himself on free trade early in his career. This would be understandable as a natural growth—only Roosevelt never had any real conviction on the tariff, one way or another. His attitude, when President, was "Let Taft change the tariff when I'm gone"; but when Taft compromised with Aldrich and the Bourbons of the Senate, Roosevelt lapsed into an unholy rage. He denounced the "corrupt" Blaine; but when Blaine was nominated, in 1884, the willing worker in the vineyard decided that Cleveland, the friend of Civil Service reform, was the real instrument of Satan. And when Blaine became Harrison's Secretary of State, Roosevelt was quite willing to play up to him for a job.

Again, though Roosevelt admitted his agnosticism in the realms of economics, he contradicted his expressed friendship for the frontiersman by echoing his smart friends in denunciation of Bryan. Altgeld he refused to meet; he was afraid he might be compelled to fire on the Illinois "anarchist" some day at the head of a battalion. Yet Altgeld was one of the first of the "Progressives"—if the word is to have any meaning at all. Free silver might have been a nostrum (and the discovery of the cyanide process for extracting gold cheaply from ore makes it seem so in retrospect), but Roosevelt didn't think the matter out for himself in 1896—he took Mark Hanna's word for it. Yet the deflation of the post-Civil War period had meant grinding poverty for the sons of the frontier whom "Colonel" Roosevelt invited to storm San Juan Hill with him. On labor, the Progressive knight showed himself to have no grasp of the situation. His decisions as an Albany assemblyman were those of a young Goo-goo out of Edith Wharton's *Age of Innocence*. He opposed a bill in 1882 requiring New York and Buffalo to pay laborers $2 a day. At a later period he made the statement that if he, instead of Wilson, had been President he would not have signed the Adamson eight-hour bill. His apologists suggest it may have been the Wilson-hater speaking here—but it is no apology that a man allows personal hatreds to come between himself and professed humanitarian principles.

Roosevelt could always take a high moral tone; he repeatedly showed himself on the side of righteousness, even though humanity might, at times, go hang. But even in the matter of morality, expediency altered cases. The young Governor of New York State temporized on the Erie Canal frauds. As President, Roosevelt was perfectly willing to use party machinery to dictate Taft's nomination, yet in 1912 he called

Elihu Root a thief for exercising the same prerogative in throwing out the Roosevelt delegates. When John Hay negotiated the Hay-Pauncefote treaty, Roosevelt didn't like it, and argued that a government had the right to abrogate a treaty in a "solemn and official manner." But when Colombia refused to accept the Hay-Herran treaty, Roosevelt quickly doubled on his tracks and denounced the Bogatà "dagoes," as he called them, for "breach of faith." And as for arbitration, he could urge it at Christiania before the Nobel Prize Committee in 1910, and later denounce Taft for suggesting a treaty for arbitration with France. France, it seemed, was not sufficiently "civilized" to be treated with.

But perhaps the most damaging give-away of Roosevelt's pretensions to morality involved the invasion of Belgium. H. L. Mencken has shown, in an essay that was written immediately after Roosevelt's death while the flood of eulogy was at its height, that Roosevelt had no immediate experience of shock when the Germans tore up the "scrap of paper" and marched through Luxembourg and across the Belgian frontier. The moral reaction didn't reach Oyster Bay until the temper of the country had changed; Roosevelt simply shifted to meet the demands of public opinion. His course, after the *Outlook* article that "explained" and justified the invasion of Belgium, was vacillating to the extreme—and well might Roosevelt vacillate in view of his own "ethical" trampling of Colombia in 1903!

All the chopping and changing, the roaring invocations to morality and the sudden descents to political bargaining, simply prove to me that Roosevelt was a surface swimmer—not so brave a man as Grover Cleveland, and neither so honest as Boies Penrose on the one hand, nor as La Follette, on the other. He was, it is clear, the perfect *representative* of the middle class of pre-War America. His class philosophy, however, was inchoate—in no way so clearly formulated as La Follette's. Indeed, on the score of possessing an articulate middle-class, democratic philosophy, La Follette deserved to be the leader of the middle-class movement. But the most conspicuous attribute of the middle-class of 1900-09 was its confusion; it had delusions about rising into the plutocracy, and yet it feared being forced into the ranks of labor. It wanted to curb the trusts, yet it wanted to leave an opening at the top—the good old American right to succeed! Therefore it was in the dilemma of Mr. Facing-Both-Ways. La Follette saw this, Lincoln Steffens saw this, and both labored to make clear the vitiating nature of the desire and the fear. But Roosevelt perfectly represented the confusion, as his attitude toward the trusts shows. Mr. Dooley summed it up when he put words into Roosevelt's mouth: "'Th' thrusts,' says he, 'are heejous monsthers built up be th' enlightened intherprize iv th' men that have done so much to advance progress in our beloved country,' he says. 'On wan hand I wud stamp thim unher fut; on th' other hand, not so fast.'"

The result of equivocation on Roosevelt's part, and on the part of those he represented, is that the middle sort of man now finds himself, more than ever before, between the upper Fascist millstone and the nether stone of Communism. Had La Follette's views been heeded, had industrial development been halted at the single corporation, had the combination of corporations been prevented in John Sherman's time or in Roosevelt's (impossibilist dream though it may be), the vision of a middle-class democracy of farmers and shopkeepers and small manufacturers, all obeying the laws of trade formulated at Manchester, might have been made a reality.

What were the accomplishments of Theodore Roosevelt as a statesman? There was the matter of forcing England and Germany to back down in Venezuela. Good evidence exists to show that Roosevelt exaggerated his use of the "big stick" in bringing this incipient conflict to a peaceful conclusion. But Roosevelt was always shaking the big stick—a stick which often, as Gilson Gardner says, turned out to be a "stuffed club." In his early years Roosevelt was an unmitigated jingo. He believed that an occasional war was a good thing for "the moral fiber of the nation"—a view that has been adapted to the current depression. He wrote to Lodge, in 1895, when the earlier Cleveland controversy was raging about Venezuela: "I most earnestly hope that our people won't weaken in any way on the Venezuela matter. The antics of the bankers, brokers and Anglo-maniacs generally are humiliating to a degree.... As for the editors of the *Evening Post* and the *World*, it would give me great pleasure to have them put in prison the minute hostilities began...."

The young jingo is to blame for the present embarrassing possession of the Philippine Islands by the United States. He and Henry Cabot Lodge cooked up the attack on Manila before hostilities in 1898 had begun. The order which eventually sent Dewey to the Philippines was issued by Assistant Secretary of the Navy Roosevelt one day after Secretary Long had gone home to sleep—and Long never quite dared countermand it. It would make him look like a fool! But at the time it was issued McKinley had not given a thought to the Philippines, and most Americans didn't know of their existence. Before the Spanish-American War came to provide Roosevelt with his taste of glory in the field, the young fire-eater was spoiling for a fight with England. "We would take Canada," he wrote to Henry Cabot Lodge. All that the full martial program of the fledgling Roosevelt contained was the annexation of Canada, the abolishing of all European powers from the Western Hemisphere, and the taking of Cuba, Porto Rico, Hawaii and the Philippines. Peace advocates were molly-coddles. A big navy was needed to police the world in the interests of American morality. If this is "world-mindedness," give us La Follette's "Little American" program any day. Even when Roosevelt's "world-mindedness" was of the peaceful sort, he blundered into war traps. There was the Moroccan crisis, for instance; here Roosevelt, through Henry White, helped France to complete the encirclement of Germany which led to the Great War. And the "taking of Panama," after the comic-opera intrigue which featured the wily William Nelson Cromwell—who made lobbying one of the Seven Lively Arts—and the connivance of Roosevelt himself, might have led to bloodshed if the "revolution," carried out under the guns of American ships, hadn't gone off without a hitch.

Roosevelt's domestic achievements were more ethical than the Panama intrigue. But his two administrations were more talk than effort; Taft's "progressive record" is fully as clean as Roosevelt's own. The coal-strike compromise of 1902 was an undoubted temporary feather in the Rough Rider's hat, yet, after all, it merely settled *one* coal dispute—as Harlan and Bell Counties and both bituminous and anthracite Pennsylvania are still with us to testify. The Elkins Rebate Law was good, but the Hepburn Act—as we have seen—was only an indication that a fight against railroad abuses had started. The Hepburn Act was in reality a victory for the "crafty Aldrich," since it limited rate-making to fixing maximum charges after complaint had been made, and offered no provision for valuation. The so-called modified "broad court" review clause played into the very hands of the judges whose decisions Roosevelt wanted subject to "recall" in 1912. Conservation and the beginnings of pure-food legislation were the great Roosevelt accomplishments. One might also include the Alaska Boundary settlement, the Russo-Japanese War arbitration, the appointment of Justice Holmes to the Supreme Court (it is amusing that the Holmes decision in the Northern Securities case nettled Roosevelt considerably), and the creation of the Department of Commerce and Labor.

But didn't T. R., whose first term resounded to the war-whoops of "trust-busting," do *something* about certain particular trusts? Well, there were 149 trusts in 1900, representing four billion dollars in approximate capitalization. When Roosevelt went out of office, there were 10,020 trusts with a capitalization of virtually thirty-one billion dollars, seventy per cent of which was estimated as pure water. And Roosevelt was only nominally victorious in the Northern Securities case by which he set such store. The dissolution decree did not by any means restore competition between the two Northwestern railroads—the Northern Pacific and the Great Northern. The order of the Supreme Court had been phrased so that the bond issue floated against the two companies remained intact. Charles G. Dawes compared the issue to a stepladder with one leg in one road and the other in another road. And Philander C. Knox, Roosevelt's "crackerjack" Attorney General, had permitted the decree to be so written. The dissolution wording actually enabled James J. Hill to squeeze E. H. Harriman out of the control of the Northern Pacific, since the original stock was not returned to those who had come in on the holding company scheme. Harriman got as much value as he had turned over to the Northern Securities Company, but it was split between Northern Pacific and Great Northern securities. He had a majority control in neither railroad when the dust cleared away. The ultimate dissolution of the oil and tobacco trusts was to come in Taft's time, but the letter has been more altered than the spirit, and the results have been barren. The existence of the "power-trust" to-day is a commentary on the effectiveness of the whole cloudy program of the pre-war trust-busting.

A final estimate of Roosevelt, I think, will be that expressed by Senator Aldrich: he was the greatest politician of his time. Not, mind you, the greatest statesman—not even by the test of action, which John Carter makes the one test of statesmanship. And no one has succeeded in endowing Roosevelt with economic sense; the judgment of Gardner, that he kept himself an economic moron in order to remain in politics, must stand. So let him rest—as a great politician and an astounding, charming, effervescent character. But what an ironic rôle to be played by a moralist!

WHEN La Follette rose to address the eight hundred guests at the Periodical Publishers' dinner in Philadelphia on February 2, 1912, he was a tired man. He had just completed a speaking trip. Little by little he had come to realize that the Pinchots, Gilson Gardner of the Scripps papers, and others who had sworn to the support of his candidacy, were using him as a stalking horse for Roosevelt. William Allen White had deserted him; the *Emporia Gazette,* barometer of the corn lands, had registered editorially on the tenth of January for "Roosevelt or Bust"! And money was calling the turn. Frank Munsey, heavy investor in United States Steel, was backing the Oyster Bay candidacy. George W. Perkins, formerly a Morgan partner, and an important figure in the International Harvester Company, was busy behind the scenes providing the sinews of war for the embryonic Roosevelt boom.

And what could La Follette do against such a combination? Who was this Perkins? Friends say he was a sincere man, desirous of obtaining the best good for his country. No one challenges his integrity in his own eyes. But the fatal community of interests that Perkins represented, willy-nilly, was not propitious to Progressive government. He was, Amos Pinchot says, instrumental in cutting the anti-trust plank from the Progressive platform. This same Perkins had been indicted by a New York grand jury for forgery in connection with donations of life insurance funds to the Republican National Committee. He had been involved in the United States Steel gulping of the Tennessee Coal and Iron Company. As an officer of the International Harvester Company, he had persuaded Roosevelt to halt the prosecution of the harvester trust for violation of the Sherman Act. Mr. Perkins' partner in the Progressive financing business, Frank Munsey, was—as William Allen White has pointed out in a notable editorial—a newspaper man who had the ideals of a corner grocer; he bought and sold newspapers as a butcher would meat. A Progressive? Ask the former managing editor of Mr. Munsey's New York *Herald* if he was a Progressive.

La Follette's nerves were raw. But the loss of support had been taken for granted by January 29, when his campaign manager issued a statement that the Wisconsin Senator did not contemplate withdrawing from the race; he "never has been and is not now a quitter." Of more import on the night of February 2, 1912, was the condition of La Follette's small daughter, who was, the following morning, to go under the surgeon's knife. The seriousness of the operation could not be predicted.

Owen Wister, one of Philadelphia's finer snobs, has told the story of the La Follette speech that night, of how the Senator shuffled the pages of his manuscript attacking journalists and trusts, of how he ran on and on, compelling the guests in the home of the *Saturday Evening Post* to swallow the bitter medicine. Coherence, said Wister, departed. At half-past twelve, after speaking for two hours and a half, La Follette sank forward on the table. It is not true that a nervous breakdown followed, although his enemies were assiduous in spreading the report that his health had failed and his candidacy had come to an end. He was up the next morning, and by his daughter's side in the hospital. But the Progressive cause collapsed, not in November at the polls, not in 1916, not with the Harding normalcy—but with that slow fall forward to the table in Philadelphia, "the corrupt and contented."

CHAPTER NINE

"The Technique of Liberal Failure"

☆

"THE fiddles are tuning...all over America." So wrote Van Wyck Brooks in 1916, quoting J. B. Yeats, and adding: "A fresh and more sensitive emotion seems to be running up and down the old Yankee backbone—that unblossoming stalk."

The fiddles could be heard, lightly, tentatively, sweetly, as early as 1912 and 1913, the years of Great Expectations when the Millennium, Woodrovian-fostered, seemed just around the corner. For those who have grown up this side the War it takes considerable of an effort of the imagination to attempt to recreate the mood of that day. Could any note of hope, any time, any place, have been so universal? Yet—there it was, as people as diverse in temperament as Elmer Davis and Genevieve Taggard can explain. To Mr. Davis, 1913 with its tango teas, its delicate chaffing of the conventions, was the very peak year of human felicity. To Miss Taggard, things may have been wrong in 1913, but "not terribly wrong." "Just wrong enough to insure a holiday" of "zealous social work backed by optimistic social theory."

Ten years of political and social agitation, touched off by the sons of Populism and by the muck-rakers of the *McClure's* staff of 1902, had had their effect. The churnings of the political atmosphere, the growth of the Socialist Party, the restlessness of the middle classes, the incredible increase in mechanical aids to pleasant existence, such as the automobile, the phonograph, the electric light, had created a vague itch in the American psyche. Far-off, divine events moved closer behind the mysterious veil that shrouded the future. The intellectual climate of a nation was altering. Minds had been liberated, categories had been broken down. America was ripe for a youth movement. And the movement came.

It came, at first, in seemingly unrelated trickles. Out in Chicago a young Irishman, Francis Hackett, was waging effective warfare in the pages of the *Evening Post* on the dry-rot which, outside of the muck-rake magazines and the muck-rake novels, could be discerned at the heart of American expression. Hackett, who became the first literary editor of the *New Republic,* was the spiritual progenitor of a long line of lively and disputatious Chicago critics of life and letters—a line that would include the Burton Rascoe who, with Mencken, was to sell Dreiser, Cabell and, inadvertently, the novel of flaming youth to a skeptic land. And to the Chicago of Hackett came two contrasted figures, the brooding, serious George Cram Cook, the idea of the Provincetown Players as yet unformed in his head, and Floyd Dell, embryonic Rousseau of the youth movement. They would, both of them, shortly desert Chicago for New York, the one to give Eugene O'Neill his chance, the other to become an editor, with Max Eastman, of the *Masses,* which commenced its savage and exhilarating career in 1911 only to run foul of the government during the War.

When Woodrow Wilson took the oath of office in 1913, the movement had gathered something approaching a real momentum. Mencken and Nathan, their brows touched by the consecrating wands of Percival Pollard and James Huneker, were beginning to work in tandem. Insatiable young souls just out of Yale, Paul Rosenfeld and Waldo Frank, had caught a glimpse of an America transformed by art from the camera work of Alfred Stieglitz. Boys and girls who had seen Isadora Duncan dance, who had listened to Emma Goldman define anarchism, who had caught the infectious dental grin of Roosevelt, became sick of the tepid loyalties of their fathers. Decorum was no word for the day. And many who would have none of decorum were congregating in Greenwich Village—not because of any Murger connotations of the place, but because the rents in that maze of crooked streets were incredibly cheap before Seventh Avenue was cut through.

The Hotel Brevoort, on the edge of the village, became a rendezvous for the young hopefuls of America who were about to pull aside the curtain on a Little Golden Day. The Liberal Club was formed. The Little Theater movement was a-borning—in Chicago, where Maurice Browne gathered his group, in New York with the Neighborhood Playhouse and the Washington Square Players. The poetry movement received important impetus with the founding of Harriet Monroe's *Poetry: A Magazine of Verse* in Chicago. Dreiser's *Jennie Gerhardt* marked the reëmergence into the sunlight of an author who had gone underground with *Sister Carrie*. Edith Wharton suddenly turned from her social satire to a story of truly tragic implications in *Ethan Frome,* and Willa Cather, deserting the tutelage of Henry James, brought out *O Pioneers!* And looking on the whole scene, catching a sense of electric change and portent from the air, was a young hunchback, Randolph Bourne, whose papers on "Youth and Life" sounded the major chord of an epoch.

Art and social change were running together in 1912, as Genevieve Taggard, the anthologist of the period's verse, has accurately observed. While the nude was descending the stairs at the Armory show in 1912, the women suffragists were parading in the streets. Socialism had long since reached the universities; it was an exciting topic at the Harvard of Walter Lippmann, and at the Vassar from which Inez Milholland was graduated in 1909. Young people, catching fire from the work and personality of Jane Addams, were going off in full force to the settlements. Inez Milholland not only caused a rumpus by shouting for "Votes for Woman" at the Taft parade down Fifth Avenue in 1908, but she also set the Vassar faculty by the ears when she organized the undergraduates for socialism and woman suffrage. A gay spirit, she walks through the pre-War epoch with a blitheness that is lost to our grimmer day, getting her friends out of jail, picketing during garment strikes, sailing on the Ford Peace Ship, and haranguing English audiences in Hyde Park during her trips to Europe. She died in 1916, from the effects of overstrain incurred while campaigning for Hughes in California in the hope that the Republican nominee would look with friendly eyes upon the suffrage movement.

"Everybody was playing," says Miss Taggard, who has a warm and sentimental regard for her memories. John Reed was playing hard in those days before his sympathies for the underdog led him to the grim business of working (and dying) for the new Soviet State. Half in earnest, half in fun, Jack wrote a pageant for the Paterson strikers in 1913, which they performed under his direction in Madison Square Garden. Half in earnest, half in fun, Reed joined the staff of the *Masses,* resigning when the magazine changed under the impact of war into the *Liberator.* But it was not even halfway amusing for the unemployed whom Frank Tanenbaum led into New York churches during the hard times of 1913 to test the honesty of a proclaimed Christianity. It was not amusing for the Lawrence and Paterson strikers, even though, as Miss Taggard says, the I. W. W. shared "the verbosity and romanticism of the time."

However, the intellectuals, the playboys of ideas, the young and hopeful baiters of the bourgeoisie, had not looked upon the death that the system under which they had been reared was capable of dealing. It looked like a good bet, in 1913, for a fairly intelligent, fairly good-natured and fairly easy transition, via the ballot, via a liberalism called to terms by radicalism, to the millennium. The *Masses* may have been gayly savage and gleefully scornful, in the pictures of Art Young, Boardman Robinson and George Bellows, of the society which Herbert Croly and the *New Republicans* hoped to convert by laying on of hands, but for all that, the extreme intellectual Left of that day hobnobbed with liberal thought. Between a Lippmann and an Eastman the hopeful bourgeois convert to reformed democracy made little distinction. Weren't both men calling for Utopia? Freedom was the watchword, not the harsher slogans of the class struggle; and "rob the robbers," had some Lenin urged it from a soapbox in Union Square, would have been welcomed as gleeful hyperbole.

FREEDOM was the watchword, and Woodrow Wilson, going about the land in 1912 as Democracy's challenge to Theodore Roosevelt and the "New Nationalism," sought to make capital of the mood of a country. *The New Freedom* was his answer to the New Nationalism—and the freedom he proposed was that urged, in the eighties and the nineties, by Henry George and later championed by the intransigent La Follette. "The truth is," Wilson proclaimed, "we are all caught in a great economic system which is heartless." The Democratic shibboleths of new freedom for the small business man differed in some respects from the shibboleths of the Progressive Party, whose members wished, not to destroy the huge corporations, but to bring them under Federal control. But for all practical purposes—as the innocents who hoped for great things toward restoring primitive competition under the Clayton Anti-trust Act were to discover—the New Freedom and the New Nationalism were two brother peas in the pod. There was no smashing and cracking up of trusts under Wilson, not even after Louis D. Brandeis moved his baggage to Washington after his appointment to the Supreme Court. There would have been nothing more than haphazard "control" under the Progressives; the men to be controlled—the George W. Perkinses and the Frank A. Munseys—would have done the controlling through their grip on the Progressive purse strings.

But the New Freedom sounded magnificent. As they have been gathered together for us in book form by William Bayard Hale, Wilson's campaign promises read to-day like the ringing assurances of a Thomas Jefferson returned to earth to dominate the industrial scene. "The old political formulas do not fit the present problems; they read now like documents out of a forgotten age . . . we are facing the necessity of fitting a new social organization, as we did once fit the old organization, to the happiness and prosperity of the great body of citizens." The sacred cow of the Supreme Court, "freedom of contract," was to receive its first effective Presidential jolt from Wilson when the Adamson Eight-Hour Bill for railroad employees became a law. In carrying through this most effective bit of legislation for the happiness of the common man (for eventually the eight-hour day was to become as much an act of general economic faith as "freedom of contract"), Wilson was redeeming a campaign pledge implicit in the New Freedom. "The employer," he had said, "is now generally a corporation or a huge company of some kind; the employee is one of hundreds or thousands brought together, not by individual masters whom they know and with whom they have personal relations, but by agents of one sort or another. . . . New rules must be devised with regard to their obligations and their rights. . . . Rules must be devised for their protection, for their compensation when injured, for their support when disabled."

In his attempts to keep up with Roosevelt, who was ruining his throat by denouncing the Barneses and the Penroses up and down the land, Wilson was to grow sarcastic about the promise of "freedom-in-control" for the corporations which the Progressive platform promised. But once the Governor of New Jersey had become President the eternal gadfly, Charles Edward Russell, remarked that his Cabinet choices revealed little will towards breaking up trustification. Brandeis was not a member of that Cabinet. The Morgan interests might have been rebuffed and affronted when Wilson broke with Colonel George Harvey, but the Morgan crowd merely gave way to Bernard Baruch and the Kuhn, Loeb crowd. It was one banker group for another, as it always must be when money is needed to provide a leverage in politics.

But when Wilson was chanting the delicious phrases of the New Freedom, a hungry people was lifting its eyes up unto the hills. Bryan, the Commoner, had swallowed the cocked-hat which Wilson had once wanted him knocked into, and had spoken for the Democratic nominee. The street called Wall had been properly rebuked. The mood of a people—and if it was not the whole people, it was a very large part of the whole, as William Howard Taft was to discover—is perhaps best expressed by John Curtis Underwood, who was to write, in 1914, that the typical American rises to the sound of a factory whistle or a fifty-cent alarm clock; gets into clothes that are to a greater or less extent shoddy, and produced by sweated labor; consumes a breakfast made by machinery and from the cold-storage warehouse whose staples are trust-made or controlled; rides to work in a conveyance owned or controlled by a ring of franchise robbers or profit parers at the community's expense; reads a yellow journal; goes to work for a trust or a concern dominated by one; eats a cold storage dinner; goes to see a machine-made drama, plays mechanical card games or reads mechanical literature; and so to bed.

Underwood, of course, was no unprejudiced observer. But granted the rôle of the trusts, was the way out for Americans to break the big corporations into a thousand quarreling and equally greedy groups? La Follette, who had imbibed his economic philosophy on the frontier, thought so, and La Follette was so constituted that, had he been elected, he would have made a sincere attempt to put his philosophy into working operation. We should have known for certain the practicability of the New Freedom under La Follette. Wilson virtually considered trust-busting to be the answer, but, unlike La Follette, he had no conception of the magnitude of the task ahead of him. He was no economist. Roosevelt, as we have seen, was divided in mind, uncertain in effect. His division, accepted at some stage in the course of his attack on large units, was that of "good" and "bad" trusts; but his distinctions were no safe guide, for manners meant more to him than facts.

Walter Lippmann, as sincere a friend, in spite of divergences, as Wilson was to have, called the turn on the general trend of the New Freedom in Wilson's first Administration. We must remember, Lippmann said, that Wilson's political grammar is "a fusion of Jeffersonian democracy with a kind of British Cobdenism. This means in practical life a conviction that the world needs not so much to be administered as to be released from control." The New Freedom, Lippmann continued, saw the "working man merely as a possible shopkeeper." Wilson's campaign utterances showed a sympathy with the "man on the make," a horror at the crimes of monopoly, but little recognition of the crimes of competition. In short, Wilson was looking both backward and forward, hoping, somehow, to restore the age of competition in an age whose technological discoveries worked irresistibly toward mass action, mass marketing, mass bargaining at the factory door. In practice, Wilson, of course, was forced to make his compromises. It was with a shrewd eye to the actualities of the situation that William Allen White made his remark about the New Freedom and the New Nationalism having all the difference between Tweedledum and Tweedledee.

What manner of man was this prophet of the New Freedom who, somehow, had picked up the jargon around 1909 which La Follette had learned on the farm border in the eighties? He was, said Colonel House, a man who loved humanity, but didn't like people. It is difficult for me to believe that he had any deep-rooted passion for a democratic way of life, such as distinguished La Follette. As a young man he used to remark, facetiously, "I'll argue that out with you in the Senate"—but the accent was on attaining to the Senate, not on the subject to be argued out. In this desire for eminence on any terms Wilson was kin to the Roosevelt who was a patron of politics. He had studied the English political thinkers of an earlier day—Edmund Burke, Walter Bagehot, William Ewart Gladstone, but he made little effort to assess the economic sub-structure of their ideas, the hundred complexities of human life on a tight little fog-bound shopkeeping island that had provided the matrix of their thought. He cared nothing whatever for the rest of Europe; comparative politics were not his politics. Like Roosevelt, he made the mistake of identifying liberalism with morality; he could not cut through the Presbyterian decalogue to the economic sanctions of that morality and compare them with the economic sanctions of other moralities. The working class, as such, meant nothing to him; it merely consisted of a group of people to be won for righteousness. The upper-class Englishman was Wilson's *beau ideal; ipso facto,* the way of life that produced this English gentleman, the type of the Arthur Balfours, must be ordained of God.

Fred Howe, who had studied under Wilson at Johns Hopkins in the nineties, remembers his old professor as he was in the days when Populism was making the West clamorous and labor troubles at Homestead and elsewhere were frightening the Hamiltonians who had come marching up to power through the Gilded Age. Wilson believed, says Howe, in "government by *noblesse oblige.*" After listening to rapt words about the disinterested fathers of the Republic, after scribbling down notes from Woodrovian lips on the superiorities of English statesmen who had been drawn from the best families and trained for the job, Howe summed up the Wilsonian formula. Wilson equaled his Church (Scotch Presbyterian and, of course, Calvinist), plus his student days (study of Magna Charta, the Bill of Rights, Petition of Rights), plus his native State (Virginia) whose university law school he had attended after graduation from Princeton. The Wilson of the Johns Hopkins days would have felt supremely at home at Westminster; he would have been ill at ease in the Washington of the Cleveland and McKinley Administrations. All the Johns Hopkins students caught from their Solon was an exalted glimpse of a ruling caste; the mechanics of how a ruling caste attains and holds power were discreetly hidden from view. There trickled through to them little inkling of the economic background of the fathers of sons at Eton and Harrow, Oxford and Cambridge. Wilson was "not interested in economics." He "esteemed great documents as the most enduring of deeds." As Walter Lippmann said, supplementing Howe, he believed the world could be set right, not by organization, but by a "communion of consciences."

All his life this most unspeculative of thinkers, this most incurious of men, this lay preacher who was utterly uninterested in science and in the arts, considered he had a first-class mind. It was, says William Allen White, his main delusion. His closest approach to fresh, if not remarkably original, work is to be found in his first book, *Congressional Government,* published in 1885 after a short and unhappy period spent as a lawyer in a Southern town. In this book he advocated the English system of a Premier and Cabinet responsible to and working with a parliament. This was *true* representative government, far more flexible than the cumbrous American check-and-balance system. It is important to remember this predilection (a sound preference on Wilson's part) to understand the President of 1913 and after, the Executive who read his own messages to Congress, who insisted on going to Paris to talk matters over with men of actual Premier positions—Lloyd George, Clemenceau, Orlando. The joker in the deck here is that Wilson was not a premier, and was not working with a Cabinet responsible to a parliament. He was working on his own, with the American equivalent of parliament ultimately against him. If we had had the English system of government, he would probably not have been in office for long in 1919. In all probability it would have been Henry Cabot Lodge who would have carried the mandate of the American people to the Hall of Mirrors before any possible American signature had been attached to the Treaty of Versailles. This is pure supposition, of course, but the irony of its possibility apparently never occurred to Wilson. He was a Calvinist, you see, and Calvinists are always elected of God.

I don't want to appear blind to Wilson's fine qualities.

He had an admirable quality of will; he could inspire grand loyalties and equally grand hatreds. He was a great poet in his way—or at least his phrases could move multitudes. His vision of the League, if not firmly based, at least threw into the arena of discussion the idea of the Parliament of Man in the Federation of the World. When antecedent economic conditions are taken care of, the resultant League may reflect eternal glory on Wilson. He may be the Copernicus of a new political system. But just because he began at the top, letting the foundations remain a matter of assumption, it is more than likely that uncouth Marxians and dirty Leninists will steal the ultimate credit from him in the Valhalla of future heroes.

Because of Wilson's anæsthesia to detail, the suspicion will not down that he admired the British system, not so much for its flexibility as for the opportunity it provided for a man of Presidential timbre to take the spotlight, to employ the graces of eloquence, to call together consciences in communion. According to John Maynard Keynes, who kept a shrewd eye on Wilson at the Peace Conference, "he had no plan . . . no constructive ideas whatever for clothing with the flesh of life the commandments he had thundered from the White House. He could have preached a sermon on any of them or have addressed a stately prayer to the Almighty for their fulfillment; but he could not frame their concrete application to the actual state of Europe."

This preacher who made political office his pulpit was the son of a preacher, and the grandson of a preacher. Thomas Woodrow Wilson was born in Staunton, Virginia, of Scotch-Irish antecedents. His paternal grandfather, "Jimmie" Wilson, who had come over from the old country in the early years of the nineteenth century, was a country editor in Steubenville, Ohio; his grandmother, stern Anne Adams, was also of immigrant stock, having met Jimmie on the ocean voyage. The God of each grandparent was the God of John Knox and the Covenanters; the God of Calvin and the predestinarians, a

God as stern, as moral, as Anne Adams herself. And from the other side of the family, from the forbears of Janet Woodrow, young "Tommy" Wilson's mother, the inheritance was also Presbyterian. An uncle of Woodrow Wilson—his mother's brother, James Woodrow—was a rather famous Southern divine, Calvinist yet modern according to his lights. They were good lights for the late nineteenth century below the Mason-Dixon line. James Woodrow was tried by his church for advocating evolution, a doctrine which he tried to square with the old faith of the covenanters. The intellectual strains that were woven into young Tommy Wilson's make-up stemmed pretty securely to his Calvinist forbears on all sides; there is no mutation here. Even the frivolous moods of the man, the moods that took him regularly to the vaudeville show and caused him to delight in his store of limericks, may be followed through his father, the Reverend Joseph Ruggles Wilson, to Jimmie Wilson, the grandparent whose Calvinism was lightened by a joy in the effervescent young world of the Ohio frontier.

The mystery of the Woodrow Wilson who became President resides, for me, not in his early wabbling over the idea of war plus the seeming later inconsistency of his harsh treatment of those who stood in his way. His childhood in Georgia and South Carolina had demonstrated to him the horrors of a dictated, victorious peace. But once Wilson had made up his mind, his very fear of violence caused him to shut down hard on the promptings of his own better nature. He knew that he had to be harsh, lest he weaken altogether. If, as Amos Pinchot has said, he put "his enemies in office and his friends in jail," this is scant cause for wonder. A man elected of God to show the world the road to righteousness, once he has won through incertitude to a conviction of that righteousness, will not scruple to cut down a Debs, to avail himself of an Espionage Act, to demand force, force to the uttermost, force without stint or limit. "Tolerance," said Wilson, "is an admirable intellectual gift, but it is of little worth in politics." The intolerant

Wilson was born of irrevocable decision to travel along the route finally dictated by his "single-track" mind, plus the Calvinist's conviction of the righteousness of the route.

The real mystery of Wilson is—when and where and why did he become a democrat? As a young professor at Bryn Mawr, Wesleyan and Princeton, he showed little interest in industrial democracy. His credo of the nineties might be found in the political philosophy of William Graham Sumner. He had accepted the American system, not suspecting or apparently caring that it had ceased to be a democracy and had become a plutocracy. His eyes were still on the England of Cobden.

But suddenly, as President of Princeton, we find him throwing himself with a covenanter's fervor into the cause of democratic education. Why? The inner course of the man remains inscrutable; he had always taken it for granted that the men on top were there because they deserved to be there. Their sons, who made the good fraternities, were part of the deserving set-up: they, too, had superior qualities. But when the muck-rakers started muck-raking the country, Wilson commenced to do his own muck-raking at Princeton. The clubs, with their special phalansteries, must go—they work for *snobisme*. A universal "quad" plan—very much along the lines that have since been followed out at Yale—must be substituted for the system of segregation by aristocratic choice. And when Dean Andrew West wished to avail himself of a gift which would enable him to build a new graduate school, *away* from the campus proper, Wilson was up in arms. The university must be maintained as a democratic whole, with each natural division helping to cross-fertilize the others.

During the course of the squabbling for democratic education at Princeton, Wilson first came into overt encounter with the power of money. The wealthy old graduate returning for the football game, was duly outraged by the tactics of the crusading president. To have his son "eat with the muckers"? Not if he could help it. And consequently the strong alumni organizations, backed by the powerful local influence of Grover Cleveland, who had settled down at Princeton, grew mighty in their wrath.

Wilson, as always, seemed to be winning—at the start. He defeated Adrian H. Joline when that representative of the plutocracy was up for trustee. He caused Procter to withdraw the offer of the gift for a separate graduate school. But a later gift, contained in the will of a Salem, Mass., millionaire, was so huge that it could not be turned down. As at Versailles, Wilson lost his battle at the very moment of his seeming triumph.

But if he lost at the university, he won before the country. During the course of his Princeton fight, he had made a number of eloquent speeches attacking the malefactors of great wealth who would pervert the Eastern centers of learning to the ends of their class. One speech in particular, made in Pittsburgh at the very headquarters of nineteenth-century Hamiltonianism, caught the fancy of a country that was already looking towards 1912. Wilson had become a national figure. And, incongruously enough, he had interested a power in Jersey politics, Colonel George Harvey, whom William Allen White has called a messenger boy for the Wall Street crowd. If Harvey didn't expect to use Wilson as a democratic blind for plutocratic action, his attachment to the president of Princeton must forever remain an anomaly, a mystery as mysterious as Wilson's conversion to the doctrines of the New Freedom.

Wilson's battle for democratic education at Princeton coincided with the invasion of New Jersey by the spirit of La Follette. Between 1906 and 1908, a body of reformers commenced sapping tactics in the Republican organization, looking forward towards the reforms that had been enthusiastically adopted in certain of the Western States. George L. Record, Everett Colby and La Follette's friend, Gilbert Roe, had carried the spirit of Progressivism into the State that was preëminently the mother of trusts. And James Smith and James Nugent, weather-wise "Jim-Jim" bosses of the New Jersey Democracy, were looking about for a man in the Democratic ranks to oppose to the George Record group within the Republican Party. Through George Harvey, James Smith had his own Wall Street connections. And it was Harvey who suggested Wilson to Smith after talking matters over with Wilson's wife, Ellen Axson. The "Jim-Jim" organization had found its man.

Reformers among the Democrats were opposed to the newcomer. They thought him an innocent, a blind for the machinations of a gang that boded reform no good. And James Smith himself considered Wilson amenable to discipline. Even when Wilson, in answering Record's pointed questionnaire, swore that he would not compromise with Smith, the boss of the "Jim-Jims" was not frightened. He knew the conditions of campaigning, and he discounted at 100 per cent the questions of Record: "Where do you stand upon the direct primary? What is your position upon the subject of the establishment of a Public Utilities Commission with the power to fix rates? ... If ... the Republican leaders are the representatives of the railroads and the utilities and other interests, which I admit, is it not a fact that the Democratic leaders, such as Jim Smith, also represent the same interests? And if so, what do you propose to do about it?"

Wilson proposed to do away with his patron and maker, James Smith, whom he threw down after the election had swung New Jersey into the Democratic column. James Martine had been named primary nominee of the Democrats for the United States Senate, and the State Legislature was morally bound to accept him. But Smith, who had once been Senator, wanted to return to Washington. He commenced his own campaign by ignoring the primary mandate. Wilson, he considered, would be a docile partner to the crime. But events proved otherwise; Smith was beaten by Martine, with the help of Wilson, of James Kerney of the Trenton *Times* and Joseph Tumulty, who became Wilson's secretary in Washington.

Had Wilson committed himself to Smith? Did he owe him his support? The question will probably be argued from now to doomsday. However, the ease with which Wilson smashed his benefactor is disconcerting. He broke, later, with Colonel George Harvey, when the latter had gathered with Thomas Fortune Ryan and Henry Watterson at the Manhattan Club in 1911 to ask guarantees in the event the Democratic nomination for President should devolve upon Wilson. The break with Harvey made Wilson in a national sense; it brought Bryan to his side, at least tacitly. But Harvey had led Wilson to Smith, and he was junked at the expedient moment. The smashed friendships are a *leitmotif* in the Wilsonian career; he had broken with Andrew West after persuading him to remain at Princeton; he had broken with John Grier Hibben. He was to use Bryan, and break with Bryan. Ultimately he broke with his most faithful retainer and friend, Colonel House. The record is not envious; doubtless it proves something. The most one can say for Wilson is that Smith had double-crossed Martine, and had laid himself open to attack; that if Harvey was trying to use Wilson he got paid in his own coin; that circumstances altered cases when Bryan, a pacifist, found himself compromised with the war technique as Secretary of State; and that Wilson was a sick, irresponsible and woman-ridden man when House was dropped into outer darkness.

What the story of the sundered relationships seems to prove is that Wilson was the soul of ingratitude, lacking even the excuse that he was working from the start for an idea. There is good reason to believe his progressivism as Governor of New Jersey was something of a "gotten-up" product. It was not wholly synthetic, for Wilson was undoubtedly working his way to progressivism before he left Princeton. But it was George L. Record, the liberal Republican, who drafted the planks of the Democratic platform into Wilson's bills. And there is more than a little evidence that without Colonel Edward Mandell House Wilson would never have made so enviable a record as a progressive President in his first term.

The meeting with House marked the turning point in

Wilson's aspirations for the Presidency. It was House, the courteous, the smiling, the smooth, who made Bryan a potential ally of the Wilson forces. In a famous letter, written to Adrian Joline back in 1907, Wilson had ventured the hope that Bryan would be knocked "once and for all into a cocked hat." As a tactical measure to embarrass Wilson, the letter had been released. But it proved a boomerang. Bryan may have had his private reservations, but there was no estrangement, since the letter had been given out by the Wall Street group. House explained it all. And at Baltimore, after the long deadlock with Champ Clark, Wilson was put over as the nominee when Bryan swung his influence to the late schoolmaster of Princeton. Wilson was virtually President of the United States.

During the Wilsonian ascendancy the relationship between House and the President was a matter for much curious comment. House had written a romance, a political novel called *Philip Dru—Administrator,* published anonymously in 1912, which contained, in essence, a prophecy of the course of the first Wilson Administration. Dru was an American dictator whose faith was that of a Bryanite who had become a State socialist; by force, he had seized the government, and had put through a series of reforms including labor insurance, a progressive income tax, old-age pensions, a tax board, and a banking system analogous to what the Federal Reserve was to be. Like Louis Brandeis, House, as the creator and manipulator of Dru, wished to smash the credit trust which the Pujo investigation was to expose. Like Roosevelt, he wished to rob the Supreme Court of its function. In the field of foreign affairs, Philip Dru, true to the imagination of Colonel House, worked for a league of Western nations—possibly the embryonic sketching of the League of Geneva.

Commentators have pointed out similarities between the fictive reforms of Dru and the actual reforms of Wilson. Recently, in a remarkably sensitive book, *The Strangest Friendship in History,* George Sylvester Viereck has stressed the parallel again. Did House hold a position in national affairs equivalent to the one held by George L. Record in New Jersey when Wilson was Governor? This is a matter for fascinating conjecture, as Mr. Viereck has proved. But did not Clemenceau, who was always shrewd, say that House was the window through which light came to Wilson?

House has recently outlined his purpose in hitching his wagon to the star of Wilson. He wished, so he has told Mr. Viereck, "to translate into legislation certain liberal and progressive ideas. Texas, under Governor Hogg and Governor Culberson, was the pioneer Progressive among the States. The Progressive movement in the United States was fathered by Hogg, not by La Follette or Roosevelt. Many of the laws which we wrote on the statute books of Texas were subsequently adopted by the nation at large. The regulation of railroads, for instance, was first attempted in our State. I wanted to carry the Texas idea into national politics."

Thus, through the offices of a Texas honorary colonel who stood with Bryan on most issues except free silver, the spirit of Hogg and Culberson joined with the spirit of Record and Colby and La Follette to give the first Democratic Administration since Cleveland a firmly progressive tone. There followed the Underwood Tariff and the launching of the Federal Reserve System—the latter made palatable to Bryan, who was satisfied by House that the new banking régime had been preserved for the people and kept from the domination of the group which Aldrich and his National Monetary Commission had represented. There followed, too, the creation of the Federal Trade Commission, and the amendment of the Sherman law known as the Clayton Anti-Trust Act—an act which Gompers, in a moment of unfounded eloquence, hailed as "labor's Magna Charta." The Federal Farm Loan Act came in 1916, and in the same year the Adamson eight-hour bill became a law. Wilson also signed La Follette's Seamen's bill, designed to free the men in the forecastle from intolerable conditions at sea.

In all of this may be glimpsed the intelligence of Philip

Dru, as well as the work of a decade of Progressive activity. The quest for social justice seemed nearing its end, and the end appeared happy. Even Wilson's chaotic Mexican policy—which Hugh Neal ("Wells") Wells has scanned in search of the development of Philip Dru's ideas pointing toward a league of Western nations under Washington's hegemony—could not make Wilson seem illiberal. The dreams of La Follette, of Bryan, of countless thousands of foot-sloggers in the Progressive ranks, seemed about to be made flesh.

But in the meantime Europe had gone to war. And Wilson, the war-hater, who adjured his countrymen to remain neutral in thought and deed alike, found himself slowly compromised with the Allied forces, and drawn into the orbit of Armageddon.

The situation confronting Wilson in 1914 and after was heavily weighted in favor of the Allies. In an excellent and unread book, *Why We Fought,* C. Hartley Grattan has drawn up the balance sheet making for our entrance into the conflict on England's side, even though the War was a fight between mutually black sheep. London controlled the cable services; the British censor controlled all but a minimum of war news appearing in the American papers, American bankers were largely pro-Ally, even at the outset of the War, as were certainly our Ambassadors to England and France, Walter Page and Myron Herrick. Thomas W. Lamont, speaking for the Morgan interests, has written of 1914: "Those were the days when American citizens were being urged to remain neutral in action, in word, even in thought. But our firm had never for one moment been neutral; we didn't know how to be. From the very start we did everything that we could to contribute to the cause of the Allies." And when the banking house of Morgan became the British purchasing agent in America, with vast sums at its disposal, the community of interest between American industrialists and the Allied forces was made even more water-tight than it had been. Wilson was forced to confuse the Allies with righteousness; full information was denied him. He knew when a *Lusitania* had gone down; he heard nothing of tubercular babies in blockaded Germany.

There is good evidence to show that Wilson had committed himself to the Allies as early as February of 1916, when a "gentleman's agreement" was entered upon by Colonel House, representing the President in Europe, Sir Edward Grey of the British Foreign Office, and the French. On October 17, 1915, we find House informing Grey: "In my opinion it would be a world-wide calamity if the War should continue to a point where the Allies could not, with the aid of the United States, bring about a peace along the lines you and I have so often discussed. What I want to know is that, whenever you consider the time is propitious for this intervention, I will propose it to the President. He may then desire me to go to Europe in order that a more intimate understanding as to procedure may be had.

"It is in my mind that, after conferring with your Government, I should proceed to Berlin and tell them that it was the President's purpose to intervene and stop this destructive war, provided the weight of the United States, thrown on the side that accepted our proposal, could do it.... I would not let Berlin know, of course, of any understanding with the Allies, but would rather lead them to think our proposal would be rejected by the Allies. This might induce Berlin to accept the proposal, but, if they did not do so, it would nevertheless be the purpose to intervene. If the Central Powers were still obdurate, it would *probably* [my italics] be necessary to join the Allies and force the issue."

This is not an open promise to aid the Allies in a peace movement that would be satisfactory to Downing Street and the Quai d'Orsay; and Wilson was canny in insisting that House include the italicized word "probably" in the memorandum. But it was disingenuous, to say the least, to make certain of the agreeableness of Grey before proceeding openly to the

Kaiser. On February 23, 1916, the cords linking us to the Allied cause grew tighter, as Grey dictated a memorandum: "Colonel House told me that President Wilson was ready, on hearing from France and England that the moment was opportune, to propose that a conference should be summoned to put an end to the War. Should the Allies accept this proposal, and should Germany refuse it, the United States would probably enter the War against Germany.

"Colonel House expressed the opinion that, if such a conference met, it would secure peace on terms not unfavorable to the Allies; and, if it failed to secure peace, the United States would leave the conference as a belligerent on the side of the Allies, if Germany was unreasonable. Colonel House expressed an opinion decidedly favorable to the restoration of Belgium, the transfer of Alsace and Lorraine to France, and the acquisition by Russia of an outlet to the sea, though he thought that the loss of territory incurred by Germany in one place would have to be compensated to her by concessions to her in other places outside Europe...."

Once again Wilson insisted on the use of "probably," this time making a sentence read, "the United States would *probably* leave the conference." In so doing, he provided himself with a legal out. But, as Mr. Grattan and Mr. Viereck have demonstrated, the moral commitment had been made—and by the very President who was shortly to defeat Hughes by running for reëlection on the slogan, "He kept us out of war."

However, even after the tacit commitment, Wilson fought off an irrevocable decision. Did he want *his* war, with the United States playing trumps at the peace conference, as Mr. Hugh Neal Wells has so cogently insisted? Or was he afraid of the violence whose results he had glimpsed as a child in the Southern cotton States? Whatever may be the truth (and it is probably compounded of both guesses), we find him uttering a most prophetic reservation to Frank Cobb, editor of the New York *World,* as late as April 1, 1917:

"I have never been so uncertain about anything in my life as that decision. A declaration of war would mean that Germany would be beaten and so badly beaten that there would be a dictated peace, a victorious peace. It means an attempt to reconstruct a peace-time civilization with war standards, and at the end of the War there will be no bystanders with sufficient power to influence the terms. There won't be any peace standards left to work with. There will be only war standards. It would mean that we should lose our heads, along with the rest, and stop weighing right and wrong. It would mean that a majority of people on this hemisphere would go war mad, quit thinking and devote their energies to destruction.

"We couldn't fight Germany and maintain the ideals of government that all thinking men share. I shall try it but it will be too much for us. Once lead this people into war and they'll forget there ever was such a thing as tolerance. To fight, you must be brutal... and the spirit of ruthless brutality will enter into the very fiber of our national life, infecting Congress, the courts, the policeman on the beat, the man in the street. Conformity will be the only virtue. And every man who refuses to conform will have to pay the penalty."

In that statement, so clairvoyant, so sane, the better Wilson spoke. And it is a matter for cosmic irony to note that every line and word of it foreshadowed what Randolph Bourne had to say a few weeks later in the pages of the *Seven Arts* after Wilson had capitulated to the war technique and was calling for force, force to the uttermost, force without stint or limit. The statement to Cobb makes the hardness of the war President explicable. This hardness, which liberal commentators—Gilson Gardner, Amos Pinchot, Fred Howe—have insisted upon, was the product, we must believe, of Wilson's own essential weakness. He was afraid to let up for a minute, lest the truth he had himself proclaimed sap his terrible will. And the country must be made to conform—conformity had become the only virtue.

But there was one person in the United States who took Wilson's words to Frank Cobb almost out of his mouth, and who threw them back into the public discussion after the declaration of war. This person was Randolph Bourne, the hunchback, a great spirit in a twisted body.

Bourne lives to-day mainly as a beautiful memory in the minds of his very good friends. He died on December 22, 1918, after a short life and after hardly a decade of writing. His first book, *Youth and Life* (1913), fabricated out of the assembled facets of the vision of existence which was his by virtue of his apprenticeship to the pragmatism of James and Dewey, is a young man's performance; the only remarkable thing about it was its youthful sensitiveness. American essayists in 1913 had not been noted for that quality. In *Youth and Life* Bourne was exploring the possibilities of life in America, his own "constant susceptibility to the new, this constant eagerness to try experiments." He was disgusted with the "crass waste" of human personality in the world about him. Radicalism attracted him, and he was feeling his way along towards a fruitful state of revolt, as were so many of that pre-War decade—Brooks, Joel Spingarn, Frank. Always the accent was on experiment, experiment; always the phrases of revolt were the tentative ones taught by John Dewey. But of one thing Bourne was sure: "that life will have little meaning for me except as I am able to contribute toward some ideal of social betterment, if not in deed, then in word."

When Van Wyck Brooks, Waldo Frank, Louis Untermeyer and Paul Rosenfeld commenced editing the *Seven Arts,* it gave Bourne his great opportunity. But at first he shied away from the non-pragmatic point of view of the editors; he had not finished with liberal pragmatism. He still put his hopes in an instrumentalism that would transform the world into a radiant democracy. His own rebelliousness made no distinction between a revolutionary and an evolutionary approach to that society to which he aspired.

But with the entrance of America into the War, the iron

entered into Bourne's soul. He had always had a horror of regimentation and exploitation for inhumane ends; and like the Woodrow Wilson of April 1, 1917, he knew that war would kill any chance of maintaining the ideas of government that all thinking men share. At the age of eighteen, when he was living at home, he had first come into contact with the commercial spirit which made the War inevitable in Europe. He had left school to go to work for a musician who had a machine on which to cut perforated music-rolls for the player-pianos which were then becoming popular. From eight to five each day he worked in the home of that musician, doing piece work. For every foot of paper that he perforated he got five cents. The musician got fifteen cents from the manufacturers with whom he had a contract. While Bourne was working the musician composed symphonies. For a time the relationship went along smoothly. But when Bourne became skillful at the job, the musician reduced his rate to four and one-half cents a foot. The hunchback flared into an innocent rebellion, and the musician said he could stay or go—he was "perfectly free." But Bourne returned "cravenly to my bench." However, he had learned; he enlarged that musician into "the employing class." He had become a socialist.

The spirit of pragmatism would do away with exploitation, Bourne felt sure. It was only after Wilson, the liberal, had decided to play the old game, no matter from what motives, and had called for war; it was only after the pragmatic idols—Dewey, the editors of the *New Republic*—began to make excuses justifying that war, that Bourne, who could see no tangible good gained by adherence to the war technique, broke openly with his masters. The shock of the War, as James Oppenheim has said, set Bourne free. The War, as Waldo Frank has said, drove most men mad, but it drove Bourne sane.

The sanity of Bourne may be found in a small volume, published in 1919, called *Untimely Papers*. Most of these papers were printed in the *Seven Arts* during America's first Summer of the War, when even a number of the socialists had fallen into line behind Wilson. Men who, presumably, had pondered the words of Marx about the seeds of destruction within the framework of international capitalism had lost sight of the common enemy. William English Walling, Upton Sinclair, Charmian London, Charles Edward Russell, John Spargo—all of them had moved into the orbit of the pragmatic acquiescence, splitting with their party's majority group. But Bourne, with the courage of desperation, continued to attack the war-minded liberals and socialists until September, when the subsidy of the *Seven Arts* was withdrawn. He had with him, at first, two plaintive liberal voices, those of Robert L. Duffus and Lewis S. Gannett, both of whom were displeased with Wilson's course. Duffus, a Californian, was outraged that a President who had won California's vote on the slogan, "He kept us out of war," should so quickly decide for fighting without consulting the will of the people as a whole, California included. Gannett asked—with a note of supplication in his question—just what those who believed that it was an "unrighteous war" were to do?

The answer to that question was—they could do what Bourne did, and be hounded, as Bourne was hounded, by the Department of Justice, or they could shut up for the duration of the fighting, or they could cynically apply to George Creel for a job in Washington. Bourne himself slashed fiercely, with all the outraged horror of the suddenly betrayed, at the umbilical cord that had bound him to pragmatism. Long before the relative strengths of the British and the German propaganda had been explored and documented by Harold Lasswell and Mr. Grattan, Bourne had sensed that "the reputable opinion of the American intellectuals became more and more either what could be read pleasantly in London, or what was written in an earnest effort to put Englishmen straight on their war-aims and war-technique." "Whence," Bourne wrote in June of 1917, "our confidence that history will not unravel huge economic and imperialist forces upon which our rationalizations float like bubbles?"

Like La Follette, with whom his name should be linked, Bourne considered that America's rich and generous emotions were needed for the work of democratization of society at home. The War, he knew with Jane Addams, would set progress back a generation. He doubted the dogma that insisted the world was about to be made safe for democracy by a war to end war; if Wilson's words were true, then why the need for a "selective service" act by which all could be compelled to do the will of the leader, why the need for an Espionage Act? A righteous cause supposedly needs no compulsion.

Like the Wilson of April 1, 1917, Bourne predicted a victorious peace, a peace that would saddle the world with all that he had hoped, sitting at the feet of John Dewey, to escape. The War came as a numbing experience. "One has a sense," Bourne wrote, "of having come to a sudden, short stop at the end of an intellectual era." "To those of us who have taken Dewey's philosophy almost as our American religion, it never occurred that values could be subordinated to technique. We were instrumentalists, but we had our private utopias so clearly before our minds that the means fell always into its place as contributory."

What did Dewey, what did the Herbert Croly whose magazine printed editorials "In Defense of the Atlantic World" (as if Hamburg were not an Atlantic port), what did Walter Lippmann, what did the anti-Kaiser socialists, hope to gain from the War? The word "democracy" in their mouths, Bourne demonstrated, was an "unanalyzed term, useful as a call to battle, but not an intellectual tool." "Is it the political democracy of a plutocratic America that we are fighting for," Bourne asked, "or is it the social democracy of the new Russia?" "Which do our rulers really fear more, the menace of Imperial Germany or the liberating influence of a socialist Russia?" "War," Bourne insisted, "always undermines values"—but the *New Republic* editors went on speaking as if the Allies could be held to a peace without victory. And Wilson himself, although we know now that he knew of the secret treaties when he was ostensibly battling for open covenants and the League at Paris, talked on about a really democratic peace.

Bourne, of course, was not heeded. When the *Seven Arts* failed, he was thrown upon the literary market, unfriended and unwanted. He made a living reviewing bad novels. At the time of his death he was at work on an analysis of the State, the American and Wilsonian exemplification of which had done for him. "War," he wrote, "is the health of the State." The State he defined as a mystical concept, used by the dominant power groups, organized as the government, to fuse the citizens of the nation for a common, if often specious, purpose. The definition is Veblenian; and it is true. The idea of the State is a red herring, used to divert citizens from a contemplation of values. When the aims of the "inner circle" of its governors need to be hidden, it is trotted forth, implemented with Draft Acts and Espionage Acts, and used to stop the processes of thoughtful analysis.

The liberals who followed Wilson to Paris discovered the cogency, the apt prophecy, of Bourne's unheeded words. One by one they have confessed their disillusion; one by one they have commented upon what Harold Stearns has scarified as Wilson's "technique of liberal failure." Fred Howe, Walter Weyl, William Bullltt, Lincoln Steffens, Herbert Croly—all of them were vastly disappointed by the return at Versailles to the old diplomacy, a diplomacy in which oil was trumps. Upton Sinclair, one of the war-minded socialists, publicly recanted his stand of 1917. For Wilson permitted himself to be mulcted of all he had insisted upon—all, that is, but a crippled League, designed, in actuality, to preserve the fruits of victory to France and England. The promise to the German people—that it was to be a peace without victory—was rudely dashed by the provision leading to fantastic reparations. Wilson himself considered the peace a muffed opportunity. He knew he had thrown down the opinion he claimed to represent. He said, on one occasion, that he ought not to have signed, and then added, piteously, "But what could I do?" Here again it was the better Wilson speaking, but when he came home for the last time, to face the irreconcilables of the Senate and a country suddenly grown weary and cynical, just as he had predicted it would, he chose to stand by the best of all possible peaces. The League would justify him. And he refused to admit even to his closest friends that he had failed. And the strain of the deception broke him.

"It is obvious," Mr. Stearns has written in a now forgotten book, *Liberalism in America,* "that we would have got a more democratic peace, if we had not handed over the entire resources of the country to President Wilson and then allowed him to put through an Espionage law which prevented any effective public criticism of either his military or diplomatic methods. If President Wilson had had to *fight* for men to wage his war, had had to *fight* to make his ideals of the settlement prevail, the chances are that the peace settlement would not have seen quite so many broken promises."

Stearns may have been unduly under the sway of the Great Man theory when he wrote that paragraph; it may be that Wilson, as Walter Weyl has said, will appear, a generation from now, "as a straw dike carried away by the flood." But Versailles killed the hopes for a world made safe for democracy, just as the War had diverted American's rich and generous impulses from the quest for social justice and burned them out in a hunt for German witches. Wilson himself exemplified the uselessness of a liberalism that trusts to phrases for salvation. "You cannot lay down fourteen general formulas without raising innumerable questions in political casuistry," wrote Weyl of the Fourteen Points after the return from Paris. Wilson went into "the jungle with a map of the world but without a compass." He permitted the Italians to engulf a goodly slice of territory inhabited by people of German blood—and "self-determination" went by the board. He knew nothing of Shantung, Fiume, Dalmatia, Silesia, Macedonia, and cared little, so long as his principles prevailed. And in the end not even his principles prevailed.

In his college days Tommy Wilson had entered a debating contest. It was the usual affair, with the contestants putting their hands in a hat to draw forth the slips placing them upon one side of the question or another. The sole purpose of the debate was to sharpen minds, to familiarize the participants with the principles of logical coherence. But Wilson drew a slip committing him to the protection side of the tariff question. Angrily, he ripped the paper into bits and left the room. In his later years he recalled the incident with some pride.

At Versailles, in April of 1919, he had found himself committed to a peace which he could not, in the core of his heart, approve. So he took a leaf out of his college notebook, and prepared, once more, to leave the room. When he announced that he had cabled for the *S.S. George Washington,* thinking to quit the conference and leave the United States morally unbound by the intrigue of Clemenceau and Lloyd George, liberals like Weyl went to bed hoping at last that Wilson would stand firm. But it was all a bluff; Wilson didn't leave the room. The upright young Solon who had refused to compromise with his own innermost convictions when it was all a game could not go through with the gesture when it was reality that confronted him. He was, as Weyl said, adapting Bismarck's conception of Salisbury, "a lath painted to look like iron." He had no ballast. A vicious treaty, said Weyl, "must of necessity destroy the League to which it is in principle opposed." And Weyl's prophecy seems on the verge of coming true. Japan, a member of the League, has successfully played the old game to date in Manchuria. The League, too, seems a lath structure, painted to look like iron.

The Walter Weyl who saw through Wilson came home from Paris to write a paper on "Tired Radicals." The tired radical, he noted, with perhaps a rueful glimpse into his own heart, passes from a grand passion for universal housekeeping to a microscopic farm. "He who aspired to overturn Society... ends by fighting in a dull Board of Directors of a village library for the inclusion of certain books." The tired radical knows too much; he has seen all tactics fail. And he ceases to be of any propulsive use to the younger radical, the fledgling who has the courage of his inexperience.

Mr. Weyl himself may be taken as a symbol of radicalism in post-war America, the America of the extirpation of the "Wobblies," of the Red hunts of Wilson's Attorney General, A. Mitchell Palmer, of the Sacco-Vanzetti case, of the oil scandals, of the New Era. The old *Masses,* rippling organ of protest, had been killed by the decision of a Federal judge. John Reed was dead. The "social conscience" departed from American fiction; the personal document usurped its place with the publication of *This Side of Paradise.* And the strange new presence of an actual socialist State in Soviet Russia, appalling in some respects to American socialists of the W. J. Ghent, John Spargo or William English Walling type, split the American Marxians and Marxian revisionists further apart after the election of 1920 and virtually crushed the Second Internationale. Normalcy returned as the New York *Call* died, and business took over the slogans of the radicals and the progressives of the Rooseveltian and Wilsonian days. Poverty was to be abolished; a living wage was to be guaranteed to all. But the peace to which Wilson had been an important party, the peace which Randolph Bourne foresaw, with its burden of impossible debt loaded down upon the defeated power, was to boomerang upon the one real beneficiary of the War. The New Era, like Wilson, like the League to date, was also a lath structure, painted to look like iron.

WHAT was the "technique of liberal failure"? It was, so Mr. Stearns said, the unwillingness of the liberal to continue with analysis once the process of analysis had become uncomfortable. La Follette had been willing to continue with the analysis of the War; so had Bourne. But liberalism in general couldn't stand the gaff. It suddenly, before April of 1917, ceased to be critical; it contented itself with following the drift of events. It took its eyes from the heritage of all past wars of history, and looked weakly to the New Jerusalem in the clouds. This war, liberalism said, would be different. And so it idealized the drift of events, calling the drift decision. With what results, we know.

CHAPTER TEN

Foray

☆

AND so we come to the end of the Progressive trail. What have the years left with us? Their reverberations have bequeathed to us what might be called, with proper obeisance to Lewis Mumford, a Little Golden Day of general culture, with satire at its base. This culture has been the more adventurous because of the spirit of general dissent and inquiry that begot it. But since this book is concerned only with that culture which, on the plane of ideas, has served as carrier of the notions shaping the direct development of the politics of the Progressive epoch, the end-product of the Little Golden Day need not concern us here.

The results, or lack of results, of the Progressive years in government and interrelated business are, however, our direct concern. There are some—such as the good William Allen White, and Charles Edward Russell—who consider that American industry has been suffused with Progressive shibboleths; we have been saved, they aver, from a harsh industrial tyranny by the stirrings of the Rooseveltian and Wilsonian years. This is not an opinion to be dismissed with a sneer. Al Smith's factory legislation, the pure food laws, workmen's compensation, and so on, have done some humanizing. The Morgan trick of taking in the public as investors, the idea of which had a grand burgeoning after the success of the government in floating the Liberty Loan bond issues, is beneficent in one sense, although in a larger sense it is unfortunate, since it paralyzes the will to radical action when radical action is needed. There have been honest efforts directed toward instituting a humane science of industrial management, notably in the Procter and Gamble Company, the Hart, Schaffner and Marx Company, the Baltimore and Ohio railroad equipment shops, the manufacturing company of Henry Dennison of Framingham, Mass. Mr. E. A. Filene, given his way, could, no doubt, do much to integrate the spirit of humane rationalism with the spirit of business.

But the ghost of the Veblen who knew, better than Lippmann, the import of the phrase, "well-meaning but unmeaning," will not down; the very nature of business, which is, fundamentally, based on the desire for profits, works to undermine the advance guard of the Filenes and the Dennisons. Faced with a loss, only the most Quixotic man of business can indulge in positive humanitarian tactics. Consciences may be salved by the practice of hiring outside efficiency experts to do firing and wage cutting, but the results are the same. Work may be "shared" and staggered, but sharing on the basis of stationary or diminished total wages per week does not increase purchasing power. The Progressive business man, individually humane, is caught in a complicated net of aggregate weave. He cannot cut clear by himself. In business, in time of trouble, the most unscrupulous inevitably set the pace for the whole machine, just as in good times the ones out for the immediate gain set the pace.

As for Progressive government, the results of the three decades of strife antecedent to 1919 are, perhaps, minimal. Oswald Garrison Villard thinks we are no further along the road than we were in 1900. This, I think, is susceptible of proof—and, to boot, we are on the wrong road. If you think the tariff is at the bottom of our troubles, it is to be noted that the tariff is still sky-high. But even if we had a low tariff, it is doubtful that it could have stemmed the down-thrust of depression. The Underwood tariff of 1913 did not prevent us from limping industrially until the War created a market for

American goods. Free trade, in the long run, cannot prevent a dynamic capitalistic industrial machine from glutting markets as the upcurve of greed succeeds the downcurve of fear in the psychological cycle that is the concomitant of the business cycle.

The pet political solutions of the Progressives, designed to make government more responsible to the will of the electorate, have notoriously been weak reeds. The initiative and the referendum have produced nothing. Women suffrage has only added, in direct proportion, to Republican and Democratic totals. Direct primaries have proved not even a palliative; they have worked against strong labor and independent party organization, which is the only hope of labor and the consumer in the political field. As Paul Douglas says, where parties are closed organizations, as in England, nominations are made by local nuclei of party workers who know what they want. If a group dislikes the candidates of existing party machines, the only recourse is to put a candidate of its own in the field. The direct primary seemingly weakens the necessity for this; it creates the illusion that an inert "people," spasmodically led, can be aroused to holding the machine politician in line by the threat that they may turn on him at the primary polls. The result is . . . the machine politician promises much, does little . . . and the people are let down. During a two, or four, or six, year period of office-holding, there is much time for an electorate to forget.

The popular election of Senators, instituted in 1913, has made very little actual difference. The real difference between the type of Senator that flourished in the days of the McKinley plutocracy and the type of the present is one of demagoguery; the modern Senator, representing the same interests as his legislature-elected predecessor, is compelled to be a master of the art of obfuscation. Senator Nelson Aldrich, in the 1890 dispensation, could afford to leave the obfuscation to his local manipulator, General Brayton, who kept the legislature in line while his master attended to more important business.

The real human gain of Woodrow Wilson's Administration was the domestication of the eight-hour day in many areas of industry, made possible by the Adamson Law rendering it compulsory on the railroads. The Federal Reserve system is, beyond doubt, better than the previous banking system. It is flexible, it is an instrument which, through its control of the rediscount rate, can take up the slack between productive activity, and speculation at any time *if it is properly run*. But, in setting down these gains, we have about exhausted the really important positive legislation of thirty years. The business cycle remains; until that is done away with, all legislation looking to the welfare of the common man must appear in the light of small, temporary oscillations along the course of a major graph.

This brings us to the definition of "reform," and its alternative, revolution. Now, revolution (change of structure and aims) inevitably carries with it connotations of untoward happenings, of barricades or whatever may be their twentieth-century equivalent, of whatever modern ingenuity can devise as substitute for the guillotine, of the reign of terror induced by the menace of counter-revolution. To Stuart Chase, it means a sudden sharp disruption of the distributive mechanism of an entire nation.

Personally, I experience none of the psychological thrill which hopes of "the revolution" send tingling through the born radical. I am as timorous in the face of physical violence as Mr. Bernard Shaw. Because of this fact, it may be that I am indulging in wishful thinking when I say that I am not persuaded that votes will not do. It seems to me that, in a nation of forty-eight organized State governments, with forty-eight militias, votes *must* do. I am mindful of the good old revolutionary axiom that no owning class ever gave up its property and preferred position without a struggle. Yet there are revolutions *and* revolutions; and there are ways *and* ways of confiscation, even in the face of the Fifth and Fourteenth Amendments. There is the revolution advocated (but not worked out in its implications) by Mr. Kenneth Burke—the revolution by indirection. An income of six per cent may be shaved to the vanishing point by a five per cent system of taxation, as will be necessary if the toll of technological unemployment in agriculture and industry grows. Such a system of taxation would sorely cripple the re-investment process—which, in turn, would help bring closer the day of total legal confiscation of productive private property (with the exception of small farm holdings). In the light of the possibilities which the Sixteenth (Income Tax) Amendment, one of the negative triumphs of the Progressive epoch, has opened up for bloodless revolution in this country, I affirm the hope, in bidding farewell to reform, that parliamentary processes will not fail in the interim leading up to the necessary class shifts in control.

But, one fancies the reader asking, are not parliamentary methods the very essence of reform? This depends upon the definition of the word. In the United States, "reform"—apart from the meaning pumped into it by the Anti-Saloon Leaguers and other specifically "moral" reformers, who are beyond the scope of this inquiry—has always had a "return" connotation. By "reform," a host of political leaders, Bryan, La Follette, Wilson, Theodore Roosevelt at times, and Franklin D. Roosevelt to-day, have hoped to "return" to the ways of their fathers—to the methods and possibilities of a more primitive capitalism. As Walter Lippmann remarked of the Wilson of *The New Freedom,* they have seen the laborer as a possible shopkeeper. That is why Progressivism and Liberalism in this country are, at the moment, preparing the ground for an American Fascism; they have been identified with the shopkeeper instincts of the common citizen, who is willing to make his trade with the "big fellow" if he can retain a privilege or two.

The curbing of the "money power," the abolition of "privilege," the opening up of opportunity by the Single Tax, the redemption of the promises of the New Freedom, all of these have been made the basis for a "return" demand—a demand for the evocation and reëstablishment of a vanished, and somehow more "moral" and "honest" *status quo.* And all economic reforms that have been undertaken in the spirit of Bryan, of La Follette, of Wilson, have worked in a way precisely against the grain of Progressive or neo-democratic hopes; instead of "freeing" the common man within the capitalistic system, these reforms have made the system, as a long-run proposition, more difficult of operation; and this, in turn, has reacted upon the common man as employee, as small bondholder, as savings-account depositor, as insurance-policy owner. The value of reforms, as I see it, is that they fail to achieve what they are sanguinely intended to achieve; and in so failing they help make the sytem which they are intended to patch up only the more unpatchable. In other words, every vote for reform, entered upon intelligently, is a Jesuitical vote for revolution. Conservatives like Nicholas Murray Butler know this; that is why they fear the growth of a bureaucracy intended to administer a "return"; that is why they fear the retention of the anti-trust acts.

Illustration is called for. Let us begin by taking the first of the "return" reforms that resulted from the agitation of the Farm Border: the Interstate Commerce Commission. This Commission was instituted at the repeated request of the shippers, who had their own capitalistic economic interest in getting the railroads "down." The Commission has had whatever real success it can claim because two wary, strongly entrenched economic classes have fought for its control. If the fight had been merely consumer versus exploiter, the latter would inevitably have won by superiority of pressure. As things have worked out, what with the development of motor transportation, the shipper has been able to bring pressure a little stronger than that of the railroad owners. I do not question the shipper's "right" to the victory; in fact, my sympathy is all with the shipper, since he has represented the underdog in the game of grab to which William Graham Sumner so strenuously objected. But—as a long-run proposition—the efforts of the shipper will be defeated, for, indirectly, they have worked to undermine the system of which the shipper is a part.

What is now left to the railroad capitalists after three or four decades of "reform" is a limited right to management, a limited right to profits. Under the present dispensation, as Walter J. Shepard has pointed out, the railroad shareholder (often synonymous with the shipper and the small business man, either directly or through the ownership of insurance policies) is reduced to the position of a mere investor in securities, indistinguishable from the bondholder, save that his right is contingent within limits instead of being fixed. Directors and managers, again as Professor Shepard says, function within the limits of a circumscribed plan that leaves little scope for initiative. Because of the partial control involved in the supervision of the railroads, the howl of "unfair" discrimination goes up. We are faced with either a general weakening of the railroads or the extension of control to bus lines, trucking companies and airplanes in the interests of "fairness" to all. Beyond this looms the control of electric power and of gasoline, or the substitutes for gasoline, inasmuch as they supply the dynamic food of the carriers. The result—a general limitation of profits, a cutting of dividends, less money to reinvest. The shipper will win—and lose. He will transport his goods the more cheaply, but cutthroat competition in his own field will inevitably work to squeeze out the weakling, and the investment structure open to the big fellow will be impaired by the very legislation he has brought into effect. A congealing capitalism, I suspect, is of no benefit, ultimately, to any capitalist, no matter what his immediate interest may be. It produces the racketeer, brought in to maintain the *status quo* against extension of competition. It limits the scope of possible profit; it thereby limits new enterprise. It creates business bureaucracy, which is more horrible to contemplate than political bureaucracy.

More illustration is called for. Let us take the second of the reforms that grew out of the agitation sired on the Farm

Border—the anti-trust legislation. Under capitalism, we are damned if we accept this legislation, and damned if we don't. If we accept it, and endeavor to enforce it, the resources of business in a technological age are crippled. If we remove the restrictions, there is no assurance that open trustification will result in a benefit to labor and the consumer. In any case, the Sherman and the Clayton Acts have served only as a latent threat; they have notoriously failed to break up large units. Anti-trust legislation failed in all but name when the Northern Securities Company was ordered dissolved; it failed to halt the ingestion of the Tennessee Coal and Iron Company by United States Steel; it has failed to halt the inevitable push toward railroad consolidation; and it has failed, recently, to prevent radio trustification. The "genius" of the machine is clearly against anti-trust laws.

The impotence of the anti-trust legislation (save as a living reminder that oppression in the matter of exorbitant charges and reduced wages invites reprisal, however unintelligent it may be) is illustrated by the career of the Federal Trade Commission, which was instituted under Wilson to supersede Roosevelt's ineffective Bureau of Corporations. The Federal Trade Commission was supposed to check trust growth at the source; it was set up to administer the Clayton Act. What has actually happened? Huston Thompson, once a member of the Commission, has told of its failure, in 1919, when the price of coal advanced to a point where price-fixing was suspected. The Commission investigated production costs, discovering that West Virginia coal, which cost four dollars a ton at the mouth of the mine, was sold for twenty-two dollars or more a ton in Norfolk. But before the Commission had an opportunity to announce that the price was due to manipulation, it was called off by a court proceeding. Ultimate judgment held that the Commission had no power to demand cost facts of mining within a State, as that did not come under the heading of "interstate commerce."

The cross-purposes, the effect of bringing industries to a

Mexican stand-off, the ineptitude at policy-making of a government half the creature of small business men, and half the creature of large, might be traced out in other legislation of "return" bias—legislation designed to preserve the fiction of small-unit competition. The Farm Board is a notorious example. Those who wish to investigate the chameleon quality of the present facing-both-ways dispensation are referred to the books of Stuart Chase and George Soule. I have merely tried to indicate here the congealing effects of the "return" reform legislation.

Both Mr. Chase and Mr. Soule are intelligent appraisers of the gyrations of American business men in the magnetic field of our individualist traditions. The contradictions, the hopelessness, of running a system half-planned, half-controlled, and half "free," have been apparent to them for some time, as they have been apparent to Charles A. Beard and John Dewey, two other spiritual descendants of the Progressives of the Rooseveltian and Wilsonian days. These men have seen us "backing into" control by Farm Boards, Federal Reserve Systems, Federal Trade Commissions, Federal Radio Commissions, Reconstruction Finance Corporations. They have seen the *laissez faire* proudly championed by William Graham Sumner failing bit by bit. They have grasped the need of control from a fixed point at the top. And so they have proclaimed the virtues of a Central Planning Board.

But they have not, at least in their books and articles on a planned economy, examined the political incidence of their beliefs. They have not seen that fixed control requires a priesthood to administer it. And this fixed control entails a society of one consensus of aim and will—not a classless society, as individualists fear, but a society without horizontal classes of proletariat, small and upper bourgeosie, all of whom have different aims. The classes in the society of the future will be vertical classes, of farmers, miners, technicians, and so on. Bœotia versus Athens will remain to make life interesting.

The Soules and the Chases propose a Central Planning

Board—but they fail explicitly to realize that such a board, once set up, would merely amount to the definition of the boundaries of the battlefield. The fight for the control of the Board would still go on, between the various "interests" in contemporary society, just as the fight for the control of the Interstate Commerce Commission, and for control of the Federal Reserve System, has gone on. The creation of a Board, even a master Board, does not mean the coördination which Mr. Chase seems to think it does. The Interstate Commerce Commission, for instance, wavers in its policy according to pressure; it failed to raise freight rates in the good years before 1930, with the result that the railroads had no surplus with which to combat the lean years that have followed; and lately the I. C. C. has felt compelled to raise rates when everything else is being reduced. The Federal Reserve Board, which was supposed by Bryan to have been kept within the control of a virtuous people, failed to raise the rediscount rate in 1928, thus encouraging the speculation. And a gambling public approved. There is every reason to believe that a Central Planning Board, overseeing investment, stock flotations, mergers, prices, wages, and so on, would fall a prey to the same forces that have used the Federal Reserve System, the Interstate Commerce Commission, the Federal Trade Commission, and other central agencies, for their own ends. Confusion would be thus compounded.

Every dilemma that Soule, Chase and Beard uncover in the course of their demonstration—the dilemma of the engineer in a profit economy, the dilemma of traditional liberalism in a situation that requires a new corrective approach—seems to ray out into politics. Yet these men, with the possible exception of Soule, who has made his effort in the past to organize a farmer-labor alignment, won't work with the stuff of politics, with men, with blocs, with groups, with classes. Chase calls himself the world's worst politician—which argues his irrelevance in a revolutionary situation. He is the doctor who should be called in *after* a revolutionary change; he should not be heeded, as he is so earnestly heeded, during the interregnum, save insofar as it is valuable to keep ideas alive at all times.

The works of Chase, Soule, Beard and company are like magnificent machines with no dynamos attached; there is nothing to start the conveyor belts moving. One comes out of their blueprints for the future society in a state of reverie. "Yes," one muses, thinking of a four-day week, of a ten-month year, of a guaranteed sabbatical year, of an assured monthly draught upon an adequate common stock of food and clothing, of hours on the tennis court and in the sun, "it would be a fine thing to have a planned society; it would be nice, as these men suggest, to have a National Economic Board at the top, representing the whole public." It would be good, too, as Mr. Soule specifies, to have a Board composed, not of "bargaining representatives of various interests, but of qualified experts representing the nation as a whole."

But the Board which Mr. Soule proposes would have to be appointed under the present dispensation by the equivalent of the Republican and Democratic leaders. It could not, therefore, represent the nation as a whole; it would have to be a compromise between warring interests in a society of horizontal classes. For what, under capitalism, is the nation as a whole? Going back to primer politics, we may answer that it is a collection of various interests, none of which goes to make up its part of a functioning whole until its bargaining power has been satisfied. In advocating a central planning board under capitalism to represent *the nation as a whole,* Soule, Chase and Beard are simply not talking in terms of human material—farmers, shippers, mechanics, miners, rentiers, bank directors, newspaper owners, advertising men, Senator Borah, Senator Fess, "Alfalfa Bill" Murray, Huey Long, William Z. Foster, white-collar workers, loafers, Goo-goos and Purchasables. They are talking in the terms of Plato, who believed in the disinterested philosopher-king. Only in modern terms, the philosopher-king has become a man with the ability of Henry Ford and the values of Stuart Chase, which somehow can't be found in one and the same corporeal body.

Mr. Soule goes beyond Mr. Chase and beyond John Dewey, for he admits the necessity of a Board with "teeth" in it. But what are these teeth? They must inevitably depend on Congress—on permission to initiate and enforce plans on recalcitrant industries, and on legislation required to put phases of planning in operation. Which, of course, brings us back to where we stand at present: to the collection of various interests which are represented in Congress, none of which (despite the admonitions of the professional monitor, Walter Lippmann) goes to make up its part of a functioning whole until its bargaining power has been satisfied. If we had a national will to plan, Congress could do it without a planning board, simply by requisitioning data and experts.

I believe that Mr. Soule really knows this. And that is why I think he is disingenuous when he says: "The Board should not be limited in its ultimate choice by any bias in favor of 'private enterprise' on the one hand or in favor of 'socialism' on the other." Mr. Soule knows that such "disinterestedness" doesn't exist; that any Board at the top, in 1932, would represent the congeries of interests which put it at the top, and nothing else. It would have to have certain objectives in mind, which would imply a "bias." Mr. Soule says: "It should choose the form which, after thorough examination, seemed best suited to the ends in view." But this involves us in the same circular reasoning which vitiates the control of the railroads by the Interstate Commerce Commission. The "ends in view" would, quite naturally, dictate the form.

The "economic planners" start from the wrong end. They are fond of demolishing the "Utopians," including the Marxists, and then they proceed to create economists' Utopias. Their "ends in view" imply the prior existence of a radical party, dominated by labor (including the white-collar worker) and the mortgage-ridden small farmer, to say nothing of the 11,000,000 unemployed, which would be compelled to put a majority in Congress before the creation of any "Board at the top" is undertaken. Otherwise, planning will go on as at present. And it will be capitalist planning, done piecemeal, depending on the Sixteenth Amendment and ultimately invoking the dole on a broad scale. It will continue the Reconstruction Finance Corporation, with its "dole" to capital.

The Chase-Soule group gets around the immediate necessity of considering politics by positing the "organizing man." This man, they say, following the lead thrown out by Veblen, may save society because the industrial set-up demands that he be given a free rein lest we all perish. But what is the "organizing man" but our old friend, man, the "political animal"? Politics is, in simplest definition, the art of organizing and preserving for the organizers the means of existence and the way of life these organizers prefer. The "organizing man" works very well in single industries as things are at present. The minute it becomes a question of organizing two competing industries the "organizing man" becomes a politician, attempting to gain consensus to suit his own side. If he is a representative of the so-called public-at-large, he becomes a politician in favor of either one of two things: preserving profits and productive property in favor of some group-alignment that has elected him, or of managing the industrial machine for the benefit of everybody. The only sort of organizing man (human psychology being what it is) who can be trusted with the second choice is the man who has nothing to lose by it, and everything to gain. And this brings us back to the necessity (not to the inevitability) of a radical party, dominated by labor, skilled and otherwise, the white-collar worker, the unemployed, and the poorer farmer. The "inner circle" of this party, once it had attained to office, would make use of the engineer, it would commandeer Howard Scott's Technocracy group at Columbia University, for example, but it would not, if it is to be wise, let the engineering mind (which is a non-qualitative mind) dictate to it. Engineers are notoriously careless of the master whom they work for, whether he be a red tyrant, a black tyrant or a butter-and-egg man. They are interested primarily in means, or they would not be engineers.

The situation begs for a "demand" politics along socialist lines, with propaganda playing a prominent part in the necessary political organization. The "social planners" who are for a "planned society" under capitalism can help; but not in the way they think they can. If they succeed in embodying their proposals for a control and "management" of money, for a regulated investment, for publicity of business processes and account books (as William Z. Ripley advocates), for a super-cabinet to correlate industry, something may be gained; but it will not be the gain along the "third road" that Mr. Chase expects. The gain will be—a further congealing of capitalism, a further check upon the system. Prosperity, it must not be forgotten, is a function of a rising market. Because the issue between preservation of individual profits and fulfillment of mass desires would not be clear, a national economic council under capitalism would tend to waver, depending upon the strength of relative pressures brought to bear on it. Thus such a council would do the work of the Rooseveltian and Wilsonian reforms; it would make the system upon which it is grafted so much the more unpredictable and unpatchable. Regulated investment, for example, would create more graft. At first it would make capital timid, conduce to hoarding, send money abroad. For, under regulation, withdrawal of capital would be as difficult as investment of capital; otherwise it would not be regulation. And who would be willing to tie up a fortune—unless that fortune is to be guaranteed by the government that ties it up, an intolerable situation for the tax payer? That is, who would be willing to tie up a fortune unless the men to be controlled are to do their own controlling? And if they are to do the controlling to make profits for themselves, what sort of social control would it be?

Buying into control would, as a political corollary, follow inevitably, just as buying into control of our political parties—even our Progressive political parties—has followed inevitably in a democracy. This would, I think, work to kill new enterprise—perhaps a desirable thing, but hardly contemplated by Mr. Chase in his prospectus for the Investment Board of his New Jerusalem. Inevitably the men whose money is tied up in a *status quo* would tend to cut off competition in the form of new industries that might threaten the income of their regulated capital. A Board with the power to control investment could, by easy alliance through politics with the top economic planning board, also control obsolescence. A new alloy—"lighter than aluminum and stronger than steel"—would find it hard sledding to get a chance from a Board whose money connections were with either aluminum or steel. A favored class would be created, a class interested in maintaining itself on a certain favored plane. The Rockefellers and the Carnegies of the future would find themselves faced by an intrenched priesthood of investors.

Here Mr. Chase, if he is to run true to form, would step in to reply to Mr. Redbonnet. The system could not be humanly disastrous, he would say, because under machine technology and mass production, the masses must be paid sufficient money to buy back the goods they turn out. A *status quo* would have a proprietary interest in paying high wages and in spending all high salaries and incomes. This sounds very enticing. But is it psychologically sound? Does it take into consideration the emulative factor? A group of favored spenders, an inner circle of Lorenzos, gorgeous in their open-handed welcome to the arts, would be the object of the invidious comparison which Veblen has so urbanely satirized in *The Theory of the Leisure Class*. The worker, naturally, would tend to save some of his high wages, that he might the better seize the elusive opportunity to buy his way into the favored group. The hierarchy of owners, human nature being what it is, would let him in, increasing the capitalization of existing industries in order that more money might be made to spend. Short of police-dictated consumption to infinity, the system, running on spending power, would thus be thrown out of kilter, its life-blood partially withdrawn. Inflation would be the remedy, as now. And inflation is the very dislocation that Mr. Chase wants, really, to avoid. It fails to consider the sections of society that have made no provision for it in their calculations.

So planned capitalism, being a contradiction in terms, seems no permanent way out. Mr. Chase is valuable only insofar as his efforts to point out the desirability of a planned society tend to show up the inner inconsistencies of capitalism. Political organization looking towards a socialist America, or an "industrial democracy," as Oscar Ameringer, with his sound instinct for the telling Americanism, prefers to call it, is the *sine qua non* of any alternative to the present chaotic order. This does not mean a reliance upon strict Marxist doctrine; for, as Mr. Soule has so cogently pointed out in his analysis of theories of social revolution, the group of men whom the Marxians are in the habit of regarding as the "industrial proletariat" (those who work with their hands and receive wages) is tending to decrease. The advance of industrial technique means more and more products turned out with less and less physical labor. Workers in factories, mills, railroads and mines fail to keep pace with the increase in population, or even decrease in relation to a static population. And at the same time sales and office forces grow, or did grow before 1930. As direct labor goes down, overhead rises. In good times, amusement occupations increase. And the result is that a group of human material which is not good "revolutionary" material in the original Marxist sense tends to grow up at the base of society. The increase in unemployment, too, is not material for the classic Marxist revolution. Marx expected as little from the "rotting" masses of the unemployed as he did from employees with a petty bourgeois psychology. The unemployed man is usually a potential scab. And a dole buys him.

Mr. Soule regards all this as very damaging to the Marxian

hopes—that is, unless a war or a catastrophe occurs which would give a small determined inner circle the opportunity which Lenin and Trotsky had in Russia. But, in a larger sense, is it as damaging as he thinks? Does it not call for a redefinition of the phrases of the class struggle, a re-application of Marxian dogma to American conditions? If Marx is any good, he can stand the tampering. If capitalism cannot get back to its pre-1914 basis on a world stage (and who believes that it can?), is not the field open in America for a decade of re-application? A *milieu,* a climate of opinion, is being created. Literature, after a decade of pure individualism split off from any "social consciousness," is returning to its function of 1902-17, and with its return, the whole general field of pamphleteering and propaganda will be re-opened to discussion of these matters and possibly advanced beyond the state of 1902-17.

Somewhere, within the jostling alignment of the disaffected of America, whether within the ranks of the striking farmers, the forces of Foster or Thomas, or the 11,000,000 unemployed who have made experiments with councils of their own, there is the nucleus of an American party which will include not only the traditional "industrial proletariat," which tends to diminish, but the groups which Mr. Soule has singled out for mention, and the groups which have, traditionally, followed the star of Bryanism. The course of the present depression will determine the chances for the immediate cohesion and the rise of this party. The danger is, of course, that the American set-up will tend to force a division of the disaffected into the Fascist and socialist camps, with Ku Kluxism, American Legion "buddy" patriotism, and bloody intolerance congregating under the device of the fasces. I venture no prophecies here, but fear the worst.

However, any development of American radicalism, whether Red or Black, to impressive proportions must depend on the course of the depression. If capitalism survives the crisis and moves on toward another upgrade, the coming to grips will be postponed. You cannot talk to a man with hopes.

Socialism, as W. E. Woodward says, is based on pessimism; it assumes that human nature cannot change. It assumes, too, that man cannot work the complicated credit structure he has reared without getting fingers caught in the machinery. It is a last-ditch refuge, stormed by hungry men who prefer to live on terms of economic equity rather than starve on terms of hopes for economic superiority. Its mass appeal, as distinct from its individual appeal, like the appeal of all other political systems, is a belly appeal.

But the next half-century should witness the convergence of forces. There may be, as the economic parrot says, new markets to be uncovered, new wants to be exploited, new famines to create new farmer-purchasing power, even new sources of gold.

But...there is Russia. The hopes for eternal capitalism are all predicated on the course of events in the Soviet Union. What will be the rôle of Russia in the forthcoming years? A nation whose industries have no six per cents to pay to investors will, inevitably, become a favored nation in some quarters; it can undersell. And underselling that you don't just happen to like is dumping. The menace of Russian dumping will lead to the adoption of the quota system of imports and exports in many countries. Is this propitious for capitalist expansion?

No, however we look at it, eventual constriction stares us in the face. And that is why a contemplation of "reform" in America—the reform that has talked, endlessly, about going back to the primitive capitalism of our fathers while an economic revolution has been beating about our ears—is productive of no further hopes in its tenets. The situation, looked upon with intelligence and considered as a long-range proposition, can lead to but one of two personal conclusions: it can make one either a cynic or a revolutionist. Even if an American Fascist régime intervenes in the future, one, two or ten years from now, it can only postpone the inevitable day when one must decamp into cynicism, facing endless trouble, with the assurance that we are born to trouble, or concur. For Fascism implies the development of the labor-syndicate idea; and it would be only a question of opportunity before the syndicates attempted their own march to power.

Index

QUADRANGLE PAPERBACKS

History

Frederick Lewis Allen. *The Lords of Creation.* QP35
William Sheridan Allen. *The Nazi Seizure of Power.* QP302
Lewis Atherton. *Main Street on the Middle Border.* QP36
Thomas A. Bailey. *Woodrow Wilson and the Lost Peace.* QP1
Thomas A. Bailey. *Woodrow Wilson and the Great Betrayal.* QP2
Charles A. Beard. *The Idea of National Interest.* QP27
Carl L. Becker. *Everyman His Own Historian.* QP33
Ray A. Billington. *The Protestant Crusade.* QP12
John Chamberlain. *Farewell to Reform.* QP19
Alice Hamilton Cromie. *A Tour Guide to the Civil War.*
Chester McArthur Destler. *American Radicalism, 1865-1901.* QP30
Elisha P. Douglass. *Rebels and Democrats.* QP26
Herman Finer. *Road to Reaction.* QP5
Felix Frankfurter. *The Commerce Clause.* QP16
Lloyd C. Gardner. *A Different Frontier.* QP32
Ray Ginger. *Altgeld's America.* QP21
Raul Hilberg. *The Destruction of the European Jews.* QP301
Frederic C. Howe. *The Confessions of a Reformer.* QP39
Louis Joughin and Edmund M. Morgan. *The Legacy of Sacco and Vanzetti.* QP7
Edward Chase Kirkland. *Dream and Thought in the Business Community, 1860-1900.* QP11
Adrienne Koch. *The Philosophy of Thomas Jefferson.* QP17
Walter LaFeber. *John Quincy Adams and American Continental Empire.* QP23
David E. Lilienthal. *TVA: Democracy on the March.* QP28
Arthur S. Link. *Wilson the Diplomatist.* QP18
Huey P. Long. *Every Man a King.* QP8
Gene M. Lyons. *America: Purpose and Power.* QP24
Jackson Turner Main. *The Antifederalists.* QP14
Ernest R. May. *The World War and American Isolation, 1914-1917.* QP29
Henry F. May. *The End of American Innocence.* QP9
George E. Mowry. *The California Progressives.* QP6
Frank L. Owsley. *Plain Folk of the Old South.* QP22
David Graham Phillips. *The Treason of the Senate.* QP20
Julius W. Pratt. *Expansionists of 1898.* QP15
David A. Shannon. *The Socialist Party of America.* QP38
Richard W. Van Alstyne. *The Rising American Empire.* QP25
Willard M. Wallace. *Appeal to Arms.* QP10
Norman Ware. *The Industrial Worker, 1840-1860.* QP13
Albert K. Weinberg. *Manifest Destiny.* QP3
Bernard A. Weisberger. *They Gathered at the River.* QP37
Bell I. Wiley. *The Plain People of the Confederacy.* QP4
William Appleman Williams. *The Contours of American History.* QP34
Esmond Wright. *Causes and Consequences of the American Revolution.* QP31

Philosophy

James M. Edie. *An Invitation to Phenomenology.* QP103
James M. Edie. *Phenomenology in America.* QP105
Moltke S. Gram. *Kant: Disputed Questions.* QP104
George L. Kline. *European Philosophy Today.* QP102
Pierre Thévenaz. *What Is Phenomenology?* QP101

Social Science

George and Eunice Grier. *Equality and Beyond.* QP204
Charles O. Lerche, Jr. *Last Chance in Europe.* QP207
David Mitrany. *A Working Peace System.* QP205
Martin Oppenheimer and George Lakey. *A Manual for Direct Action.* QP202
Clarence Senior. *The Puerto Ricans.* QP201